What people are saying about …

On Guard

and

William Lane Craig

"In these pages, you'll learn the most compelling arguments in favor of Christianity. Not only that, but you'll also find out how to respond to the most popular objections to those arguments. You'll discover that *On Guard* is solidly factual, winsomely personal, consistently practical, and ultimately convincing in its presentation of the case for Christianity."

Lee Strobel, former skeptic and author of
The Case for Christ and *The Case for the Real Jesus*

"There is probably no greater defender of the Christian faith alive today than William Lane Craig. *On Guard* is Craig's introduction to the wealth of information, logic, and evidence that powerfully point to the truth of our Christian beliefs. Read it to deepen your own faith and to embolden your confidence in sharing that faith with others."

Mark Mittelberg, author of *Faith Path, Choosing Your
Faith,* and coauthor of *The Unexpected Adventure*

"*On Guard* is an excellent summation of how the Christian faith makes sense of the real world in which we all live. 'Speaking the truth in love,' once again William Lane Craig proves we don't have to be abrasive to be persuasive."

Jim Thomas, pastor at the Village Chapel, Nashville, and
author of *Coffeehouse Theology and Streetwise Spirituality*

"William Lane Craig is arguably one of the finest Christian philosophers of our time. His knowledge and skill have placed him on platforms on every continent, engaging the most notable skeptics in dialogue and debate."

Ravi Zacharias, founder and chairman of Ravi Zacharias International Ministries

"It is hard to overstate the impact that William Lane Craig has had for the cause of Christ. He is simply the finest Christian apologist of the last half century, and his academic work justifies ranking him among the top 1 percent of practicing philosophers in the Western world. Besides that, he is a winsome ambassador for Christ, an exceptional debater, and a man with the heart of an evangelist. I know him well and can say that he lives a life of integrity and lives out what he believes. I do not know of a single thinker who has done more to raise the bar of Christian scholarship in our generation than Craig. He is one of a kind and I thank God for his life and work."

J. P. Moreland, distinguished professor of philosophy at Talbot School of Theology

"Today is not a world where blind faith is accepted. You need faith with backup. *On Guard: Defending Your Faith with Reason and Precision* is a guide to using reason to defend one's beliefs in today's world when discussing matters of faith and religion. For those who want to talk Christianity with grace and poise, *On Guard* is a highly useful read."

Library Bookwatch, September 2010

ON GUARD

Defending Your Faith with
Reason and Precision

WILLIAM LANE CRAIG

David C Cook®
transforming lives together

ON GUARD
Published by David C Cook
4050 Lee Vance Drive
Colorado Springs, CO 80918 U.S.A.

Integrity Music Limited, a Division of David C Cook
Brighton, East Sussex BN1 2RE, England

The graphic circle C logo is a registered trademark of David C Cook.

The Web site addresses recommended throughout this book are offered as a resource to you. These Web sites are not intended in any way to be or imply an endorsement on the part of David C Cook, nor do we vouch for their content.

Scripture quotations, unless otherwise noted, are taken from the New Revised Standard Version Bible, copyright 1989, Division of Christian Education of the National Council of the Churches of Christ in the United States of America. All rights reserved. Scripture quotations marked RSV are taken from the Revised Standard Version Bible, copyright 1952 [2nd edition, 1971], Division of Christian Education of the National Council of the Churches of Christ in the United States of America. All rights reserved; NIV are taken from the *Holy Bible, New International Version®. NIV®.* Copyright © 1973, 1978, 1984 International Bible Society. All rights reserved; ESV are taken from *The Holy Bible, English Standard Version.* Copyright © 2000; 2001 by Crossway Bibles, a division of Good News Publishers. All rights reserved; NLT are taken from the *Holy Bible, New Living Translation,* copyright © 1996, 2004 by Tyndale Charitable Trust; NASB are taken from the *New American Standard Bible,* © 1960, 1995 by The Lockman Foundation; KJV are taken from the King James Version of the Bible. (Public Domain.) All versions used by permission. The author has added italics to Scripture quotations for emphasis.

LCCN 2009943352
ISBN 978-1-4347-6488-1
eISBN 978-1-4347-0188-6

The cartoon by Mary Chambers in chapter one is reprinted with the artist's permission.

The Team: Brian Thomasson, Karen Lee-Thorp, Jaci Schneider, and Karen Athen
Cover Design: Amy Kiechlin
Cover Photos: iStockphotos, royalty-free
Interior Portraits: Dan Schultz
Interior Sketches: Luke Flowers

Printed in the United States of America
First Edition 2010

15 16 17 18 19 20 21 22 23 24

070219

To the Defenders

CONTENTS

FOREWORD

BY LEE STROBEL

William Lane Craig is, in my opinion, among the very best defenders of Christianity in this generation. With doctorates in philosophy and theology, a sharp and incisive mind, and the passionate heart of an evangelist, Bill travels the globe debating some of the most ardent and articulate atheists. Invariably, their arguments against God wither in the face of Bill's affirmative evidence for the existence of a Creator and the truth of the Christian faith.

For example, in 2009 Bill debated Christopher Hitchens, author of the best seller *God Is Not Great* and one of the so-called "four horsemen of the new atheism." Bill built an impressive case for the existence of God—a case that Hitchens absolutely failed to refute—while at the same time artfully exposing Hitchens' empty rhetoric. What was the result? Well, here's how an *atheist* commentator summed up the event: "Frankly, Craig spanked Hitchens like a foolish child."

I first met Bill several years ago when a friend of mine, who was the national spokesman for American Atheists, Inc., said to me, "Wouldn't it be great if we could lay out the case for atheism and your side could lay out the case for Christianity, and we could just let the audience decide for themselves?"

I jumped at the opportunity. "You go out and find the strongest defender of atheism you can—your best and brightest," I said. "We'll go out and get a top-notch proponent of Christianity, and we'll have an intellectual shoot-out!"

The atheists chose Frank Zindler, a colleague of renowned atheist Madalyn Murray O'Hair and a former professor of geology and biology. We chose Bill Craig to present the Christian case.

The news media—amazed that a church was unafraid to confront the toughest objections by skeptics—was quickly abuzz. Soon I began getting calls from radio stations across the country. "Can we broadcast this debate live?" they would ask. "Uh, sure," I'd say. To our astonishment, pretty soon we had 117 stations from coast to coast.

On the night of the debate, traffic became gridlocked around the church. When we opened the doors, people ran down the aisles to get a seat. When is the last time you saw people run *into* a church? In all, 7,778 people showed up for the event. The atmosphere was electric!

Bill began by spelling out five powerful arguments for God and Christianity. First, the beginning of the universe clearly points toward a Creator ("Whatever begins to exist has a cause; the universe began to exist; therefore, the universe has a cause"). Second, the universe's incredible fine-tuning defies coincidence and exhibits the handiwork of an intelligent designer. Third, our objective moral values are evidence that there is a God, since only He could establish a universal standard of right and wrong. Fourth, the historical evidence for the resurrection—including the empty tomb, eyewitness accounts, and the origin of the Christian faith—establish the divinity of Jesus. And, fifth, God can be immediately known and experienced by those who seek Him.

Despite Bill's repeated challenges, Zindler balked at offering an affirmative case for atheism. Instead, he charged that biological evolution "is the death knell of Christianity"; that there's no convincing evidence Jesus actually lived; and that the existence of evil argues against God.

To the audience's surprise, Bill promptly used Zindler's arguments against him. He pointed out that if evolution did occur despite the prohibitive odds against it, then it must have been a miracle and therefore it would be additional evidence for the existence of God!

As for evil in the world, Craig said, "No logical inconsistency has ever been demonstrated between the two statements 'God exists' and 'evil exists.'" Besides, he added, in a deeper sense the presence of evil "actually demonstrates God's existence, because without God there wouldn't be any [moral] foundation for calling anything evil."

At the end of the two-hour debate, we had the audience cast ballots on

the results. An overwhelming 82 percent of the atheists, agnostics, and other non-Christians concluded that the evidence offered for Christianity was the most compelling. And—get this!—forty-seven people walked in as unbelievers, heard both sides, and walked out as believers. What's more, not a single person became an atheist. It was a stunning affirmation that Christians have an unfair advantage in the marketplace of ideas: *We have truth on our side!*

You may never debate an atheist. Nevertheless, the Bible says in 1 Peter 3:15 that *all* Christians should be prepared to explain why they believe what they believe—and to do so, as Bill Craig unfailingly does, with gentleness and respect.

In a world where the media often trumpet claims by skeptics, best-selling books hawk atheism, and many university professors seem bent on destroying the beliefs of young Christians, it's increasingly important for all of us to be able to articulate the reasons why our faith makes sense. And that's why this book is so absolutely vital.

In these pages, you'll learn the most compelling arguments in favor of Christianity. Not only that, but you'll also find out how to respond to the most popular objections to those arguments. You'll discover that *On Guard* is solidly factual, winsomely personal, consistently practical, and ultimately convincing in its presentation of the case for Christianity.

So devour this book. Read and reread it. Underline and highlight it. Make notes in the margins. Study and debate it with friends. Become conversant with its logic and teachings. Try out its points with some of your skeptical friends.

In the end, here's my prediction: You'll emerge stronger in your own faith and much more confident in sharing Christ with others.

Lee Strobel, former skeptic and author of *The Case for Christ* and *The Case for the Real Jesus*

CHAPTER I

WHAT IS APOLOGETICS?

Always be prepared to make a defense to any one who calls you to account for the hope that is in you. (1 Peter 3:15 RSV)

I teach a Sunday school class called "Defenders" to about one hundred people, from high schoolers to senior adults, at our home church in Atlanta. We talk about what the Bible teaches (Christian doctrine) and about how to defend it (Christian apologetics). Sometimes people who aren't in our class don't understand what we do. One fine Southern lady, upon hearing that I teach Christian apologetics, remarked indignantly, "I'll never apologize for my faith!"

Apologetics Means a Defense

The reason for her misunderstanding is obvious: "Apologetics" sounds like "apologize." But apologetics is not the art of telling somebody you're sorry that you're a Christian! Rather *apologetics* comes from the Greek word *apologia*, which means a defense, as in a court of law. Christian apologetics involves making a case for the truth of the Christian faith.

The Bible actually commands us to have such a case ready to give to any unbeliever who wants to know why we believe what we do. Just as the contestants in a fencing match have learned both to parry each attack as well as to go on the offensive themselves, so we must always be "on guard." First Peter 3:15 says, "Always be prepared to make a defense [*apologia*] to anyone who asks you for a reason for the hope that is in you; yet do it with gentleness and respect" (author's translation).

APOLOGETICS
_____

Apologetics comes from the Greek word *apologia*, which means a defense, as in a court of law. Christian apologetics involves making a case for the truth of the Christian faith.

Notice the attitude we're supposed to have when giving our defense: We should be gentle and respectful. Apologetics is also not the art of making somebody else sorry that you're a Christian! We can present a *defense* of the Christian faith without becoming *defensive*. We can present *arguments* for Christianity without becoming *argumentative*.

When I talk in this book about arguments for the Christian faith, it's vital to understand that I don't mean quarreling. We should never quarrel with a nonbeliever about our faith. That only makes people mad and drives them away. As I'll explain later in this chapter, an argument in the philosophical sense is not a fight or a heated exchange; it's just a series of statements leading to a conclusion. That's all.

Ironically, if you have good arguments in support of your faith, you're less apt to become quarrelsome or upset. I find that the better my arguments, the less argumentative I am. The better my defense, the less defensive I am. If you have good reasons for what you believe and know the answers to the unbeliever's questions or objections, there's just no reason to get hot under the collar. Instead, you'll find yourself calm and confident when you're under attack, because you know you have the answers.

I frequently debate on university campuses on topics like "Does God Exist?" or "Christianity vs. Atheism." Sometimes students in the audience get up during the Q&A period and attack me personally or go into an abusive rant. I find that my reaction to these students is not anger, but rather simply feeling sorry for them because they're so mixed up. If you have good reasons for what you believe, then instead of anger you'll feel a genuine compassion for the unbeliever, who is often so misled. Good apologetics involves "speaking the truth in love" (Eph. 4:15).

Is Apologetics Biblical?

Some people think that apologetics is unbiblical. They say that you should just preach the gospel and let the Holy Spirit do His work! But I think that the example of Jesus and the apostles affirms the value of apologetics. Jesus appealed to miracles and to fulfilled prophecy to prove that His claims were true (Luke 24:25–27; John 14:11). What about the apostles? In dealing with other Jews, they used fulfilled prophecy, Jesus' miracles, and especially Jesus' resurrection to prove that He was the Messiah. Take, for example, Peter's sermon on the day of Pentecost recorded in the second chapter of Acts. In verse 22, he appeals to Jesus' miracles. In verses 25–31 he appeals to fulfilled prophecy. In verse 32 he appeals to Christ's resurrection. By means of these arguments the apostles sought to show their fellow Jews that Christianity is true.

In dealing with non-Jews, the apostles sought to show the existence of God through His handiwork in nature (Acts 14:17). In Romans 1, Paul says that from nature alone all men can know that God exists (Rom. 1:20). Paul also appealed to eyewitness testimony of Jesus' resurrection to show further that Christianity is true (1 Cor. 15:3–8).

So it's clear that both Jesus and the apostles were not afraid to give evidence for the truth of what they proclaimed. This doesn't mean they didn't trust the Holy Spirit to bring people to God. Rather they trusted the Holy Spirit to *use* their arguments and evidence to bring people to God.

> ## TALK ABOUT IT
>
> What kinds of arguments does Paul use in Acts 17:22–31 to persuade non-Jews that the gospel is true? How are his arguments like and unlike those Peter uses when talking to Jews in Acts 2:14–29? What do you learn about the place of apologetics in evangelism?

Why Is Apologetics Important?

It's vitally important that Christians today be trained in apologetics. Why? Let me give three reasons.

1. *Shaping culture.* We've all heard of the so-called culture war going on in American society. Some people may not like this militaristic metaphor, but the truth is that a tremendous struggle for the soul of America is raging right

now. This struggle is not just political. It has a religious or spiritual dimension as well. Secularists are bent on eliminating religion from the public square. The so-called New Atheists, represented by people like Sam Harris, Richard Dawkins, and Christopher Hitchens, are even more aggressive. They want to exterminate religious belief entirely.

American society has already become post-Christian. Belief in a sort of generic God is still the norm, but belief in Jesus Christ is now politically incorrect. How many films coming out of Hollywood portray Christians in a positive way? How many times do we instead find Christians portrayed as shallow, bigoted, villainous hypocrites? What is the public perception of Bible-believing Christians in our culture today?

The above cartoon poignantly depicts the perception of Christians by the cultural elite in American society today: goofy curiosities to be gawked at by normal people. But notice, they're also *dangerous*. They mustn't be allowed positions of influence in society. Maybe that's why they even need to be penned up.

Why are these considerations of culture important? Why can't we Christians just be faithful followers of Christ and ignore what is going on in the culture at large? Why not just preach the gospel to a dark and dying world?

The answer is, because *the gospel is never heard in isolation.* It is always heard against the backdrop of the culture in which you've been born and raised. A person who has been raised in a culture that is sympathetic to the Christian faith will be open to the gospel in a way that a person brought up in a secular culture will not. For a person who is thoroughly secularized, you may as well tell him to believe in fairies or leprechauns as in Jesus Christ! That's how absurd the message of Christ will seem to him.

To see the influence of culture on your own thinking, imagine what you would think if a Hindu devotee of the Hare Krishna movement, with his shaved head and saffron robe, approached you at the airport or shopping mall, offering you a flower and inviting you to become a follower of Krishna. Such an invitation would likely strike you as bizarre, freakish, maybe even a bit funny. But think how differently someone in Delhi, India, would react if he were approached by such a person! Having been raised in a Hindu culture, he might take such an invitation very seriously.

If America's slide into secularism continues, then what awaits us tomorrow is already evident today in Europe. Western Europe has become so secularized that it's hard for the gospel even to get a fair hearing. As a result, missionaries must labor for years to win even a handful of converts. Having lived for thirteen years in Europe in four different countries, I can testify personally to how hard it is for people to respond to the message of Christ. Speaking on university campuses around Europe, I found that the students' reaction was often bewilderment. *Christianity is supposed to be for old women and children,* they would think. *So what's this man with two earned doctorates from European universities doing here defending the truth of the Christian faith with arguments we can't answer?*

Once, when I was speaking at a university in Sweden, a student asked me during the Q&A following my talk, "What are you doing here?" Puzzled, I said, "Well, I've been invited by the Religious Studies Department to give this lecture." "That's not what I mean," he insisted. "Don't you understand how unusual this is? I want to know what motivates you personally to come

SECULARISM

Secularism is a worldview that allows no room for the supernatural: no miracles, no divine revelation, no God.

and do this." I suspect he had never seen a Christian philosopher before—in fact, a prominent Swedish philosopher told me that there are no Christian philosophers at any university in Sweden. The student's question gave me the chance to share the story of how I came to Christ.

The skepticism on European university campuses runs so deep that when I spoke on the existence of God at the University of Porto in Portugal, the students (as I learned later) actually telephoned the Higher Institute of Philosophy at the University of Louvain in Belgium, where I was affiliated, to see if I was an imposter! They thought I was a fake! I just didn't fit into their stereotype of a Christian.

If the gospel is to be heard as an intellectually viable option for thinking men and women today, then it's vital that we as Christians try to shape American culture in such a way that Christian belief cannot be dismissed as mere superstition. This is where Christian apologetics comes in. If Christians could be trained to provide solid evidence for what they believe and good answers to unbelievers' questions and objections, then the perception of Christians would slowly change. Christians would be seen as thoughtful people to be taken seriously rather than as emotional fanatics or buffoons. The gospel would be a real alternative for people to embrace.

I'm not saying that people will become Christians *because* of the arguments and evidence. Rather I'm saying that the arguments and evidence will help to create a culture in which Christian belief is a reasonable thing. They create an environment in which people will be open to the gospel. So becoming trained in apologetics is one way, a vital way, of being salt and light in American culture today.

2. *Strengthening believers.* The benefits of apologetics in your personal Christian life are huge. Let me mention three.

First of all, knowing *why* you believe as well as *what* you believe will make you more confident in sharing your faith with others. I see this happen all the time on university campuses when I have a public debate with a non-Christian professor. My experience is that while these professors may be very knowledgeable in their area of specialization, they are almost clueless when it comes to the evidence for Christianity. The Christian position in these debates usually comes out so far ahead of the non-Christian position that unbelieving students often complain that the whole event was a setup, staged to make the non-Christian position look bad! The truth is that we try to get the best opponents, who are often picked by the atheist club on campus.

Christian students, by contrast, come away from these debates with their heads held high, proud to be Christians. One Canadian student remarked to me following a debate, "I can't wait to share my faith in Christ!" People who lack training in apologetics are often afraid to share their faith or speak out for Christ out of fear that someone might ask them a question. But if you know the answers, then you're not afraid to go into the lion's den—in fact, you'll enjoy it! Training in apologetics will help to make you a bold and fearless witness for Christ.

Second, apologetics can also help you to keep the faith in times of doubt and struggle. Emotions will carry you only so far, and then you're going to need something more substantial. When I speak in churches around the country, I often meet parents who say something like, "If only you'd been here two or three years ago! Our son (or daughter) had questions about the faith which no one could answer, and now he's far from the Lord." In fact, there seem to be more and more reports of Christians abandoning their faith. A Christian minister at Stanford University recently told me that 40 percent of Christian high school students in church youth groups will quit church involvement altogether after graduation. Forty percent! It's not just that they lose their faith in a hostile university environment. Rather, many have already abandoned faith while still in the youth group but continue to

TALK ABOUT IT

Why do you think so many students abandon their faith during or just after high school? Who or what is to blame for this?

Relativism is the view that something is relative rather than absolute. That is to say, the thing in question (a truth, a moral value, a property) is the case only in relation to something else. For example, being rich is relative. Relative to most Americans, you're probably not rich. But relative to the people of the Sudan, you are fabulously rich! By contrast, it is not just relatively true that the Cubs did not win the 2009 World Series. It is absolutely true that they did not win. Many people today think that moral principles and religious beliefs are at best relative truths: true, as they say, for you, but not true for me.

go through the motions until they're out from under their parents' authority.

I think the church is really failing these kids. Rather than provide them training in the defense of Christianity's truth, we focus on emotional worship experiences, felt needs, and entertainment. It's no wonder they become sitting ducks for that teacher or professor who rationally takes aim at their faith. In high school and college, students are intellectually assaulted with every manner of non-Christian philosophy conjoined with an overwhelming relativism and skepticism. We've got to train our kids for war. How dare we send them unarmed into an intellectual war zone? Parents must do more than take their children to church and read them Bible stories. Moms and dads need to be trained in apologetics themselves and so be able to explain to their children simply from an early age and then with increasing depth why we believe as we do. Honestly, I find it hard to understand how Christian couples in our day and age can risk bringing children into the world without being trained in apologetics as part of the art of parenting.

Of course, apologetics won't *guarantee* that you or your children will keep the faith. There are all kinds of moral and spiritual factors that come into play, too. Some of the most effective atheist Web sites feature ex-believers who were trained in apologetics and still abandoned the faith. But when you look closely at the *arguments* they give for abandoning Christianity, they are often confused or weak. I recently saw one Web site where the person provided a list of the books that had persuaded him that Christianity is bunk—followed by the remark that he hopes to read them someday! Ironically, some of these folks come to embrace positions that are more extreme and require more gullibility—such as that Jesus never existed—than the conservative views they once held.

But while apologetics is no guarantee, it can help. As I travel, I also meet many people who have been brought back from the brink of abandoning their faith by reading an apologetics book or watching a debate. Recently I had the privilege of speaking at Princeton University on arguments for the existence of God, and after my lecture a young man approached me who wanted to talk. Obviously trying to hold back the tears, he told me how a couple of years earlier he had been struggling with doubts and was almost to the point of abandoning his faith. Someone then gave him a video of one of my debates. He said, "It saved me from losing my faith. I cannot thank you enough."

I said, "It was the Lord who saved you from falling."

"Yes," he replied, "but He used you. I can't thank you too much." I told him how thrilled I was for him and asked him about his future plans. "I'm graduating this year," he told me, "and I plan to go to seminary. I'm going into the pastorate." Praise God for the victory in this young man's life! When you're going through hard times and God seems distant, apologetics can help you to remember that our faith is not based on emotions, but on the truth, and therefore you must hold on to it.

TALK ABOUT IT

How could apologetics help you?

Finally, the study of apologetics is going to make you a deeper and more interesting person. American culture is so appallingly superficial, fixated on celebrities, entertainment, sports, and self-indulgence. Studying apologetics is going to take you beyond all that to life's deepest questions, questions about the existence and nature of God, the origin of the universe, the source of moral values, the problem of suffering and evil, and so on. As you wrestle with these deep questions, you yourself will be changed.

You will become more thoughtful and well-rounded. You'll learn how to think logically and to analyze what other people are saying. Instead of saying sheepishly, "This is how I *feel* about it—it's just my opinion, that's all," you'll be able to say, "This is what I *think* about it, and here are my reasons...." As a Christian, you'll begin to have a deeper appreciation of Christian truths about God and the world and see how they all fit together to make up a Christian worldview.

3. *Winning unbelievers.* Many people will agree with what I've said about the role of apologetics in strengthening believers, but they deny that it's of any use in winning unbelievers to Christ. "No one comes to Christ through arguments!" they'll tell you.

To a certain extent, I think that such people are just victims of false expectations. When you realize that only a minority of people who hear the gospel respond positively to it and place their faith in Christ, we shouldn't be surprised that most people will refuse to be persuaded by our arguments and evidence. By the very nature of the case, we should expect that most unbelievers will remain unconvinced by our apologetic arguments, just as most remain unmoved by the preaching of the cross.

And remember, no one knows for sure about the cumulative effect of such arguments, as the seed is planted and then watered again and again in ways we can't even imagine. We shouldn't expect that the unbeliever, when he first hears our apologetic case, will just roll over and play dead! Of course he'll fight back! Think of what's at stake for him! But we patiently plant and water in hopes that over time the seed will grow and bear fruit.

But why bother, you might ask, with that minority of a minority with whom apologetics is effective? First, because every person is precious to God, a person for whom Christ died. Like a missionary called to reach an obscure

people group, the Christian apologist is burdened to reach that minority of persons who will respond to rational argument and evidence.

But second, this people group, though relatively small in numbers, is huge in influence. One of these persons, for example, was C. S. Lewis. Think of the impact that one man's conversion continues to have! I find that the people who resonate most with my apologetic arguments tend to be engineers, people in medicine, and lawyers. Such persons are among the most influential in shaping our culture today. So reaching this minority of persons will yield a great harvest for the kingdom of God.

In any case the general conclusion that apologetics is ineffective in evangelism is just not true. Lee Strobel recently remarked to me that he has lost count of the number of people who have come to Christ through his books *The Case for Christ* and *The Case for Faith*. Nor has it been my experience that apologetics is ineffective in evangelism. We continually are thrilled to see people committing their lives to Christ through presentations of the gospel coupled with apologetics.

After giving a talk on arguments for the existence of God or evidence for the resurrection of Jesus, I'll sometimes conclude with a prayer of commitment to give one's life to Christ, and the comment cards indicate those who have registered such a commitment. Just recently I did a speaking tour of universities in central Illinois, and we were thrilled to find that almost every time I gave such a presentation, students indicated decisions for Christ. I've even seen students come to Christ just through hearing a defense of the cosmological argument (which I'll explain in this book)!

It has been thrilling, too, to hear stories of how people have been drawn to Christ through reading something I've written on apologetics. Since the attacks of September 11, 2001, I've had the privilege of being involved in debates with Islamic apologists on various university campuses in Canada and the States. Recently, early one Saturday morning, we received a telephone call. The foreign voice on the other end announced, "Hello! This is Sayd al-Islam calling from Oman!" He went on to explain that he had secretly lost his Muslim faith and

THE APOSTLE TO THE SKEPTICS

C. S. Lewis (1898–1963) rejected Christianity as a teenager for both personal and intellectual reasons. However, as an English professor at Oxford in his twenties and early thirties, Lewis was exposed to writers and friends who offered convincing reasons first for theism and eventually for Christianity. Lewis became a Christian and began to use his intellectual and literary talents to articulate and defend a Christian view of the world. He became one of the most influential Christian apologists of his generation. His books have sold more than one hundred million copies worldwide.

had become an atheist. But now by reading various Christian apologetic works, which he was ordering on Amazon.com, he had come to believe in God and was on the verge of making a commitment to Christ.

He was impressed with the evidence for Jesus' resurrection and had called me because he had several questions he still needed to settle. We talked for an hour, and I sensed that in his heart he already believed; but he wanted to be cautious and be sure he had the evidence in place before he consciously made that step. He explained to me, "You understand that I cannot tell you my real name. In my country I must lead a sort of double life because otherwise I would be killed." I prayed with him that God would continue to guide him into truth, and then we said good-bye. You can imagine how full of thanks my heart was to God for using these books—and the Internet!—in the life of this man! Stories like this could be multiplied, and, of course, we never hear of most of them.

When apologetics is persuasively presented and sensitively combined with a gospel presentation and a personal testimony, the Spirit of God is pleased to use it to bring people to Himself.

How to Get the Most out of This Book

This book is intended to be a sort of training manual to equip you to fulfill the command of 1 Peter 3:15. So this is a book to be *studied*, not just read. You'll find several arguments that I've put into easily memorizable steps. In discussing each argument, I'll present a reason (or several reasons) to think that each step in the argument is true. Then I'll discuss the usual objections to each step and show you how to answer them. In that way you'll be prepared in advance for possible questions you might meet in sharing your faith.

For example, suppose we have the following argument:

1. All men are mortal.

2. Socrates is a man.

3. Therefore, Socrates is mortal.

This is what we call a logically valid argument. That is to say, if steps 1 and 2 are true, then the conclusion, 3, is also true.

Logic is an expression of the mind of God (John 1:1). It describes how a supremely rational being reasons. There are only about nine basic rules of logic. So long as you obey the rules of logic, they *guarantee* that if the steps of your argument are true, then the conclusion is true as well. We then say that the truth of the conclusion *follows logically* from the argument's steps.

So the question then becomes: Are steps 1 and 2 in the above argument *true?* In support of step 1, we might present scientific and medical evidence for the fact that all men are mortal. In support of step 2 we might turn to historical evidence to prove that Socrates was a man. Along the way, we'd want to consider any objections to 1 or 2 and seek to answer them. For example, someone might deny step 2 because he believes that Socrates is just a mythical figure and not a real man. We'd have to show why the evidence suggests that this belief is mistaken.

Steps 1 and 2 in this argument are called *premises*. If you obey the rules of logic and your premises are true, then your conclusion must be true as well.

Now the determined skeptic can deny any conclusion simply by denying one of the premises. You can't force someone to accept the conclusion if he's willing to pay the price of rejecting one of the premises. But what you can do is raise the price of rejecting the conclusion by giving good evidence for the truth of the premises.

For example, the person who denies premise 2 of the above argument is embracing a historical skepticism that the vast majority of professional historians would find unjustified. So he can reject premise 2 if he wants to, but he pays the price of making himself look like a kook. Such a person can hardly condemn as irrational someone who *does* accept the truth of premise 2.

So in presenting apologetic arguments for some conclusion, we want to raise the price of denying the conclusion as high as we can. We want to help the unbeliever see what it will cost him intellectually to resist the conclusion. Even if *he* is willing to pay that price, he may at least come to see why *we*

The steps of an argument that lead to the conclusion are called the *premises* of the argument.

are not obliged to pay it, and so he may quit ridiculing Christians for being irrational or having no reasons for what we believe. And if he's *not* willing to pay the price, then he may change his mind and come to accept the conclusion we're arguing for.

In presenting the arguments and evidence in this book, I've tried to be *simple* without being *simplistic.* I'll consider the strongest objections to my arguments and offer answers to them. Sometimes the material may be new and difficult for you. I'd encourage you to consider it in small bites, which are easier to digest. You might find it helpful to be part of a small group, where you can discuss the arguments. Don't feel bad if you disagree with me on some points. I want you to think for yourself.

At the end of most chapters you'll find an argument map or outline of the case presented in that chapter. Let me explain how to use the argument map. The map has a "swim lane" format that exhibits my argument in the left-hand lane labeled "Pro." The right-hand lane labeled "Con" exhibits the objections that might be raised by an opponent of the argument. The arrows moving back and forth across the lanes trace the various Pro and Con responses that might be given. These maps will help you to see the big picture.

Consider, for example, the argument map on the facing page:

In the left-hand lane we see the first premise of the argument: "All men are mortal." Following the arrow, we find the evidence given in support of that premise. In this case no response to this premise is offered, and so the "Con" lane remains blank. Next in the "Pro" lane comes the second premise: "Socrates is a man." Here the skeptic does have a response, and so in the "Con" lane we see the objection that "Socrates was just a mythological figure." Following the arrow, we find the answer to this objection, which states succinctly the historical evidence for Socrates' being a real man. Notice that only a very terse summary is provided; reading the argument maps will be no substitute for studying the arguments themselves as they are presented in the text. The argument maps just help you to see the big picture.

SAMPLE ARGUMENT MAP

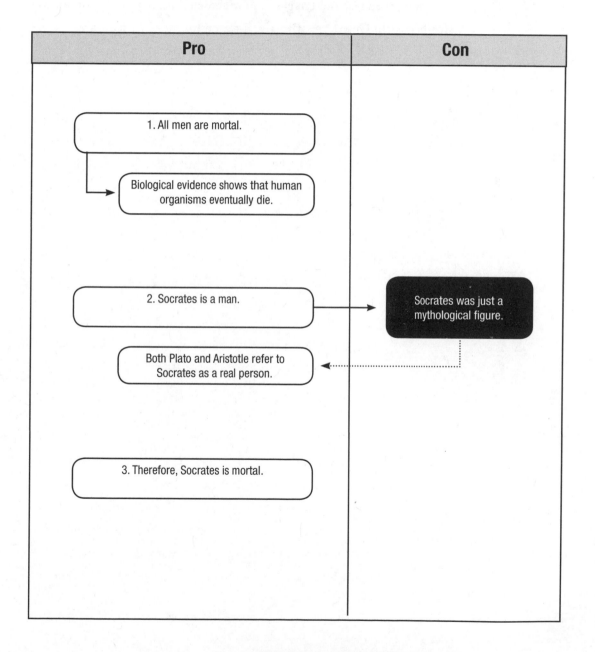

Pro	Con

1. All men are mortal.

Biological evidence shows that human organisms eventually die.

2. Socrates is a man.

Socrates was just a mythological figure.

Both Plato and Aristotle refer to Socrates as a real person.

3. Therefore, Socrates is mortal.

Wouldn't you like to be able to defend your faith intelligently? Wouldn't you like to have some arguments at your fingertips to share with someone who says Christians have no good reasons for what they believe? Aren't you tired of being afraid and intimidated by unbelievers?

If so, then read on! I'm glad you've chosen this book, and I commend you for being On Guard, ready to give a reason for the hope within.

CHAPTER 2

WHAT DIFFERENCE DOES IT MAKE IF GOD EXISTS?

*I considered all that my hands had done and the toil I had spent in doing
it, and again, all was vanity and a chasing after wind. (Eccl. 2:11)*

Jan and I were living in Belgium when the Soviet Union collapsed and the Iron Curtain fell. It was an exciting time to be speaking on university campuses throughout Europe, when such historic, world-changing events were happening before our eyes. On a trip to St. Petersburg (formerly Leningrad) shortly after "the Change," I visited the famous Russian cosmologist Andrei Grib. As we strolled through the Hermitage, viewing its splendid treasures from Russia's czarist past, I asked Andrei about the massive turning to God in Russia that immediately followed the fall of Communism. "Well," he said to me in his thick Russian accent, "in mathematics we have something called 'proof by the opposite.' You can prove something to be true by showing its opposite is false. For seventy years we have tried Marxist atheism in this country, and it didn't work. So everybody figured the opposite must be true!"

Part of the challenge of getting American people to think about God is that they've become so used to God that they just take Him for granted. They never think to ask what the implications would be if God did *not* exist. As a result they think that God is irrelevant. It doesn't matter whether God exists or not.

So before we share with people evidence for God's existence, we may need to help them see why it matters in the first place. Otherwise they just won't care. By showing them the implications of atheism, we can help them to see that the question of God's existence is so much more than merely adding another item to our inventory of things—rather it's an issue that lies at the very center of life's meaning. It therefore touches each of us at the core of his being.

Professor Grib's "proof by the opposite" is also known as *reductio ad absurdum* (reduction to

Reductio ad absurdum,
or reduction to absurdity,
is a form of argument
that proves a statement
by demonstrating that its
opposite is absurd.

_____

Meaning has to do with
significance, why something
matters. *Value* has to do
with good and evil, right
and wrong. *Purpose* has to
do with a goal, a reason for
something.

OBJECTIVE VERSUS
SUBJECTIVE

Something is *objective* if it's
real or true independent of
anyone's opinion about it.
"Water is H_2O" is an objective
fact.
Something is *subjective* if
it's just a matter of personal
opinion. "Vanilla tastes better
than chocolate" is subjective.
You can keep these terms
straight by remembering that
"objective" is like an *object*
that is really there, whereas
"subjective" is like a *subject*
or a person on whose opinion
something depends.

absurdity). This label is especially appropriate when it comes to atheism. Many philosophers, like Jean-Paul Sartre and Albert Camus, have argued that if God does not exist, then life is absurd. Admittedly, Sartre and Camus didn't take this to be a proof of the opposite, namely, that God exists. Rather they concluded that life really *is* absurd. Nevertheless, their analysis of human existence shows us clearly the grim implications of atheism.

The absurdity of life without God may not prove that God exists, but it does show that the question of God's existence is the most important question a person can ask. No one who truly grasps the implications of atheism can say, "Whatever!" about whether there is a God.

Now when I use the word *God* in this context, I mean an all-powerful, perfectly good Creator of the world who offers us eternal life. If such a God does not exist, then life is absurd. That is to say, life has no ultimate meaning, value, or purpose.

These three notions—meaning, value, and purpose—though closely related, are distinct. *Meaning* has to do with significance, why something matters. *Value* has to do with good and evil, right and wrong. *Purpose* has to do with a goal, a reason for something.

My claim is that if there is no God, then meaning, value, and purpose are ultimately human illusions. They're just in our heads. If atheism is true, then life is really objectively meaningless, valueless, and purposeless, despite our subjective beliefs to the contrary.

This point is worth underscoring, since it's so frequently misunderstood. I'm not saying that atheists experience life as dull and meaningless, that they have no personal values or lead immoral lives, that they have no goals or purpose for living. On the contrary, life would be unbearable and unlivable without such beliefs. But my point is that, given atheism, these beliefs are all subjective illusions: the mere *appearance* of meaning, value, and purpose, even though, objectively speaking, there really isn't any. If God does not exist, our lives are ultimately meaningless, valueless, and purposeless despite how desperately we cling to the illusion to the contrary.

The Absurdity of Life without God

If God does not exist, then both man and the universe are inevitably doomed to death. Man, like all biological organisms, must die. With no hope of immortality, man's life leads only to the grave. His life is but a spark in the infinite blackness, a spark that appears, flickers, and dies forever.

Therefore, everyone must come face-to-face with what theologian Paul Tillich has called "the threat of nonbeing." For though I know now that I exist, that I am alive, I also know that someday I will no longer exist, that I will no longer be, that I will die. This thought is staggering and threatening: to think that the person I call "myself" will cease to exist, that I will be no more!

I remember vividly the first time my father told me that someday I would die. Somehow as a child the thought had just never occurred to me. When he told me, I was filled with fear and unbearable sadness. And though he tried repeatedly to reassure me that this was a long way off, that didn't seem to matter. Whether sooner or later, the undeniable fact was that *I was going to die*, and the thought overwhelmed me.

Eventually, like all of us, I grew to simply accept the fact. We all learn to live with the inevitable. But the child's insight remains true. As Sartre observed, several hours or several years make no difference once you have lost eternity.

And the universe, too, faces a death of its own. Scientists tell us that the universe is expanding, and the galaxies are growing farther and farther apart. As it does so, it grows colder and colder as its energy is used up. Eventually all the stars will burn out, and all matter will collapse into dead stars and black holes. There will be no light; there will be no heat; there will be no life; only the corpses of dead stars and galaxies, ever expanding into the endless darkness and the cold recesses of space—a universe in ruins.

This is not science fiction: This is *really going to happen*, unless God intervenes. Not only is the life of each individual person doomed; the entire human race and the whole edifice and accomplishment of human civilization is doomed. Like prisoners condemned to death, we await our unavoidable execution. There is no escape. There is no hope.

A MAN SAID TO

THE UNIVERSE

Stephen Crane

A man said to the universe:
"Sir I exist!"
"However," replied the
    universe,
"The fact has not created
    in me
A sense of obligation."

And what is the consequence of this? It means that life itself becomes absurd. It means that the life we do have is without ultimate significance, value, or purpose. Let's look at each of these.

No Ultimate Meaning

If each individual person passes out of existence when he dies, then what ultimate meaning can be given to his life? Does it really matter in the end whether he ever existed at all? Sure, his life may be important *relative* to certain other events, but what's the ultimate significance of any of those events? If everything is doomed to destruction, then what does it matter that you influenced anything? Ultimately it makes no difference.

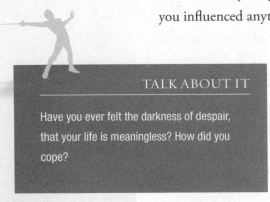

TALK ABOUT IT

Have you ever felt the darkness of despair, that your life is meaningless? How did you cope?

Mankind is thus no more significant than a swarm of mosquitoes or a barnyard of pigs, for their end is all the same. The same blind cosmic process that coughed them up in the first place will eventually swallow them all again. The contributions of the scientist to the advance of human knowledge, the researches of the doctor to alleviate pain and suffering, the efforts of the diplomat to secure peace in the world, the sacrifices of good people everywhere to better the lot of the human race—all these come to nothing. This is the horror of modern man: Because he ends in nothing, he is nothing.

But it's important to see that man needs more than just immortality for life to be meaningful. Mere duration of existence doesn't make that existence meaningful. If man and the universe could exist forever, but if there were no God, their existence would still have no ultimate significance. I once read a science-fiction story in which an astronaut was marooned on a barren chunk of rock lost in outer space. He had with him two vials, one containing poison and the other a potion that would make him live forever. Realizing his predicament, he gulped down the poison. But then to his horror, he discovered he had swallowed the wrong vial—he had drunk the potion for

immortality! And that meant he was cursed to exist forever—a meaningless, unending life.

Now if God does not exist, our lives are just like that. They could go on and on and still be utterly without meaning. We could still ask of life, "So what?" So it's not just immortality man needs if life is to be ultimately significant; he needs God and immortality. And if God does not exist, then he has neither.

Thus, if there is no God, then life itself becomes meaningless. Man and the universe are without ultimate significance.

No Ultimate Value

If life ends at the grave, then it makes no ultimate difference whether you live as a Stalin or as a Mother Teresa. Since your destiny is ultimately unrelated to

TALK ABOUT IT

Name some characters in films who have exemplified the absurdity of life. How do they convey the idea that life is absurd?

your behavior, you may as well just live as you please. As the Russian writer Fyodor Dostoyevsky put it: "If there is no immortality … then all things are permitted."

The state torturers in Soviet prisons understood this all too well. Richard Wurmbrand, a pastor who was tortured for his faith, reports,

> The cruelty of atheism is hard to believe when man has no faith in the reward of good or the punishment of evil. There is no reason to be human. There is no restraint from the depths of evil which is in man. The Communist torturers often said, "There is no God, no hereafter, no punishment for evil. We can do what we wish." I have heard one torturer even say, "I thank God, in whom I don't believe, that I have lived to this hour when I can express all the evil in my heart." He expressed it in unbelievable brutality and torture infl[i]cted on prisoners.[1]

Given the finality of death, it really does not matter how you live. So what do you say to someone who concludes that we may as well just live as we please, out of pure self-interest?

Somebody might say that it's in our best self-interest to adopt a moral lifestyle. You scratch my back, and I'll scratch yours! But clearly, that's not always true: We all know situations in which self-interest runs smack in the face of morality. Moreover, if you're sufficiently powerful, like a Ferdinand Marcos or a Papa Doc Duvalier or even a Donald Trump, then you can pretty much ignore the dictates of conscience and safely live in self-indulgence.

Historian Stewart C. Easton sums it up well when he writes, "There is no objective reason why man should be moral, unless morality 'pays off' in his social life or makes him 'feel good.' There is no objective reason why man should do anything save for the pleasure it affords him."[2]

But the problem becomes even worse. For, regardless of immortality, if there is no God, then there is no objective standard of right and wrong.

All we're confronted with is, in Sartre's words, "the bare, valueless fact of existence." Moral values are either just expressions of personal taste or the by-products of biological evolution and social conditioning.

After all, on the atheistic view, there's nothing special about human beings. They're just accidental by-products of nature that have evolved relatively recently on an infinitesimal speck of dust called the planet Earth, lost somewhere in a hostile and mindless universe, and which are doomed to perish individually and collectively in a relatively short time. Richard Dawkins' assessment of human worth may be depressing, but why, given atheism, is he mistaken when he says, "There is at bottom no design, no purpose, no evil, no good, nothing but pointless indifference.... We are machines for propagating DNA.... It is every living object's sole reason for being"?[3]

In a world without God, who's to say whose values are right and whose are wrong? There can be no objective right and wrong, only our culturally and personally relative, subjective judgments. Think of what that means! It means it's impossible to condemn war, oppression, or crime as evil. Nor can you praise generosity, self-sacrifice, and love as good. To kill someone or to love someone is morally equivalent. For in a universe without God, good and evil do not exist—there is only the bare, valueless fact of existence, and there is no one to say you are right and I am wrong.

TALK ABOUT IT

How would you live if you believed that humans are simply machines for propagating their DNA?

No Ultimate Purpose

If death stands with open arms at the end of life's trail, then what is the goal of life? Is it all for nothing? Is there no reason for life? And what of the universe? Is it utterly pointless? If its destiny is a cold grave in the recesses of outer space, the answer must be, yes—it is pointless. There is no goal, no purpose for the universe. The litter of a dead universe will just go on expanding and expanding—forever.

And what of man? Is there no purpose at all for the human race? Or will it simply peter out someday, lost in the oblivion of an indifferent universe? The English writer H. G. Wells foresaw such a prospect. In his novel *The Time Machine*, Wells' time traveler journeys far into the future to discover the destiny of man. All he finds is a dead earth, except for a few lichens and moss, orbiting a gigantic red sun. The only sounds are the rush of the wind and the gentle ripple of the sea. "Beyond these lifeless sounds," writes Wells, "the world was silent. Silent? It would be hard to convey the stillness of it. All the sounds of man, the bleating of sheep, the cries of birds, the hum of insects, the stir that makes the background of our lives—all that was over."[4] And so Wells' time traveler returned.

But to what?—to merely an earlier point on the same purposeless rush toward oblivion. When as a non-Christian I first read Wells' book, I thought, *No, no! It can't end that way!* But if there is no God, it *will* end that way, like it or not. This is reality in a universe without God: There is no hope; there is no purpose.

What is true of mankind as a whole is true of each of us individually: We are here to no purpose. If there is no God, then your life is not qualitatively different from that of an animal. As the ancient writer of Ecclesiastes put it: "The fate of the sons of men and the fate of beasts is the same. As one dies so

OZYMANDIAS

PERCY BYSSHE SHELLEY

I met a traveller from an antique land
Who said: Two vast and trunkless legs of stone
Stand in the desert. Near them on the sand
Half sunk, a shatter'd visage lies, whose frown
And wrinkled lip and sneer of cold command
Tell that its sculptor well those passions read
Which yet survive, stamp'd on these lifeless things,
The hand that mock'd them and the heart that fed.
And on the pedestal these words appear:

"My name is Ozymandias, king of kings:
"Look on my works, ye Mighty, and despair!"
Nothing beside remains. Round the decay
Of that colossal wreck, boundless and bare,
The lone and level sands stretch far away.

dies the other; indeed, they all have the same breath and there is no advantage for man over beast, for all is vanity. All go to the same place. All came from the dust and all return to the dust" (Eccl. 3:19–20 NASB).

In this ancient work—which reads more like a piece of modern existentialist literature than a book of the Bible—the author shows the futility of pleasure, wealth, education, political fame, and honor in a life doomed to end in death. His verdict? "Vanity of vanities! All is vanity" (1:2 NASB). If life ends at the grave, then we have no ultimate purpose for living.

But more than that, even if life did not end in death, without God life would still be without purpose. For man and the universe would then be simply accidents of chance, thrust into existence for no reason. Without God the universe is the result of a cosmic accident, a chance explosion. There is no reason for which it exists. As for man, he's a freak of nature—a blind product of matter plus time plus chance. If God does not exist, then you are just a miscarriage of nature, thrust into a purposeless universe to live a purposeless life.

So if God does not exist, that means that man and the universe exist to no purpose—since the end of everything is death—and that they came to be for no purpose, since they are only blind products of chance. In short, life is utterly without reason.

I hope you begin to understand the gravity of the alternatives before us. For if God exists, then there is hope for man. But if God does not exist, then all we are left with is despair. As one writer has aptly put it, "If God is dead, then man is dead too."

Living in Denial

Unfortunately, most people don't realize this fact. They continue on as though nothing has changed. I'm reminded of the story told by the nineteenth-century atheist philosopher Friedrich Nietzsche of a madman, who in the early morning hours burst into the marketplace, lantern in hand, crying, "I seek God! I seek God!" Since many of those standing about did not believe in God, he provoked much laughter. "Did God get lost?" they taunted him.

There is no advantage for man over beast, for all is vanity. All go to the same place. All come from the dust and all return to the dust.
—Eccl. 3:19–20 NASB

"Or is He hiding? Or maybe He has gone on a voyage or emigrated!" Thus they yelled and laughed. Then, writes Nietzsche, the madman turned in their midst and pierced them with his eyes.

> "Whither is God?" he cried, "I shall tell you. We have killed him—you and I. All of us are his murderers. But how have we done this? How were we able to drink up the sea? Who gave us the sponge to wipe away the entire horizon? What did we do when we unchained this earth from its sun? Whither is it moving now?… Away from all suns? Are we not plunging continually? Backward, sideward, forward, in all directions? Is there any up or down left? Are we not straying as through an infinite nothing? Do we not feel the breath of empty space? Has it not become colder? Is not night and more night coming on all the while? Must not lanterns be lit in the morning? Do we not hear anything yet of the noise of the gravediggers who are burying God?… God is dead.… And we have killed him. How shall we, the murderers of all murderers, comfort ourselves?"[5]

The crowd stared at the madman in silence and astonishment. At last he dashed his lantern to the ground. "I have come too early," he said. "This tremendous event is still on its way—it has not yet reached the ears of man."

People did not yet comprehend the consequences of the death of God; but Nietzsche predicted that someday modern man would realize the implications of atheism, and this realization would usher in an age of nihilism—the destruction of all meaning and value in life.

Most people still do not reflect on the consequences of atheism and so, like the crowd in the marketplace, go unknowingly on their way. But when we realize, as did Nietzsche, what

TALK ABOUT IT

Are the people you know willing to face up to the consequences of atheism? Why are they or aren't they?

atheism implies, then his question presses hard upon us: How shall we, the murderers of all murderers, comfort ourselves?

The Practical Impossibility of Atheism

About the only solution the atheist can offer is that we face the absurdity of life and live bravely. The British philosopher Bertrand Russell, for example, believed that we have no choice but to build our lives upon "the firm foundation of unyielding despair." Only by recognizing that the world really is a terrible place can we successfully come to terms with life. Camus said that we should honestly recognize life's absurdity and then live in love for one another.

The fundamental problem with this solution, however, is that it's impossible to live consistently and happily within the framework of such a worldview. If you live consistently, you will not be happy; if you live happily, it is only because you are not consistent.

Francis Schaeffer has explained this point well. Modern man, says Schaeffer, resides in a two-story universe. In the lower story is the finite world without God; here life is absurd, as we have seen. In the upper story are meaning, value, and purpose. Now modern man lives in the lower story because he believes there is no God. But he cannot live happily in such an absurd world; therefore, he continually makes leaps of faith into the upper story to affirm meaning,

ALBERT CAMUS (1913–1960)

French existentialist novelist. Since there is no God, Camus regarded life as absurd. Life is not merely meaningless but twisted and cruel. Suicide is the only serious philosophical question. Despite life's absurdity, Camus argued against suicide and for promoting human brotherhood.

value, and purpose, even though he has no right to, since he does not believe in God.

Let's look again, then, at each of the three areas in which we saw that life was absurd without God, to see how difficult it is to live consistently and happily with an atheistic worldview.

Meaning of Life

First, the area of meaning. We saw that without God, life has no meaning. Yet philosophers continue to live as though life does have meaning. For example, Sartre argued that one may create meaning for his life by freely choosing to follow a certain course of action. Sartre himself chose Marxism.

Now this is totally inconsistent. It is inconsistent to say life is objectively absurd and then to say you may create meaning for your life. If life is really absurd, then you're trapped in the lower story. To try to create meaning in life represents a leap to the upper story. But Sartre has no basis for this leap. Sartre's program is actually an exercise in self-delusion. For the universe doesn't really acquire a meaning just because *I* happen to give it one. This is easy to see: Suppose I give the universe one meaning, and you give it another. Who's right? The answer, of course, is neither one. For the universe without God remains objectively meaningless, no matter how *we* happen to regard it. Sartre is really saying, "Let's *pretend* the universe has meaning." And this is just fooling yourself.

The point is this: If God does not exist, then life is objectively meaningless; but man cannot live consistently and happily knowing that life is meaningless; so in order to be happy he pretends life has meaning. But this is, of course, entirely inconsistent—for without God, man and the universe are without any real significance.

Value of Life

Turn now to the problem of value. Here is where the most blatant inconsistencies occur. First of all, atheistic humanists are totally inconsistent in affirming the traditional values of love and brotherhood. Camus has been rightly criticized for inconsistently holding *both* to the absurdity of life *and* the ethics of human love and brotherhood. The view that there are no values is logically incompatible with affirming the values of love and brotherhood. Bertrand Russell, too, was inconsistent. For though he was an atheist, he was an outspoken social critic,

---

JEAN-PAUL SARTRE (1905–1980)

French existentialist philosopher. Taking Nietzsche's proclamation of God's death as given, Sartre denied that there are any objective values or meaning to life to be discovered. Rather each person is free to invent for himself whatever values and purposes he chooses. Sartre struggled to reconcile this apparent libertinism with his opposition to Nazi anti-Semitism.

denouncing war and restrictions on sexual freedom. Russell admitted that he could not live as though ethical values were simply a matter of personal taste, and that he therefore found his own views "incredible." "I do not know the solution," he confessed.[6]

The point is that if there is no God, then objective right and wrong do not exist. As Dostoyevsky said, "All things are permitted." But man cannot live this way. So he makes a leap of faith and affirms values anyway. And when he does so, he reveals the inadequacy of a world without God.

The horror of a world devoid of value was brought home to me with new intensity several years ago as I watched a BBC television documentary called *The Gathering*. It concerned the reunion of survivors of the Holocaust in Jerusalem, where they rediscovered lost friendships and shared their experiences. One former prisoner, a nurse, told of how she was made the gynecologist at Auschwitz. She observed that pregnant women were grouped together by the soldiers under the direction of Dr. Josef Mengele and housed in the same barracks. Some time passed, and she noted that she no longer saw any of these women. She made inquiries. "Where are the pregnant women who were housed in that barracks?" "Haven't you heard?" came the reply. "Dr. Mengele used them for *vivisection*."

Another woman told of how Mengele had bound up her breasts so that she could not suckle her infant. The doctor wanted to learn how long an infant could survive without nourishment. Desperately this poor woman tried to keep her baby alive by giving it pieces of bread soaked in coffee, but to no avail. Each day the baby lost weight, a fact that was eagerly monitored by Dr. Mengele. A nurse then came secretly to this woman and told her, "I have arranged a way for you to get out of here, but you cannot take your baby with you. I have brought a morphine injection that you can give to your child to end its life." When the woman protested, the nurse was insistent: "Look, your baby is going to die anyway. At least save yourself." And so this mother felt compelled *to take the life of her own baby*. Dr. Mengele was furious when he learned of it because he had lost his experimental specimen, and he searched among the dead to find the baby's discarded corpse so that he could have one last weighing.

My heart was torn by these stories. One rabbi who survived the camp summed it up well when he said that at Auschwitz it was as though there existed a world in which all the Ten Commandments were reversed. Mankind had never seen such a hell.

And yet, if God does not exist, then in a sense, our world *is* Auschwitz: There is no right and wrong; *all things* are permitted.

But no atheist, no agnostic, can live consistently with such a view. Nietzsche himself, who proclaimed the necessity of living beyond good and evil, broke with his mentor Richard Wagner precisely over the issue of the composer's anti-Semitism and strident German nationalism. Similarly, Sartre, writing in the aftermath of the Second World War, condemned anti-Semitism, declaring that a doctrine that leads to mass extermination is not merely an opinion or matter of personal taste of equal value with its opposite. In his important essay "Existentialism Is a Humanism," Sartre struggles vainly to elude the contradiction between his denial of divinely preestablished values and his urgent desire to affirm the value of human persons. Like Russell, he could not live with the implications of his own denial of ethical absolutes.

Neither can the so-called New Atheists like Richard Dawkins. For although he says that there is no evil, no good, nothing but pitiless indifference, he is an unabashed moralist. He vigorously condemns such actions as the harassment and abuse of homosexuals, religious indoctrination of children, the Incan practice of human sacrifice, and prizing cultural diversity over the interests of Amish children. He even goes so far as to offer his own amended Ten Commandments for guiding moral behavior, all the while marvelously oblivious to the contradiction with his ethical subjectivism.

TALK ABOUT IT

Why do you suppose that even smart atheists often don't care that their ideas about right and wrong are inconsistent?

Indeed, one will probably never find an atheist who lives consistently with his system. For a universe without moral accountability and devoid of value is unimaginably terrible.

Purpose of Life

Finally, let's look at the problem of purpose in life. The only way most people who deny purpose in life live happily is either by making up some purpose—which amounts to self-delusion, as we saw with Sartre—or by not carrying their view to its logical conclusions. The temptation to invest one's own petty plans and projects with objective significance and thereby to find some purpose to one's life is almost irresistible.

For example, the outspoken atheist and Nobel Prize–winning physicist Steven Weinberg, at the close of his much-acclaimed book *The First Three Minutes,* writes,

> It is almost irresistible for humans to believe that we have some special relation to the universe, that human life is not just a more-or-less farcical outcome of a chain of accidents reaching back to the first three minutes, but that somehow we were built in from the beginning.… It is very hard to realize that this all is just a tiny part of an overwhelmingly hostile universe. It is even harder to realize that this present universe has evolved from an unspeakably unfamiliar early condition, and faces a future extinction of endless cold or intolerable heat. The more the universe seems comprehensible, the more it also seems pointless.

> But if there is no solace in the fruits of our research, there is at least some consolation in the research itself. Men and women are not content to comfort themselves with tales of gods and giants, or to confine their thoughts to the daily affairs of life; they also build telescopes and satellites and

accelerators, and sit at their desks for endless hours working out the meaning of the data they gather. The effort to understand the universe is one of the very few things that lifts human life a little above the level of farce, and gives it some of the grace of tragedy.[8]

There's something strange about Weinberg's moving description of the human predicament: *Tragedy* is not a neutral term. It expresses an *evaluation* of a situation. Weinberg evidently sees a life devoted to scientific pursuits as truly meaningful, and therefore it's tragic that such a noble pursuit should be extinguished. But why, given atheism, should the pursuit of science be any different from slouching about doing nothing? Since there is no objective purpose to human life, none of our pursuits has any objective significance, however important and dear they may seem to us subjectively. They're no more significant than shuffling deck chairs on the *Titanic*.

The Human Predicament

The dilemma of modern man is thus truly terrible. The atheistic worldview is insufficient to maintain a happy and consistent life. Man cannot live consistently and happily as though life were ultimately without meaning, value, or purpose. If we try to live consistently within the atheistic worldview, we shall find ourselves profoundly unhappy. If instead we manage to live happily, it is only by giving the lie to our worldview.

TALK ABOUT IT

Think of a movie you've seen recently. If you asked the main character, "Why does your life matter?" what do you think he or she would say?

Confronted with this dilemma, modern man flounders pathetically for some means of escape. In a remarkable address to the American Academy for the Advancement of Science in 1991, Dr. L. D. Rue, confronted with the predicament of modern man, boldly advocated that we deceive ourselves by means of some "Noble Lie" into thinking that we and the universe still have value.

According to Rue, "The lesson of the past two centuries is that intellectual and moral relativism is profoundly the case." He says that the consequence of this realization is that the quest for self-fulfillment and the quest for social coherence fall apart. This is because on the view of relativism the search for self-fulfillment becomes radically privatized: Each person chooses his *own* set of values and meaning.

So what are we to do? Rue says there is on the one hand "the madhouse option": We just pursue self-fulfillment regardless of social coherence. On the other hand, there is "the totalitarian option": The state imposes social coherence at the expense of people's personal fulfillment. If we're to avoid these two options, he says, then we have no choice but to embrace some Noble Lie that will inspire us to live beyond selfish interests and so voluntarily achieve social coherence. A Noble Lie "is one that deceives us, tricks us, compels us beyond self-interest, beyond ego, beyond family, nation, [and] race." It is a lie because it tells us that the universe is infused with value (which is a great fiction), because it makes a claim to universal truth (when there is none), and because it tells me not to live for self-interest (which is evidently false). "But without such lies, we cannot live."

This is the dreadful verdict pronounced over modern man. In order to survive, he must live in self-deception.

My Story

The absurdity of life is more than just an academic affair. It touches us at the core of our being. I know. As a teenager I felt deeply the meaninglessness of life and the despair that it brings.

Although I had been raised in a good and loving home, we weren't a churchgoing family, much less a Christian family. But when I became a teenager, I began to ask the big questions of life: "Who am I?" "Why am I here?" "Where am I going?" In the search for answers I began to attend a large church in our community. But instead of answers, all I found was a social country club where the dues were a dollar a week in the offering plate. The other high school students who were involved in the youth group and claimed to be Christians

NOBLE LIE

A Noble Lie "is one that deceives us, tricks us, compels us beyond self-interest, beyond ego, beyond family, nation, [and] race."
—Dr. L. D. Rue

on Sunday lived for their real God the rest of the week, which was popularity. They seemed willing to do whatever it took to be popular.

This really bothered me. *They claim to be Christians, but I'm leading a better life than they are,* I thought. *Yet I feel so empty inside. They must be just as empty as I am, but they're just pretending to be something they're not. They're all just a pack of hypocrites!* I began to grow very bitter toward the institutional church and the people in it.

In time this attitude spread toward other people. *Nobody is really genuine,* I thought. *They're all just a bunch of phonies, holding up a plastic mask to the world, while the real person is cowering down inside, afraid to come out and be real.* So my anger and resentment spread toward people in general. I grew to despise people; I wanted nothing to do with them. *I don't need people,* I thought, and I threw myself into my studies. Frankly, I was on my way toward becoming a very alienated young man.

And yet—in moments of introspection and honesty, I knew deep down inside that I really did want to love and be loved by others. I realized in that moment that I was just as much a phony as they were. For here I was, pretending not to need people, when deep down I knew that I really did. So that anger and hatred turned in upon myself for my own hypocrisy and phoniness.

I don't know if you understand what this is like, but this kind of inner anger and despair just eats away at your insides, making every day miserable, another day to *get through.* I couldn't see any purpose to life; nothing really mattered.

One day when I was feeling particularly crummy, I walked into my high school German class and sat down behind a girl who was one of those types who is *always so happy* it just makes you sick! So I tapped her on the shoulder, and she turned around, and I growled, "Sandy, what are you always so happy about, anyway?"

"Well, Bill," she said, "it's because I'm saved!"

I was stunned. I had never heard language like this before.

"You're *what?*" I demanded.

"I know Jesus Christ as my personal Savior," she explained.

"I go to church," I said lamely.

"That's not enough, Bill," she said. "You've got to have Him really living in your heart."

That was the limit! "What would He want to do a thing like that for?" I demanded.

"Because He loves you, Bill."

That hit me like a ton of bricks. Here I was, so filled with anger and hate, and she said there was someone who really loved me. And who was it but the God of the universe! That thought just staggered me. To think that the God of the universe should love *me,* Bill Craig, that worm down there on that speck of dust called planet Earth! I just couldn't take it in.

That began for me the most agonizing period of soul-searching that I've ever been through. I got a New Testament and read it from cover to cover. And as I did, I was absolutely captivated by the person of Jesus of Nazareth. There was a wisdom about His teaching I had never encountered before and an authenticity in His life that wasn't characteristic of those people who claimed to be His followers in the local church I was attending. I knew that I couldn't throw the baby out with the bathwater.

Meanwhile, Sandy introduced me to other Christian students in the high school. I had never met people like this! Whatever they said about Jesus, what was undeniable was that they were living life on a plane of reality that I didn't even dream existed, and it imparted a deep meaning and joy to their lives, which I craved.

To make a long story short, my spiritual search went on for the next six months. I attended Christian meetings; I read Christian books; I sought God in prayer. Finally I just came to the end of my rope and cried out to God. I cried out all the anger and bitterness that had built up inside me, and at the same time I felt this tremendous infusion of joy, like a balloon being blown up and blown up until it was ready to burst! I remember I rushed outdoors— it was a clear Midwestern summer night, and you could see the Milky Way stretched from horizon to horizon. As I looked up at the stars, I thought, *God! I've come to know God!*

That moment changed my whole life. I had thought enough about this message during those six months to realize that if it were really the truth—really *the truth*—then I could do nothing less than spend my entire life spreading this wonderful message among mankind.

For many Christians, the main difference they find in coming to know Christ is the love or the joy or the peace it brings. All of those things were thrilling for me, too. But if you were to ask me what is the main difference Christ has made in my life, without hesitation I would say, "Meaning!" I knew the blackness, the despair, of a life lived apart from God. Knowing God suddenly brought eternal significance to my life. Now the things I did were charged with eternal meaning. Now life mattered. Now every day I could wake up to another day of walking with Him.

TALK ABOUT IT:

Do you have a deep sense that your life matters? If so, what gives you that sense? If not, why do you suppose you don't?

The Success of Biblical Christianity

Biblical Christianity thus challenges the worldview of modern man. For according to the Christian worldview, God *does* exist, and life does *not* end at the grave. Biblical Christianity therefore provides the two conditions necessary for a meaningful, valuable, and purposeful life: God and immortality. Because of this, we can live consistently and happily within the framework of our worldview. Thus, biblical Christianity succeeds precisely where atheism breaks down.

Now none of this shows that biblical Christianity is true. The atheist might smugly say that I have embraced a Noble Lie and am self-deceived. So we'll examine the arguments for and against the existence of God in the following chapters. But for the time being, at least what we've done is to clearly spell out the alternatives. If God does not exist, then life is futile. If God does exist, then life is meaningful. Only the second of these two alternatives enables us to live happily and consistently. Therefore, it makes a huge *difference* whether God exists.

Moreover, it seems to me that even if the evidence for these two options were absolutely equal, a rational person ought to choose to believe in God. That is, if the evidence is equal, it seems to me positively irrational to prefer death, futility, and destruction to life, meaningfulness, and happiness. As Pascal said, we have nothing to lose and infinity to gain.

But my goal in this chapter is actually more modest than that. By sharing the absurdity of life without God, I only hope to have gotten you *to think* about these issues, to realize that the question of God's existence has profound consequences for our lives and that therefore we cannot afford to be indifferent about it. If we can achieve that much in sharing with an unbeliever, we are well on our way.

1. Richard Wurmbrand, *Tortured for Christ* (London: Hodder & Stoughton, 1967), 34.
2. Stewart C. Easton, *The Western Heritage*, 2nd ed. (New York: Holt, Rinehart, & Winston, 1966), 878.
3. Cited in Lewis Wolpert, *Six Impossible Things before Breakfast* (New York: W.W. Norton & Co, 2008), 215. Unfortunately, Wolpert's reference is mistaken. The quotation seems to be a pastiche from Richard Dawkins, *River out of Eden: a Darwinian View of Life* (New York: Basic Books, 1996), 133; and Richard Dawkins, "The Ultraviolet Garden," Lecture 4 of 7 Royal Institution Christmas Lectures, London 1991). Thanks to my assistant Joe Gorra for tracking down this reference!
4. H.G. Wells, *The Time Machine* (New York: Berkeley, 1957).
5. Friedrich Nietzsche, "The Gay Science," in *The Portable Nietzsche*, ed. and trans. W. Kaufmann (New York: Viking, 1954), 95.
6. Bertrand Russell, letter to the editor, *The Observer*, October 6, 1957.
7. Richard Dawkins, *The God Delusion* (New York: Houghton-Mifflin, 2006), 23, 264, 313–17, 326, 328, 330.
8. Steven Weinberg, *The First Three Minutes* (London: Andre Deutsch, 1977), 154–155.

I. If God does not exist, then all human life as well as every individual life will eventually be destroyed.

II. If there is no God and no life beyond the grave, then life itself has no objective meaning, value, or purpose.

   A. Meaning

      1. Without immortality your life has no ultimate significance and makes no difference to the world's outcome.

      2. Without God there is no broader framework within which man's life can be seen to matter.

   B. Value

      1. Without immortality there is no moral accountability, and your moral choices become inconsequential.

      2. Without God moral values are just delusions ingrained into us by evolution and social conditioning.

   C. Purpose

      1. Without immortality your only destination is extinction in death.

      2. Without God there is no purpose for which you came into this world.

III. It is impossible to live consistently and happily with an atheistic worldview.

   A. If we live happily as atheists, it is only by inconsistently affirming meaning, value, and purpose for our lives, despite the lack of foundation for them.

   B. If we live consistently as atheists, we shall be profoundly unhappy and even in despair because we know our lives are really meaningless, worthless, and purposeless.

IV. Biblical Christianity challenges the worldview of modern man.

   A. According to biblical Christianity God exists and life does not end at the grave.

B. Biblical Christianity thereby affirms the two conditions sufficient for a meaningful, valuable, and purposeful life: God and immortality.

C. Biblical Christianity therefore supplies a framework within which one can live consistently and happily.

D. So why not look into the truth of biblical Christianity?

CHAPTER 3

WHY DOES ANYTHING AT ALL EXIST?

In the beginning was the Word, and the Word was with God, and the Word was God.... All things came into being through him, and without him not one thing came into being. (John 1:1, 3)

Keokuk was a great place for a boy to grow up. On the banks of the mighty Mississippi River, in the southeastern toe of Iowa that hangs down over Missouri, Keokuk is Mark Twain territory. As kids, we had every kind of pet we could catch: frogs, toads, snakes, salamanders, rabbits, birds, stray dogs and cats that wandered by our house, even a bat and a possum. You could see the stars clearly at night in Keokuk, too. I remember as a boy looking up at the stars, innumerable in the black night, and thinking, *Where did all of this come from?* It seemed to me instinctively that there had to be an explanation why all this exists. As long as I can remember, then, I've always believed in a Creator of the universe. I just never knew Him personally.

Only years later did I realize that my boyhood question, as well as its answer, had occupied the minds of the greatest philosophers for centuries. For example, G. W. Leibniz, codiscoverer of calculus and a towering intellect of eighteenth-century Europe, wrote: "The first question which should rightly be asked is: *Why is there something rather than nothing?*"[1]

In other words, why does anything at all exist? This, for Leibniz, is the most basic question that anyone can ask. Like me, Leibniz came to the conclusion that the answer is to be found, not in the universe of created things, but in God. God exists necessarily and is the explanation why anything else exists.

Leibniz's Argument

We can put Leibniz's thinking into the form of a simple argument. This has the advantage of making his logic very clear and focusing our attention on the crucial steps of his reasoning. It also makes his

Gottfried Wilhelm Leibniz (1646–1716) was a German philosopher, mathematician, and logician. He invented differential and integral calculus at about the same time Sir Isaac Newton did. In fact, he spent the last five years of his life defending himself against the accusation that he had stolen Newton's ideas and published them. Today most historians agree that Leibniz did invent calculus independently.

argument very easy to memorize so that we can share it with others. (You'll find an argument map at the end of this chapter.)

There are three steps or premises in Leibniz's reasoning:

1. Everything that exists has an explanation of its existence.

2. If the universe has an explanation of its existence, that explanation is God.

3. The universe exists.

That's it! Now what follows logically from these three premises?

Well, look at premises 1 and 3. (Read them out loud if that helps.) If *everything that exists has an explanation of its existence* and *the universe exists*, then it logically follows that:

4. The universe has an explanation of its existence.

Now notice that premise 2 says that if the universe has an explanation of its existence, that explanation is God. And 4 says the universe does have an explanation of its existence. So from 2 and 4 the conclusion logically follows:

5. Therefore, the explanation of the universe's existence is God.

Now this is a logically airtight argument. That is to say, if the three premises are true, then the conclusion is

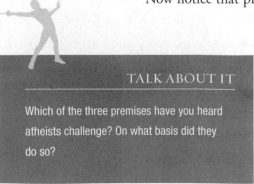

TALK ABOUT IT

Which of the three premises have you heard atheists challenge? On what basis did they do so?

unavoidable. It doesn't matter if the atheist or agnostic doesn't like the conclusion. It doesn't matter if he has other objections to God's existence. So long as he grants the premises, he has to accept the conclusion. So if he wants to reject the conclusion, he has to say that one of the three premises is false.

But which one will he reject? Premise 3 is undeniable for any sincere seeker after truth. Obviously the universe exists! So the atheist is going to have to deny either 1 or 2 if he wants to remain an atheist and be rational. So the whole question comes down to this: Are premises 1 and 2 true, or are they false? Well, let's look at them.

PREMISE I

Everything that exists has an explanation of its existence.

An Objection to Premise 1: God Must Have an Explanation of His Existence

At first blush premise 1 might seem vulnerable in an obvious way. If everything that exists has an explanation of its existence, and God exists, then God must have an explanation of His existence! But that seems out of the question, for then the explanation of God's existence would be some other being greater than God. Since that's impossible, premise 1 must be false. Some things must be able to exist without any explanation. The believer will say God exists inexplicably. The atheist will say, "Why not stop with the universe? The universe just exists inexplicably." So we seem to reach a stalemate.

Answer to the Objection: Some Things Exist Necessarily

Not so fast! This obvious objection to premise 1 is based on a misunderstanding of what Leibniz meant by an "explanation." In Leibniz's view there are two kinds of things: (a) things that exist necessarily and (b) things that are produced by some external cause. Let me explain.

(a) Things that exist necessarily exist by a necessity of their own nature. It's

NECESSARY OR

CONTINGENT

Things that *exist necessarily* exist by a necessity of their own nature. It belongs to their very nature to exist. Things that *exist contingently* can fail to exist and so need an external cause to explain why they do in fact exist.

impossible for them not to exist. Many mathematicians think that numbers, sets, and other mathematical entities exist in this way. They're not caused to exist by something else; they just exist by the necessity of their own nature.

(b) By contrast, things that are caused to exist by something else don't exist necessarily. They exist because something else has produced them. Familiar physical objects like people, planets, and galaxies belong in this category.

So when Leibniz says that everything that exists has an explanation of its existence, the explanation may be found *either* in the necessity of a thing's nature or else in some external cause. So premise 1 could be more fully stated in the following way:

> 1. Everything that exists has an explanation of its existence, either in the necessity of its own nature or in an external cause.

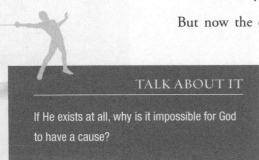

TALK ABOUT IT

If He exists at all, why is it impossible for God to have a cause?

But now the objection falls to the ground. The explanation of God's existence lies in the necessity of His own nature. As even the atheist recognizes, it's impossible for God to have a cause. So Leibniz's argument is really an argument for God as a necessary, uncaused being.

Far from undermining Leibniz's argument, the atheist's objection to premise 1 actually helps to clarify and magnify who God is! If God exists, He is a necessarily existing, uncaused being.

Defense of Premise 1: Size Doesn't Matter

So what reason might be offered for thinking that premise 1 is true? Well, when you reflect on it, premise 1 has a sort of self-evidence about it. Imagine that you're hiking through the woods and you come across a translucent ball lying on the forest floor. You would naturally wonder how it came to be there. If one of your hiking partners said to you, "Hey, it just exists inexplicably. Don't worry about it!" you'd either think that he was crazy or figure that he just wanted you to keep moving. No one would take seriously the suggestion that the ball existed there with literally no explanation.

Now suppose you increase the size of the ball in this story so that it's the size of a car. That wouldn't do anything to satisfy or remove the demand for an explanation. Suppose it were the size of a house. Same problem. Suppose it were the size of a continent or a planet. Same problem. Suppose it were the size of the entire universe. Same problem. Merely increasing the size of the ball does nothing to affect the need of an explanation.

The Taxicab Fallacy

Sometimes atheists will say that premise 1 is true of everything *in* the universe but is not true *of* the universe itself. Everything in the universe has an explanation, but the universe itself has no explanation.

But this response commits what has been aptly called the "taxicab fallacy." For as the nineteenth-century atheist philosopher Arthur Schopenhauer quipped, premise 1 can't be dismissed like a hack once you've arrived at your desired destination! You can't say everything has an explanation of its existence and then suddenly exempt the universe.

It would be arbitrary for the atheist to claim that the universe is the exception to the rule. (Recall that Leibniz does *not* make God an exception to premise 1.) Our illustration of the ball in the woods showed that merely increasing the size of the object to be explained, even until it becomes the universe itself, does nothing to remove the need for some explanation of its existence.

Notice, too, how unscientific this atheist response is. For modern cosmology (the study of the universe) is devoted to the search for an explanation of the universe's existence. The atheist attitude would cripple science.

Another Atheist Fallacy: It Is Impossible for the Universe to Have an Explanation

So some atheists have tried to *justify* making the universe an exception to premise 1. They say that it's *impossible* for the universe to have an explanation

FALLACY

A *fallacy* is an error in reasoning. Fallacies can be either formal or informal. A formal fallacy involves breaking the rules of logic. An informal fallacy involves an argumentative tactic that is illicit, such as reasoning in a circle. The "taxicab fallacy" would be an informal fallacy.

COSMOLOGY

Cosmology is the study of the large-scale structure and development of the universe. The Greek word *kosmos* means "orderly arrangement" or "world." Pythagoras may have been the first person to use this word to refer to the universe.

of its existence. Why? Because the explanation of the universe would have to be some prior state of affairs in which the universe didn't yet exist. But that would be nothingness, and nothingness can't be the explanation of anything. So the universe must just exist inexplicably.

This line of reasoning is obviously fallacious. For it assumes that the universe is all there is, so that if there were no universe there would be nothing. In other words, the objection assumes that atheism is true! The atheist is thus begging the question, arguing in a circle.

Leibniz would *agree* that the explanation of the universe must be a prior state of affairs in which the universe did not exist. But that state of affairs is God and His will, not nothingness.

So it seems to me that premise 1 is more plausibly true than false, which is all we need for a good argument.

PREMISE 2

If the universe has an explanation of its existence, that explanation is God.

Atheists Agree with Premise 2

What, then, about premise 2, that if the universe has an explanation of its existence, that explanation is God? Is it more plausibly true than false?

What's really awkward for the atheist at this point is that premise 2 is logically equivalent to the typical atheist response to Leibniz's argument. Two statements are logically

---

TALK ABOUT IT

It's hard to imagine nothing. We can imagine empty space, but empty space is something, not nothing. Try to imagine that only God exists. Not the universe, not empty space, not even time. What goes on in your head when you try to conceive of this? Now suppose that not even God exists.

LOGICAL EQUIVALENCE

Two statements are logically equivalent if it is impossible for one to be true and the other false. They are either both true or both false. One of the most important logical equivalences is called *contraposition*. It tells us that any statement of the form "If P, then Q" is logically equivalent to "If not-Q, then not-P." The example in the text of statements A and B is an example of contraposition.

equivalent if it's impossible for one to be true and the other one false. They stand or fall together. So what does the atheist almost always say in response to Leibniz's argument? As we've just seen, the atheist typically asserts the following:

A. If atheism is true, the universe has no explanation of its existence.

This is precisely what the atheist says in response to premise 1. The universe just exists inexplicably. But this is logically equivalent to saying:

B. If the universe has an explanation of its existence, then atheism is not true.

So you can't affirm (A) and deny (B).

But (B) is virtually synonymous with premise 2! (Just compare them.) So by saying in response to premise 1 that, given atheism, the universe has no explanation, the atheist is implicitly admitting premise 2, that if the universe does have an explanation, then God exists.

Another Argument for Premise 2: The Cause of the Universe: Abstract Object or Unembodied Mind?

Besides that, premise 2 is very plausible in its own right. For think of what the universe is: *all* of space-time reality, including *all* matter and energy. It follows that if the universe has a cause of its existence, that cause must be a nonphysical, immaterial being beyond space and time. Amazing!

Now there are only two sorts of things that could fit that description: either an abstract object like a number or else an unembodied mind. But abstract objects can't cause anything. That's part of what it means to be abstract. The number 7, for example, can't cause any effects. So the cause of the existence of the universe must be a transcendent Mind, which is what believers understand God to be.

I hope you begin the grasp the power of Leibniz's argument. If successful, it proves the existence of a necessary, uncaused, timeless, spaceless, immaterial, personal Creator of the universe. This is not some ill-conceived entity like the Flying Spaghetti Monster but an ultramundane being with many of the traditional properties of God. This is truly mind-blowing!

Atheist Alternative: The Universe Exists Necessarily!

What can the atheist do at this point? He has a more radical alternative open to him. He can retrace his steps, withdraw his objection to premise 1, and say instead that, yes, the universe *does* have an explanation of its existence. But that explanation is: The universe exists by a necessity of its own nature. For the atheist, the universe could serve as a sort of God-substitute that exists necessarily.

Now this would be a very radical step for the atheist to take, and I can't think of any contemporary atheist who has in fact adopted this line. A few years ago at a Philosophy of Time conference at Santa Barbara City College, I thought that Professor Adolf Grünbaum, a vociferous atheistic philosopher of science from the University of Pittsburgh, was flirting with this idea. But when I raised the question from the floor whether he thought the universe existed necessarily, he was positively indignant at the suggestion. "Of course not!" he snapped, and he went on to claim that the universe just exists without any explanation.

The reason atheists are not eager to embrace this alternative is clear. As we look about the universe, none of the things that make it up, whether stars, planets, galaxies, dust, radiation, or what have you, seems to exist necessarily. They could all fail to exist; indeed, at some point in the past, when the universe was very dense, none of them did exist.

But, someone might say, what about the matter that these things are made of? Maybe the matter exists necessarily, and all these things are just different configurations of matter. The problem with this suggestion is that, according to the standard model of subatomic physics, matter itself is composed of tiny fundamental particles that cannot be further broken down. The universe is just the collection of all these particles arranged in different ways. But now the question arises: Couldn't a different collection of fundamental particles have existed instead of this one? Does each and every one of these particles exist necessarily?

	I	II	III	
Quarks	U up	C charm	t top	γ photon
	d down	S strange	b bottom	g gluon
	νe electron neutrino	νμ muon neutrino	ντ tau neutrino	Z^0 weak force
Leptons	e electron	μ muon	τ tau	$W^{\pm}$ weak force
				Bosons

Notice what the atheist cannot say at this point. He cannot say that the elementary particles are just configurations of matter which that could have been different, but that the matter of which the particles are composed exists necessarily. He can't say this, because elementary particles aren't composed of anything! They just *are* the basic units of matter. So if a particular particle doesn't exist, the matter doesn't exist.

Now it seems obvious that a different collection of fundamental particles could have existed instead of the collection that does exist. But if that were the case, then a different universe would have existed.

To see the point, think about your desk. Could your desk have been made of ice? Notice that I'm not asking if you could have had an ice desk in the place of your wooden desk that had the same size and shape. Rather I'm asking if your very desk, the one made of wood, if *that* desk could have been made of ice. The answer seems to be obviously, no. The ice desk would be a different desk, not the same desk.

Similarly, a universe made up of different particles, even if they were identically arranged as in this universe, would be a different universe. It follows, then, that the universe does not exist by a necessity of its own nature.

Now someone might object that my body remains identical over time despite a complete exchange of its material constituents for new constituents. We're told that every seven years the matter that makes up our bodies is virtually completely recycled. Still my body is identical to the body I had before. Analogously, someone might say, various possible universes could be identical even though they're composed of wholly different collections of particles.

The crucial disanalogy, however, is that the difference between possible universes is no kind of change at all, for there is no enduring subject that undergoes intrinsic change from one state to another. So universes made up of different particles are not like the different stages of my one body. Rather they're like two bodies that have no connection with each other whatsoever.

No one thinks that every particle in the universe exists by a necessity of its own nature. It follows that neither does the universe composed of such particles exist by a necessity of its own nature. Notice that this is the case whether we think of the universe as itself an object (just as a marble statue is not identical to a similar statue made of different marble), or as a collection or group (just as a flock of birds is not identical to a similar flock made up of different birds), or even as nothing at all over and above the particles themselves.

An *analogy* is a point of similarity between two things. A *disanalogy* is a point of difference or dissimilarity between two things.

TALK ABOUT IT

Ask a physics teacher: Why do elementary particles exist? Is it impossible for them not to exist? (Be prepared for the possibility that your physics teacher doesn't want to have this conversation.)

My claim that the universe does not exist necessarily becomes even more obvious when we reflect that it seems entirely possible that the fundamental building blocks of nature could have been substances quite different from the elementary particles we know. Such a universe would be characterized by different laws of nature. Even if we take our laws of nature to be logically necessary, still it's possible that different laws of nature could have held because substances endowed with different properties and capacities than our fundamental particles could have existed. In such a case we'd clearly be dealing with a different universe.

So atheists have not been so bold as to deny premise 2 and say that the universe exists necessarily. Like premise 1, premise 2 also seems to be plausibly true.

Conclusion

Given the truth of the three premises, the conclusion is logically inescapable: *God is the explanation of the existence of the universe.* Moreover, the argument implies that God is an uncaused, unembodied Mind who transcends the physical universe and even space

TALK ABOUT IT

How has this chapter shown that God:
Is unembodied Mind?
Transcends the universe?
Created the universe?

and time themselves and who exists necessarily. This conclusion is staggering. Leibniz has expanded our minds far beyond the mundane affairs of daily life. In the next chapter our minds will be stretched further still, as we try to grasp the infinite and discover the beginning of the universe.

1. G. W. F. von Leibniz, "The Principles of Nature and of Grace, Based on Reason," in *Leibniz Selections*, ed. P. Wiener (New York: Scribner's, 1951), 527.

LEIBNIZ'S COSMOLOGICAL ARGUMENT

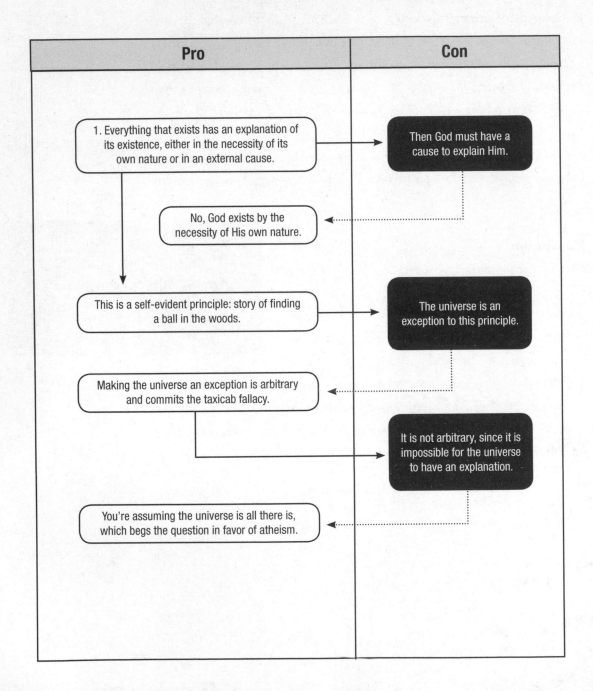

Pro	Con
1. Everything that exists has an explanation of its existence, either in the necessity of its own nature or in an external cause.	Then God must have a cause to explain Him.
No, God exists by the necessity of His own nature.	
This is a self-evident principle: story of finding a ball in the woods.	The universe is an exception to this principle.
Making the universe an exception is arbitrary and commits the taxicab fallacy.	
	It is not arbitrary, since it is impossible for the universe to have an explanation.
You're assuming the universe is all there is, which begs the question in favor of atheism.	

Pro	Con
2. If the universe has an explanation of its existence, that explanation is God.	
This is logically equivalent to the atheist's own statement that if God does not exist, the universe has no explanation	I withdraw the statement. The universe exists by a necessity of its own nature.
The universe does not exist necessarily, since different elementary particles could have existed.	
As the cause of space and time, this being must be an unembodied, transcendent Mind.	
3. The universe exists.	
4. Therefore, the universe has an explanation of its existence.	
This follows from 1 and 3.	
5. Therefore, the explanation of the existence of the universe is God.	
This follows from 2 and 4.	

A PHILOSOPHER'S JOURNEY OF FAITH,
PART ONE

Having become a Christian during my junior year in high school, I was soon faced with the decision of picking a college to attend. Sandy, the girl in my German class who had shared with me her faith in Christ, suggested that I apply to Wheaton College, where her older brother Paul was a student. Studying at a Christian college really appealed to me as a young believer, so I applied and was accepted.

You have to understand that I had never been a part of the Christian subculture before, so attending Wheaton was for me like a foretaste of heaven—professors prayed before class, there was daily chapel, you never heard swearing or filthy talk in the locker room, and so on. I was bowled over!

But the truly priceless gift that Wheaton gave to me was the integration of my faith and learning. I saw that as a Christian I didn't need to stick my brains in one pocket and my faith in the other pocket and never let them see the light of day at the same time. Rather I could have a Christian worldview—a Christian perspective on science, a Christian perspective on history, a Christian perspective on the arts, and so on. It was at Wheaton that I caught the vision of sharing my faith in the context of presenting an intellectual defense of the gospel, to appeal to the head as well as to the heart.

Unfortunately, Wheaton was at that time surprisingly weak in apologetics. My theology professor Robert Webber taught us that there are no good arguments for God's existence and that the traditional proofs had all been refuted. Though I was skeptical about his claim, I more or less bought into what he said on the basis of his authority.

Then just prior to graduating from Wheaton I picked up a copy of a book by Professor Stuart Hackett called *The Resurrection of Theism* on a clearance table at the college bookstore. I must confess that I wasn't even sure what the title meant! Later during the fall, when I got around to reading the book, I was absolutely stunned by what I read. In contrast to what I had been taught at Wheaton, Hackett, with devastating logic, was defending arguments for God's existence and providing refutations of every conceivable objection to them.

The centerpiece of Hackett's case was an argument that struck a deep chord in me: It is rationally inconceivable that the series of past events be infinite; there must have been a beginning of the universe and therefore a transcendent cause that brought it into being. Reading Hackett's book was a shocking, eye-opening experience for me. I had to find out if he was right.

During my senior year at Wheaton, a chapel speaker named John Guest had challenged us seniors to take a couple years out after graduation to share our faith full-time with university students while we were still about the same age. That made sense to me, so I decided to put off my plans to go to seminary for two years and joined the staff of Campus Crusade for Christ. I was assigned to the staff team at Northern Illinois University.

One of the other members of the team was a young, single woman named Jan Coleman, a graduate of the University of North Dakota. Vivacious and outgoing, she projected confidence, independence, and strength. She was sold out to Christ and committed to evangelism. Not only that, but with her slim figure, waist-length dark brown hair, and big brown eyes, she was—well, let's just say very attractive! She even told me she wanted to go to seminary, precisely where I was headed. Well, a girl like this was way out of my league, but I couldn't help but be attracted to her. Miracles still happen, for as I worked with the guys and she with the gals, we fell in love and were married by the end of the school year.

We then set our sights on the master's degree program in philosophy spearheaded by Dr. Norman Geisler at Trinity Evangelical Divinity School north of Chicago. One of the program's entrance requirements was the Graduate Record Exam in philosophy, so over the next year in preparation for the exam I read and took detailed notes on Frederick Copleston's monumental nine-volume *History of Philosophy*. It was there that I discovered the long

history of Jewish, Muslim, and Christian thought about the argument that Hackett was defending. I determined that if I could ever do doctoral work in philosophy, I would write my PhD dissertation on this argument.

We spent two great years at Trinity, studying under men such as Paul Feinberg, David Wolfe, John Warwick Montgomery, David Wells, John Woodbridge, J. I. Packer, Clark Pinnock, and Murray Harris. I earned twin master's degrees in philosophy of religion and in church history. Our time at Trinity turned out to be a crucial stepping-stone in the path God had set for us.

Jan and I have found that in our life together, the Lord usually shows us only enough light along the path to take the next step without knowing what lies further down the trail. So one evening as Jan and I were nearing the end of our time at Trinity, we were sitting at the supper table, talking about what to do after graduation. Neither of us had any clear idea or leading as to what we should do.

At that point Jan said to me, "Well, if money were no object, what would you really *like* to do next?"

I replied, "If money were no object, what I'd really like to do is go to England and do a doctorate under John Hick."

"Who's he?" she asked.

"Oh, he's this famous British philosopher who's written extensively on arguments for the existence of God," I explained. "If I could study with him, I could develop the cosmological argument for God's existence."

But it hardly seemed a realistic idea.

The next evening Jan handed me a slip of paper with John Hick's address on it. "I went to the library today and found out that he's at the University of Birmingham in England," she said. "Why don't you write to him and ask him if you can do a doctoral thesis under him on the cosmological argument?"

What a woman! So I did, and to our amazement and delight Professor Hick wrote back saying he'd be very pleased to supervise my doctoral work on that subject. So it was an open door! The only problem was, the University of

Birmingham required an official bank statement certifying that we had *all* of the money for *all* of the years it would take me to complete the doctoral degree. (They didn't want foreign students dropping out midway through their doctoral programs because they had run out of cash.)

Well, we didn't have that kind of money! In fact, we were as poor as church mice. Our efficiency apartment at Trinity was so small that lying on our mattress on the floor I could reach out and touch the refrigerator. We used to cut paper plates in half just to keep down expenses! (That led to an embarrassing moment once when we had Dr. Woodbridge over for dessert, and Jan, not even thinking about it, served him his pie on a half of a paper plate! Gracious to a fault, he never said a thing.)

But we really sensed that God was calling us to go to England to do this degree. There were no scholarships for foreign students at that time from the financially strapped British universities. We had to come up with the money ourselves. And so every morning and evening we began to pray that somehow the Lord would supply the funds.

We made an appointment with a non-Christian businessman whose family had supported Jan on Campus Crusade staff, and we laid out for him what we believed God was calling us to do. And this non-Christian businessman gave us—not loaned us—he *gave* us all of the money we needed to do the doctoral degree under John Hick at the University of Birmingham! It was one of the most astonishing provisions of the Lord I have ever seen. So Jan and I felt as though God had miraculously plucked us up and transported us to England to do this degree.

I did write on the cosmological argument under Professor Hick's direction, and eventually three books flowed out of that doctoral dissertation. I was able to explore the historical roots of Hackett's argument, as well as deepen and advance his analysis. I also discovered quite amazing connections to contemporary astronomy and cosmology.

Because of its historic roots in medieval Islamic theology, I christened Hackett's argument "the *kalam* cosmological argument" (*kalam* is the Arabic

word for medieval theology). Today this argument, largely forgotten since the time of Kant, is once again back at center stage. *The Cambridge Companion to Atheism* (2007) reports, "A count of the articles in the philosophy journals shows that more articles have been published about Craig's defense of the Kalam argument than have been published about any other philosopher's contemporary formulation of an argument for God's existence.... Theists and atheists alike 'cannot leave Craig's Kalam argument alone'" (p. 183).

We thank the Lord for giving us the privilege of studying this historic argument. In the next chapter I'll share it with you.

CHAPTER 4

WHY DID THE UNIVERSE BEGIN?

The heavens are telling the glory of God; and the firmament
proclaims his handiwork. (Ps. 19:1 RSV)

As a boy I not only wondered at the existence of the cosmos, I also wondered about how it began. I remember lying in bed at night trying to think of a beginningless universe. Every event would be preceded by another event, back and back into the past, with no stopping point—or, more accurately, no starting point! An infinite past, with no beginning. My mind reeled at the prospect. It just seemed inconceivable to me. There must have been a beginning at some point, I thought, in order for everything to get started.

Again, little did I suspect that for centuries—millennia, really—men had grappled with the idea of an infinite past and the question of whether there was an absolute beginning. Ancient Greek philosophers believed that matter was necessary and uncreated and therefore eternal. God may be responsible for introducing order into the cosmos, but He did not create the universe itself.

This Greek view was in contrast to even more ancient Jewish thought about the subject. Hebrew writers held that the universe has not always existed but was created by God at some point in the past. As the first verse of the Hebrew Holy Scriptures states: "In the beginning God created the heavens and the earth" (Gen. 1:1 RSV).

Eventually these two competing traditions began to interact. There arose within Western philosophy an ongoing debate that lasted for well over a thousand years about whether or not the universe had a beginning. This debate played itself out among Jews and Muslims as well as Christians, both Catholic and Protestant. It finally sputtered to something of an inconclusive finale in the thought of the great eighteenth-century German philosopher Immanuel Kant. He held, ironically, that there are rationally compelling arguments for *both* sides, thereby exposing the bankruptcy of reason itself!

Al-Ghazali's Argument

What is the argument that had caused such controversy? Let's allow one of its greatest medieval champions to speak for himself. Al-Ghazali was a twelfth-century Muslim theologian from Persia, or modern-day Iran. He was concerned that Muslim philosophers of his day were being influenced by ancient Greek philosophy to deny God's creation of the universe. They held that the universe flows necessarily out of God and therefore is beginningless.

After thoroughly studying the teachings of these philosophers, Ghazali wrote a withering critique of their views entitled *The Incoherence of the Philosophers.* In this fascinating book, he argues that the idea of a beginningless universe is absurd. The universe must have a beginning, and since nothing begins to exist without a cause, there must be a transcendent Creator of the universe.

Ghazali frames his argument simply: "Every being which begins has a cause for its beginning; now the world is a being which begins; therefore, it possesses a cause for its beginning."[1]

Once again, we can summarize Ghazali's reasoning in three simple steps:

1. Whatever begins to exist has a cause.

2. The universe began to exist.

3. Therefore, the universe has a cause.

This argument is so marvelously simple that it's easy to memorize and share with another person. It's also a logically airtight argument. If the two premises

are true, then the conclusion necessarily follows. So anybody who wants to deny the conclusion must regard either premise 1 or premise 2 as false. So the whole question is: Is it more probable that these statements are true or that they are false? Let's examine each premise in turn.

PREMISE 1

Whatever begins to exist has a cause.

I think that the first premise, that *whatever begins to exist has a cause,* is virtually undeniable for any sincere seeker after truth. For something to come into being *without any cause whatsoever* would be to come into being from nothing. That is surely impossible. Let me give three reasons in support of this premise:

1. *Something cannot come from nothing.* To claim that something can come into being from nothing is worse than magic. When a magician pulls a rabbit out of a hat, at least you've got the magician, not to mention the hat! But if you deny premise 1, you've got to think that the whole universe just appeared at some point in the past for no reason whatsoever. But nobody *sincerely* believes that things, say, a horse or an Eskimo village, can just pop into being without a cause.

This isn't rocket science. In *The Sound of Music,* when Captain Von Trapp and Maria reveal their love for each other, what does Maria say? "Nothing comes from nothing; nothing ever could." We don't normally think of philosophical principles as romantic, but Maria was here expressing

A CHRISTIAN-JEWISH-MUSLIM ARGUMENT

The *kalam* cosmological argument originated in the efforts of ancient Christian philosophers like John Philoponus of Alexandria to refute Aristotle's doctrine of the eternity of the universe. When Islam swept over Egypt, it absorbed this tradition and developed sophisticated versions of the argument. Jews lived alongside Muslims in medieval Spain and eventually mediated this tradition back to the Christian West, where it was championed by St. Bonaventura. Since Christians, Jews, and Muslims share a common belief in creation, the *kalam* cosmological argument has enjoyed great intersectarian appeal and helps to build bridges for sharing one's faith with Jews and especially Muslims.

a fundamental principle of classical metaphysics. (No doubt she had been well trained in philosophy at the convent school!)

Sometimes skeptics will respond to this point by saying that in physics subatomic particles (so-called "virtual particles") come into being from nothing. Or certain theories of the origin of the universe are sometimes described in popular magazines as getting something from nothing, so that the universe is the exception to the proverb "There ain't no free lunch."

This skeptical response represents a deliberate abuse of science. The theories in question have to do with particles originating as a fluctuation of the energy contained in the vacuum. The vacuum in modern physics is not what the layman understands by "vacuum," namely, nothing. Rather in physics the vacuum is a sea of fluctuating energy governed by physical laws and having a physical structure. To tell laymen that on such theories something comes from nothing is a distortion of those theories.

Properly understood, "nothing" does not mean just empty space. Nothing is the absence of anything whatsoever, even space itself. As such, nothingness has literally no properties at all, since there isn't anything to have any properties! How silly, then, when popularizers say things like "Nothingness is unstable" or "The universe tunneled into being out of nothing"!

When I first published my work on the *kalam* cosmological argument back in 1979, I figured that atheists would attack premise 2 of the argument, that *the universe began to exist*. But I didn't think they'd go after premise 1. For that would expose them as people not sincerely seeking after truth but just looking for an academic refutation of the argument.

What a surprise, then, to hear atheists denying premise 1 in order to escape the argument! For example, Quentin Smith of Western Michigan University responded that the most rational position to hold is that the universe came "from nothing, by nothing, and for nothing"[2]—a nice close to a Gettysburg Address of atheism, perhaps!

This is simply the faith of an atheist. In fact, I think this represents a greater leap of faith than belief in the existence of God. For it is, I repeat, literally worse than magic. If this is the alternative to belief in God, then unbelievers can never accuse believers of irrationality, for what could be more evidently irrational than this?

2. *If something can come into being from nothing, then it becomes inexplicable why just anything or everything doesn't come into being from nothing.* Think about it: Why don't bicycles and Beethoven and root beer just pop into being from nothing? Why is it only universes that can come into being from nothing? What makes nothingness so discriminatory? There can't be anything about nothingness that favors universes, for nothingness doesn't have any properties. Nor can anything constrain nothingness; for there isn't anything to be constrained!

I've heard atheists respond to this argument by saying that premise 1 is true of everything *in* the universe but not *of* the universe. But this is just the old taxicab fallacy that we encountered in chapter 3. You can't dismiss the causal principle like a cab once you get to the universe! Premise 1 is not merely a law of nature, like the law of gravity, which only applies in the universe. Rather it's a metaphysical principle that governs all being, all reality.

TALK ABOUT IT

Why do you suppose so many smart people think it makes sense that the universe may have popped into being from nothing, without a cause?

At this point the atheist is likely to retort, "All right, if everything has a cause, what is God's cause?" I'm amazed at the self-congratulatory attitude of students who pose this question. They imagine that they've said something very important or profound, when all they've done is misunderstand the premise. Premise 1 does not say that everything has a cause. Rather it says that everything *that begins to exist* has a cause. Something that is eternal wouldn't need a cause, since it never came into being.

Ghazali would therefore respond that God is eternal and uncaused. This is not special pleading for God, since this is exactly what the atheist has

TALK ABOUT IT

What would you say to someone who says that nothing ever begins to exist, since everything is made of prior material constituents?

traditionally said about the universe: It is eternal and uncaused. The problem is that we have good evidence that the universe is not eternal but had a beginning, and so the atheist is backed into the corner of saying the universe sprang into being without a cause, which is absurd.

3. *Common experience and scientific evidence confirm the truth of premise 1.* Premise 1 is constantly verified and never falsified. It's hard to understand how anyone committed to modern science could deny that premise 1 is more plausibly true than false in light of the evidence.

So I think that the first premise of the *kalam* cosmological argument is clearly true. If the price of denying the argument's conclusion is denying premise 1, then atheism is philosophically bankrupt.

Premise 2

The universe began to exist.

The more controversial premise in the argument is premise 2, that *the universe began to exist.* Let me present two philosophical arguments and two scientific arguments in defense of this premise.

First Philosophical Argument: An Actually Infinite Number of Things Cannot Exist

Ghazali argued that if the universe never began to exist, then there have been an infinite number of past events prior to today. But, he argued, an infinite number of things cannot exist. This claim needs to be carefully nuanced. Ghazali recognized that a *potentially* infinite number of things could exist, but he denied that an *actually* infinite number of things could exist. Let me explain the difference.

Potential vs. Actual Infinity

When we say that something is *potentially* infinite, infinity serves merely as an ideal limit that is never reached. For example, you could divide any

❧ On Guard

finite distance in half, and then into fourths, and then into eighths, and then into sixteenths, and so on to infinity. The number of divisions is potentially infinite, in the sense that you could go on dividing endlessly. But you'd never arrive at an "infinitieth" division. You'd never have an actually infinite number of parts or divisions.

Now Ghazali had no problem with the existence of merely potential infinites, for these are just ideal limits. But when we come to an actual infinite, we're dealing with a collection that is not growing toward infinity as a limit but is already complete: The number of members already in the collection is greater than any finite number. Ghazali argued that if an actually infinite number of things could exist, then various absurdities would result. If we're to avoid these absurdities, then we must deny that an actually infinite number of things exist. That means that the number of past events cannot be actually infinite. Therefore, the universe cannot be beginningless; rather the universe began to exist.

An Objection from Modern Math

It's very frequently alleged that this kind of argument has been invalidated by developments in modern mathematics. In modern set theory the use of actually infinite sets is commonplace. For example, the set of the natural numbers {0, 1, 2, …} has an actually infinite number of members in it. The number of members in this set is not merely potentially infinite, according to modern set theory; rather the number of members is actually infinite. Many people have mistakenly inferred that these developments undermine Ghazali's argument.

Answer to Objection: Reality vs. Fiction

These developments in modern mathematics merely show that if you adopt certain axioms and rules, then you can *talk* about actually infinite collections in a consistent way, without contradicting yourself. All this accomplishes is showing how to set up a certain *universe of discourse* for talking consistently about actual infinites. But it does absolutely nothing to show that such mathematical entities really exist or that an actually infinite number of things can really exist. If Ghazali is right, then this universe of discourse may be regarded as just a fictional realm, like the world of Sherlock Holmes, or something that exists only in your mind.

Moreover, Ghazali's claim is not that the existence of an actually infinite number of things involves a *logical* contradiction but that it is *really* impossible. To give an analogy, the claim that *something came into existence from nothing* isn't logically contradictory, but nonetheless it's really impossible. These modern mathematical developments, far from undermining Ghazali's argument, can actually strengthen it by providing us insight into the strange nature of the actual infinite.

Hilbert's Hotel

The way in which Ghazali brings out the real impossibility of an actually infinite number of things is by imagining what it would be like if such a collection could exist and then drawing out the absurd consequences. Let me share one of my favorite illustrations, called "Hilbert's Hotel," the brainchild of the great German mathematician David Hilbert.

Hilbert first invites us to imagine an ordinary hotel with a finite number of rooms. Suppose, furthermore, that all the rooms are full. If a new guest shows up at the desk asking for a room, the manager says, "Sorry, all the rooms are full," and that's the end of the story.

But now, says Hilbert, let's imagine a hotel with an infinite number of rooms, and let's suppose once again that *all the rooms are full.* This fact must be clearly appreciated. There isn't a single vacancy throughout the entire infinite hotel; every room already has somebody in it. Now suppose a new guest shows up at the front desk, asking for a room. "No problem," says the manager. He moves the person who was staying in room #1 into room #2, the person who was staying in room #2 into room #3, the person who was staying in room #3 into room #4, and so on to infinity. As a result of these

room changes, room #1 now becomes vacant, and the new guest gratefully checks in. But before he arrived, all the rooms were already full!

It gets worse! Let's now suppose, Hilbert says, that an *infinity* of new guests shows up at the front desk, asking for rooms. "No problem, no problem!" says the manager. He moves the person who was staying in room #1 into room #2, the person who was staying in room #2 into room #4, the person who was staying in room #3 into room #6, each time moving the person into the room number twice his own. Since any number multiplied by two is an even number, all the guests wind up in even-numbered rooms. As a result, all the odd-numbered rooms become vacant, and the infinity of new guests is easily accommodated. In fact, the manager could do this *an infinite number of times* and always accommodate infinitely more guests. And yet, before they arrived, all the rooms were already full!

As a student once remarked to me, Hilbert's Hotel, if it could exist, would have to have a sign posted outside: "No Vacancy (Guests Welcome)."

But Hilbert's Hotel is even stranger than the great German mathematician made it out to be. For just ask yourself the question: What would happen if some of the guests start to *check out?* Suppose all the guests in the odd-numbered rooms check out. In this case an infinite number of people has left the hotel—indeed, as many as remained behind. And yet, there are no fewer people in the hotel. The number is just infinite! Now suppose the manager doesn't like having a half-empty hotel (it looks bad for business). No matter! By moving the guests as before, only this time in reverse order, he converts his half-empty hotel into one that is bursting at the seams!

Now you might think that by these maneuvers the manager could always keep his strange hotel fully occupied. But you'd be wrong. For suppose the guests in rooms # 4, 5, 6, … check out. At a single stroke the hotel would be virtually emptied, the guest register reduced to just three names, and the infinite converted to finitude. And yet it would be true that the *same number* of guests checked out this time as when all the guests in the odd-numbered rooms checked out! Can such a hotel exist in reality?

Hilbert's Hotel is absurd. Since nothing hangs on the illustration's involving a hotel, the argument can be generalized to show that the existence of an actually infinite number of things is absurd.

Responses to Hilbert's Hotel

Sometimes people react to Hilbert's Hotel by saying that these absurdities result because the concept of infinity is beyond us and we can't understand it. But this reaction is mistaken and naive. As I said, infinite set theory is a highly developed and well-understood branch of modern mathematics. The absurdities result because we *do* understand the nature of the actual infinite. Hilbert was a smart guy, and he knew well how to illustrate the bizarre consequences of the existence of an actually infinite number of things.

Really, the only thing the critic can do at this point is just bite the bullet and say that a Hilbert's Hotel is not absurd. Sometimes critics will try to justify this move by saying that if an actual infinite could exist, then such situations are exactly what we should expect. But this justification is inadequate. Hilbert would, of course, agree that *if* an actual infinite could exist, the situation with his imaginary hotel is what we should expect. Otherwise, it wouldn't be a good illustration! But the question is whether such a hotel is really possible.

Moreover, the critics can't just bite the bullet when it comes to situations like the guests' checking out of the hotel. For here we have a logical contradiction: We subtract identical quantities from identical quantities and come up with nonidentical results. That's why subtraction of infinity from infinity is mathematically prohibited. But while we may slap the hand of the mathematician who tries to break the rules, we can't stop real people from checking out of a real hotel!

TALK ABOUT IT

Al-Ghazali shows that an infinite number of past events is impossible. What about the future? Is it actually or merely potentially infinite? How is eternity different from an infinite number of moments in time?

So I think Ghazali's first argument is a good one. It shows that the number of past events must be finite. Therefore, the universe must have had a beginning.

Second Philosophical Argument: You Can't Pass Through an Infinite Number of Elements One at a Time

Ghazali has a second, independent argument for the beginning of the universe. So those who deny that the universe began to exist have to refute not only his first argument, but his second one as well, since it's independent of the first one.

Counting to (or from) Infinity

The series of past events, Ghazali observes, has been formed by adding one event after another. The series of past events is like a sequence of dominoes falling one after another until the last domino, today, is reached. But, he argues, no series that is formed by adding one member after another can be actually infinite. For you cannot pass through an infinite number of elements one at a time.

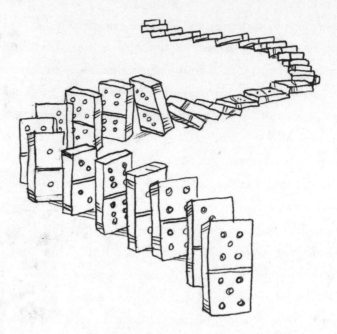

This is easy to see in the case of trying to count to infinity. No matter how high you count, there's always an infinity of numbers left to count.

But if you can't count *to* infinity, how could you count down *from* infinity? This would be like trying to count down all the negative numbers, ending at zero: …, -3, -2, -1, 0. This seems crazy. For before you could count 0, you'd have to count -1, and before you could count -1, you'd have to count -2, and so on, back to infinity. Before any number could be counted an infinity of numbers will have to have been counted first. You just get driven back and back into the past, so that no number could ever be counted.

But then the final domino could never fall if an infinite number of dominoes had to fall first. So today could never be reached. But obviously here we are! This shows that the series of past events must be finite and have a beginning.

An Objection: From Every Past Point, We Can Reach the Present

Some critics have responded to this argument by pointing out that even in a beginningless past, every event in the past is only a finite distance from the present. Compare the series of negative numbers: …, -3, -2, -1, 0. It's beginningless; nevertheless, any number you pick, say, -11 or -1,000,000 or whatever, is only finitely distant from zero. But the finite distance from any past event to the present is easily crossed, just as you can count down to zero from any negative number you pick.

Answer to Objection: The Fallacy of Composition

This objection commits a logical fallacy called the "fallacy of composition." This is the fallacy of confusing a property of *a part* with a property of *the whole*. For example, every part of an elephant may be light in weight, but that doesn't mean the whole elephant is light in weight!

In the case at hand, just because every finite *part* of a series can be crossed or counted down doesn't mean the *whole* infinite series can be crossed or counted. The critics have committed an elementary fallacy. The question is not how any finite part of the past can be formed by adding one event after another, but how the whole, beginningless past could be completed by adding one event after another.

Two More Absurdities

Ghazali sought to heighten the impossibility of forming an infinite past by giving illustrations of the absurdities that would result if it could be done. For example, suppose that for every one orbit that Saturn completes around the sun, Jupiter completes two. The longer they orbit, the further Saturn falls behind. If they continue to orbit forever, they will approach a limit at which Saturn is infinitely far behind Jupiter. Of course, they will never actually arrive at this limit.

But now turn the story around: Suppose Jupiter and Saturn have been orbiting the sun from eternity past. Which will have completed the most orbits? The answer is that the number of their orbits is exactly the same: infinity! (Don't let someone try to slip out of this argument by saying infinity is not a number. In modern mathematics it is a number, the number of

THE FALLACY OF

COMPOSITION

Each *part* of an elephant may not be heavy, but that doesn't mean the *whole* elephant isn't heavy!

elements in the set {0, 1, 2, 3,... }.) But that seems absurd, for the longer they orbit, the greater the disparity grows. So how does the number of orbits magically become equal by making them orbit from eternity past?

Another illustration: Suppose we meet someone who claims to have been counting down from eternity past and is now finishing: ... -3, -2, -1, 0! Whew! Why, we may ask, is he just finishing his countdown today? Why didn't he finish yesterday or the day before? After all, by then an infinite amount of time had already elapsed. So if the man were counting at a rate of one number per second, he's already had an infinite number of seconds to finish his countdown. He should already be done! In fact, at *any* point in the past, he's already had infinite time and so should already have finished. But then at no point in the past can we find the man finishing his countdown, which contradicts the hypothesis that he has been counting from eternity.

These illustrations only strengthen Ghazali's claim that no series that is formed by adding one member after another can be actually infinite. Since the series of past events has been formed by adding one event after another, it can't be actually infinite. It must have had a beginning. So we have a second good argument for premise 2 of the *kalam* cosmological argument, that *the universe began to exist*.

First Scientific Argument: The Expansion of the Universe

One of the most astonishing developments of modern astronomy, which Ghazali would never have anticipated, is that we now have strong scientific evidence for the beginning of the universe. Yes, science provides some of the most dramatic evidence for the second premise of the *kalam* cosmological argument. The first scientific confirmation of the universe's beginning comes from the expansion of the universe.

The "Big Bang"

All throughout history men have assumed that the universe as a whole was unchanging. Of course, things *in* the universe were moving about and changing, but the universe itself was just there, so to speak. This was also Albert Einstein's assumption when he first began to apply his new theory of gravity, called the general theory of relativity, to the universe in 1917.

But Einstein found there was something terribly amiss. His equations described a universe that was either blowing up like a balloon or else collapsing in upon itself. Perplexed, Einstein "solved" the problem by fudging his equations, adding a new term to enable the universe to walk the tightrope between exploding and imploding.

During the 1920s the Russian mathematician Alexander Friedman and the Belgian astronomer Georges Lemaître decided to take Einstein's equations at face value, and as a result they came up independently with models of an expanding universe. In 1929 the American astronomer Edwin Hubble, through tireless observations at Mount Wilson Observatory, made a startling discovery that verified Friedman and Lemaître's theory. He found that the light from distant galaxies appeared to be redder than expected.

TALK ABOUT IT

Why do you suppose Einstein might have been uncomfortable with the idea that the universe wasn't permanent and unchanging?

This "redshift" in the light was most plausibly due to the stretching of the light waves as the galaxies move away from us. Wherever Hubble trained his telescope in the night sky, he observed this same redshift in the light from the galaxies. It appeared that we are at the center of a cosmic explosion, and all of the other galaxies are flying away from us at fantastic speeds!

Now according to the Friedman-Lemaître model, we're not *really* at the center of the universe. Rather an observer in *any* galaxy will look out and see the other galaxies moving away from him. There is no center to the universe. This is because, according to the theory, it's really space itself that is expanding. The galaxies are actually at rest in space, but they recede from one another as space itself expands. To get a picture of this difficult idea, imagine a balloon with buttons glued to its surface (Fig. 1). The buttons are stuck to the surface of the balloon and so don't move across the surface. But as you blow up the balloon, the buttons will grow farther and farther and farther apart because the balloon gets bigger and bigger. Notice that there's no center of the balloon's surface. (There is a center point inside the balloon, but we're focusing just on the *surface* of the balloon.) But an observer on any button will feel as if he were at the center of the expansion because he'll look out and see the other buttons all moving away from him.

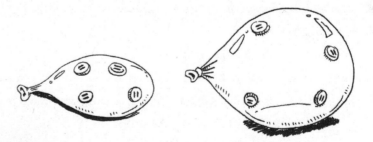

Fig. 1

Now the two-dimensional surface of the balloon serves as an illustration of our three-dimensional space, and the buttons represent the galaxies in space.

The galaxies are actually at rest in space, but they recede from one another as space itself expands. Just as there is no center of the balloon's surface, so there is no center of the universe.

The Friedman-Lemaître model eventually came to be known as the big bang theory. But that name can be misleading. Thinking of the expansion of the universe as a sort of explosion could mislead us into thinking that the galaxies are moving out into a preexisting, empty space from a central point. That would be a complete misunderstanding of the model. The big bang did not occur at some point in a preexisting, empty space.

(You might say, "But what about the central point in the interior of the balloon?" Ah, you're forgetting that it's the *surface* of the balloon that is the analogy to space! The balloon's two-dimensional surface happens to exist in a three-dimensional world, into which it is expanding. But in the Friedman-Lemaître model, there is no higher, four-dimensional world into which our three-dimensional space is expanding. So there's just nothing corresponding to the space outside or inside the balloon.)

TALK ABOUT IT

Given that the name "big bang" is misleading, why do you suppose it has caught on? What might be a better name for the theory?

So we mustn't be misled into thinking of the big bang as the explosion of a superdense pellet of matter into empty space. The theory is much more radical than that.

The Beginning of Time

As you trace the expansion of the universe back in time, everything gets closer and closer together. If our balloon had no minimum size but could just keep shrinking and shrinking, eventually the distance between any two points on the balloon's surface would shrink to zero. According to the Friedman-Lemaître model, that's what happens to space as you go back in time. Eventually the distance between any two points in space becomes zero. You can't get any closer than that! So at that point you've reached the boundary of

Try to get your mind around the idea that empty space itself is expanding right now, while you're reading this book.

space and time. Space and time can't be extended any further back than that. It's literally the beginning of space and time.

To get a picture of this we can portray our three-dimensional space as a two-dimensional surface that shrinks as you go back in time (Fig. 2).

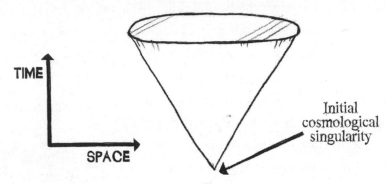

Fig. 2

Eventually, the distance between any two points in space becomes zero. So space-time can be represented geometrically as a cone. What's significant about this is that while a cone can extend indefinitely in one direction, it has a boundary point in the other direction. Because this direction represents time and the boundary point lies in the past, the model implies that past time is finite and had a beginning. Because space-time is the arena in which all matter and energy exist, the beginning of space-time is also the beginning of all matter and energy. It's the beginning of the universe.

Notice that there's simply nothing prior to the initial boundary of space-time. Let's not be misled by words, however. When I say, "There is nothing prior to the initial boundary," I do *not* mean that there is some state of affairs prior to it, and that is a state of nothingness. That would be to treat nothing as though it were something! Rather I mean that at the boundary point, it is false that "There is something prior to this point."

The standard big bang model thus predicts an absolute beginning of the universe. If this model is correct, then we have amazing scientific confirmation of the second premise of the *kalam* cosmological argument.

Is the Standard Model Correct?

So is the model correct, or, more importantly, is it correct in predicting a beginning of the universe? We've already seen that the redshift in the light from distant galaxies provides powerful evidence for the big bang. In addition, the best explanation for the abundance in the universe of certain light elements, such as helium, is that they were formed in the hot, dense big bang. Finally, the discovery in 1965 of a cosmic background of microwave radiation is best explained as a vestige of the big bang.

Nevertheless, the standard big bang model needs to be modified in various ways. The model is based, as we've seen, on Einstein's general theory of relativity. But Einstein's theory breaks down when space is shrunk down to subatomic proportions. We'll need to introduce subatomic physics at that point, and no one is sure how this is to be done. Moreover, the expansion of the universe is probably not constant, as in the standard model. It's probably accelerating and may have had a brief moment of super-rapid expansion in the past.

But none of these adjustments need affect the fundamental prediction of the absolute beginning of the universe. Indeed, physicists have proposed scores of alternative models over the decades since Friedman and Lemaître's work, and those that do not have an absolute beginning have been repeatedly shown to be unworkable. Put more positively, the only viable nonstandard models are those that involve an absolute beginning to the universe. That beginning may or may not involve a beginning *point.* But theories (such as Stephen Hawking's "no boundary" proposal) that do not have a pointlike beginning still have a finite past. The universe has not existed forever, according to such theories, but came into existence, even if it didn't do so at a sharply defined point.

In a sense, the history of twentieth-century cosmology can be seen as a series of one failed attempt after another to avoid the absolute beginning predicted by the standard big bang model. Unfortunately, the impression arises in the minds of laymen that the field of cosmology is in constant turnover, with no lasting results. What the layman doesn't understand is

"At first the scientific community was very reluctant to accept the idea of a birth of the universe."
"Not only did the Big Bang model seem to give in to the Judeo-Christian idea of a beginning of the world, but it also seemed to have to call for an act of supernatural creation.…"
"It took time, observational evidence, and careful verification of predictions made by the Big Bang model to convince the scientific community to accept the idea of a cosmic genesis."
"… [T]he Big Bang is a very successful model … that imposed itself on a reluctant scientific community."[3]
—J. M. Wersinger, Assoc. Prof. of Physics, Auburn University

that this parade of failed theories only serves to *confirm* the prediction of the standard model that the universe began to exist. That prediction has now stood for over eighty years throughout a period of enormous advances in observational astronomy and creative theoretical work in astrophysics.

Indeed, something of a watershed appears to have been reached in 2003, when three leading scientists, Arvind Borde, Alan Guth, and Alexander Vilenkin, were able to prove that *any* universe that has, on average, been expanding throughout its history cannot be infinite in the past but must have a past space-time boundary.

What makes their proof so powerful is that it holds *regardless* of the physical description of the very early universe. Because we can't yet provide a physical description of the very early universe, this brief moment has been fertile ground for speculations. One scientist has compared it to the regions on ancient maps labeled "Here there be dragons!"—it can be filled with all sorts of fantasies. But the Borde-Guth-Vilenkin theorem is independent of any physical description of that moment. Their theorem implies that even if our universe is just a tiny part of a so-called multiverse composed of many universes, the multiverse must have an absolute beginning. Vilenkin is blunt about the implications:

> It is said that an argument is what convinces reasonable men and a proof is what it takes to convince even an unreasonable man. With the proof now in place, cosmologists can no longer hide behind the possibility of a past-eternal universe. There is no escape: they have to face the problem of a cosmic beginning.[4]

We can fully expect that new theories will be proposed, attempting to avoid the universe's beginning. Such proposals are to be welcomed, and we have no reason to think that they'll be any more successful than their failed predecessors. Of course, scientific results are always provisional. Nevertheless, it's pretty clear which way the evidence points. Today the proponent of

MULTIVERSE

Some cosmologists speculate that our observable universe is just an expanding bubble in a much wider sea of energy, which is also expanding. Since this wider universe contains many other bubbles in addition to ours, it is often called a multiverse. The Borde-Guth-Vilenkin theorem also applies to the multiverse as a whole, not just to the individual bubbles within it. Thus, even if there is a multiverse, it cannot be eternal in the past but must have had a beginning. We'll return to the question of whether there is a multiverse in the next chapter.

❧ ON GUARD

the *kalam* cosmological argument stands comfortably within the scientific mainstream in holding that the universe began to exist.

Second Scientific Argument: The Thermodynamics of the Universe

As if this weren't enough, there's actually a second scientific confirmation of the beginning of the universe, this one from the second law of thermodynamics. According to the second law, unless energy is being fed into a system, that system will become increasingly disorderly. For example, if you had a bottle that was a closed vacuum inside and you injected into it some molecules of gas, the gas would spread itself evenly throughout the bottle. The chances that the molecules would all huddle together in one corner of the bottle are practically nil. This is because there are many more ways in which the molecules could exist in a disorderly state than in an orderly state.

The End of the World

Already in the nineteenth century scientists realized that the second law implied a grim prediction for the future of the universe. Given enough time, all the energy in the universe will spread itself out evenly throughout the universe, just as the gas spreads itself out evenly throughout the bottle. The universe will become a featureless soup in which no life is possible. Once the universe reaches such a state, no significant further change is possible. It is a state of equilibrium, in which the temperature and pressure are the same everywhere. Scientists called this the "heat death" of the universe.

But this unwelcome prediction raised a further puzzle: If, given enough time, the universe *will* inevitably stagnate in a state of heat death, then why, if it has existed forever, is it not *now* in a state of heat death? If in a finite amount of time, the universe *will* reach equilibrium, then, given infinite past time, it should by now *already be* in a state of equilibrium. But it's not. We're in a state of disequilibrium, where energy is still available to be used and the universe has an orderly structure.

Boltzmann's Many Worlds Hypothesis

The nineteenth-century German physicist Ludwig Boltzmann proposed a daring solution to this problem. Boltzmann suggested that perhaps the universe *is,* in fact, in a state of overall equilibrium. Nevertheless, by chance alone, there will arise more orderly pockets of disequilibrium here and there (Fig. 3). Boltzmann refers to these isolated regions of disequilibrium as "worlds." Our universe just happens to be one of these worlds. Eventually, in accord with the second law, it will revert to the overall state of equilibrium.

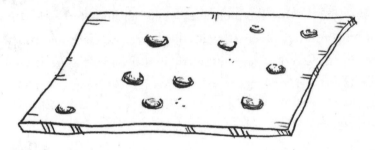

Fig. 3

Contemporary physicists have universally rejected Boltzmann's daring many worlds hypothesis as an explanation of the observed disequilibrium of the universe. Its fatal flaw is that if our world is just a chance fluctuation from a state of overall equilibrium, then we ought to be observing a much smaller region of order. Why? Because a small fluctuation from equilibrium is vastly more probable than the huge, sustained fluctuation necessary to create the universe we see, and yet a small fluctuation would be sufficient for our existence. For example, a fluctuation that formed an orderly region no bigger than our solar system would be enough for us to be alive and would be incomprehensibly more likely to occur than a fluctuation that formed the whole orderly universe we see!

In fact, Boltzmann's hypothesis, if consistently carried out, would lead to a strange sort of illusionism: In all probability we really *do* inhabit a smaller

---

EQUILIBRIUM

Equilibrium is a state in which all forces are in balance and there is therefore no change. In the case of the universe, equilibrium would be the point at which the temperature and pressure are the same everywhere in the universe. No galaxies. No stars. No planets.

❧ ON GUARD

region of order, and the stars and the planets we observe are just illusions, mere images on the heavens. For that sort of world is much more probable than a universe that has, in defiance of the second law of thermodynamics, moved away from equilibrium for billions of years to form the universe we observe.

Contemporary End-of-the-World Scenarios

The discovery of the expansion of the universe in the 1920s modified the sort of heat death predicted on the basis of the second law, but it didn't alter the fundamental question.

If the universe will expand forever, then it will never actually arrive at equilibrium. Because the volume of space is constantly growing, the matter and energy always have more room to spread out. Nevertheless, as the universe expands, its available energy is used up and it becomes increasingly cold, dark, dilute, and dead. It will eventually become a thin gas of subatomic particles endlessly expanding in absolute darkness.

By contrast, if the universe is not expanding fast enough, the expansion will slow down, come to a halt, and then gravity will begin to pull everything together again in a catastrophic big crunch. Eventually everything in the universe will coalesce into a gigantic black hole, from which the universe will never rebound.

Whether its end will be in fire or ice, the fundamental question remains the same: If, given sufficient time, the universe will reach such a state, why is it not now in such a condition, if it has existed forever?

As we enter the early decades of the twenty-first century, recent discoveries have indicated that the cosmic expansion is actually speeding up. Because the volume of space is increasing so rapidly, the universe actually moves farther and farther away from an equilibrium state in which matter and energy are evenly distributed. But the acceleration of the universe's expansion only hastens its demise. For now the different regions of the universe become increasingly isolated from one another in space, and each marooned region becomes dark, cold, dilute, and dead. So again, why isn't our region in such a state if the universe has already existed for infinite time?

The Beginning of the Universe and Attempts to Avoid It

The obvious implication of all this is that the question we're asking is based on a false assumption, namely, that the universe has existed for infinite time. Today most physicists would say that the matter and energy were simply put into the universe as an initial condition, and the universe has been following the path plotted by the second law ever since its beginning a finite time ago.

Of course, attempts have been made to avoid the beginning of the universe predicted on the basis of the second law of thermodynamics. But none of them has been successful.

Oscillating Universes. During the 1960s some theorists tried to craft oscillating models of the universe, according to which the universe has been expanding and contracting, reexpanding and recontracting from eternity past (Fig. 4).

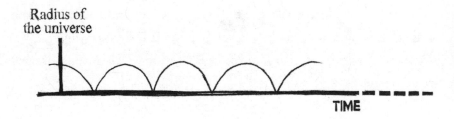

Fig. 4

But the thermodynamic properties of such models implied the very beginning they were designed to avoid. For entropy accumulates from cycle to cycle, making each cycle larger and longer than the one before it (Fig. 5). What this means is that as you trace the cycles back in time, they get smaller and smaller until you come to a first cycle and the origin of the universe. In fact, astronomers have estimated on the basis of current radiation levels in the universe that the universe cannot have gone through more than about a hundred previous cycles.

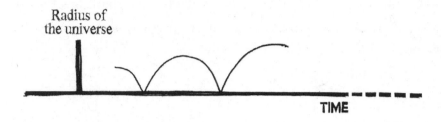

Fig. 5

Bubble Universes. More recently, other theorists have proposed that our universe is just a bubble in a much larger "multiverse" of bubble universes (Fig. 6). The claim is that the second law applies only to the bubbles, but not to the whole multiverse itself. Even if this claim were true, however, it wouldn't matter. For we have already seen that the Borde-Guth-Vilenkin theorem applies to the multiverse and requires that it have an absolute beginning.

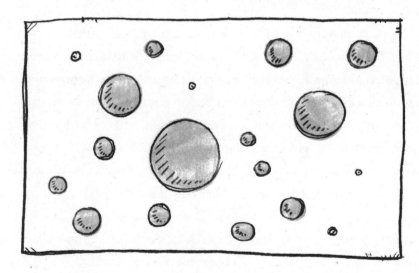

Fig. 6

Baby Universes. Finally, there have been conjectures that maybe black holes are entrances to "wormholes" in space-time through which energy could travel to spawn baby universes (Fig. 7). If the "umbilical cord" tying the mother universe to its baby pinches shut, then the baby universe becomes an independent universe. Perhaps this scenario could be extended into the infinite past, so that we're the offspring of an infinite line of ancestors?

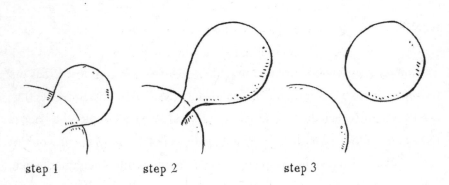

step 1   step 2   step 3

Fig. 7

Sorry, it won't work. The second law still applies, so that this process cannot have gone on for infinite time. Not only that, but the scenario contradicts subatomic physics, which requires that the information that goes down a black hole remains in our universe. This was the subject of a bet between John Preskill and Stephen Hawking, which Hawking in 2004 finally admitted he had lost. Offering his apologies to science-fiction fans everywhere, Hawking admitted, "There is no baby universe branching off."[5]

So once again the scientific evidence of thermodynamics confirms the truth of the second premise of the *kalam* cosmological argument. This evidence is especially impressive because thermodynamics is so well understood by physicists that it is practically a completed field of science. This makes it highly unlikely that these findings will be reversed.

Conclusion

On the basis, therefore, of both philosophical and scientific evidence, we have good grounds for believing that the universe began to exist. Since whatever begins to exist has a cause, it follows that the universe has a cause.

Is the Universe Self-Caused?

The prominent atheist philosopher Daniel Dennett agrees that the universe has a cause. But he thinks that the cause of the universe is: itself! Yes, he's serious. In what he calls "the ultimate boot-strapping trick,"[6] he claims that the universe created itself.

Dennett's view is nonsense. Notice that he's not saying that the universe is self-caused in the sense that it has always existed. No, he's saying that the universe brought itself into being. But this is impossible, for in order to create itself, the universe would have to already exist. It would have to exist before it existed. Dennett's view is logically incoherent.

The Personal Creator of the Universe

The cause of the universe must therefore be a transcendent cause beyond the universe. This cause must be itself uncaused because we've seen that an infinite series of causes is impossible. It is therefore the Uncaused First Cause. It must transcend space and time, since it created space and time. Therefore, it must be immaterial and nonphysical. It must be unimaginably powerful, since it created all matter and energy.

Finally, it must be a personal being. We've already seen one reason for this conclusion in the previous chapter. Only a Mind could fit the above description of the First Cause.

But let me also share a reason given by Ghazali for why the First Cause must be personal: It's the only way to explain how a timeless cause can produce a temporal effect with a beginning like the universe.

Here's the problem: If a cause is sufficient to produce its effect, then if the cause is there, the effect must be there, too. For example, water freezes when

---

EASTERN THINKING

Some people dismiss this kind of logical argument as an example of Western thinking. In the East, they say, people pursuing enlightenment can see beyond the confinements of logic. Note, though, that Ghazali was from Persia (modern Iran), and that India today is producing vast numbers of scientists and engineers who use exactly the rules of logic and the evidence of science that we have been using. Why do you suppose so many Westerners are drawn to the nonlogic of belief systems like Zen Buddhism?

the temperature is below 0 degrees centigrade; the cause of the freezing is the temperature's falling to 0 degrees. If the temperature has always been below 0 degrees, then any water around would be frozen from eternity. It would be impossible for the water to *begin* to freeze just a finite time ago. Now the cause of the universe is permanently there, since it is timeless. So why isn't the universe permanently there as well? Why did the universe come into being only 13.7 billion years ago? Why isn't it as permanent as its cause?

Ghazali maintained that the answer to this problem must be that the cause is a personal being with freedom of the will. His creating the universe is a free act that is independent of any prior conditions. So his act of creating can be something spontaneous and new. Thus, we're brought not merely to a transcendent cause of the universe but to its Personal Creator.

In my view, then, God existing alone without the universe is changeless and timeless. His free act of creation is simultaneous with the universe's coming into being. Therefore, God enters into time when He creates the universe. God is timeless without the universe and in time with the universe.

The *kalam* cosmological argument thus gives us powerful grounds for believing in the existence of a beginningless, uncaused, timeless, spaceless, changeless, immaterial, enormously powerful Personal Creator of the universe.

TALK ABOUT IT

Why do you think theologians apparently don't know the *kalam* argument? Why do you think pastors aren't taught these sorts of arguments in seminary?

When I finished my doctoral dissertation on the cosmological argument at the University of Birmingham, Professor Hick took it privately to one of the physicists on campus to have him check the scientific information. The physicist later reported back to Hick that everything I said was correct. When Professor Hick returned the dissertation to me, he looked at me quizzically and said, "Why don't the theologians know about this?" Why, indeed!

1. Al-Ghazali Kitab al-Iqtisad fi'l-I'tiqad, cited in S. de Beaurecueil, "Gazzali et S. Thomas d'Aquin: Essai sur la preuve de l'existence de Dieu proposée dans l'Iqtisad et sa comparaison avec les 'voies' Thomiste," *Bulletin de l'Institut Francais d'Archaeologie Orientale* 46 (1947): 203.
2. Quentin Smith, *Theism, Atheism, and Big Bang Cosmology* (Oxford: Clarendon Press, 1993), 135.

3. J. M. Wersinger, "Genesis: The Origin of the Universe," *National Forum* (Winter 1996), 11, 9, 12.
4. Alexander Vilenkin, *Many Worlds in One* (New York: Hill and Wang, 2006), 176.
5. S. W. Hawking, "Information Loss in Black Holes," http://arXiv:hep-th/0507171v2 (September 15, 2005): 4.
6. Daniel Dennett, *Breaking the Spell: Religion as a Natural Phenomenon* (New York: Viking, 2006), 244.

THE *KALAM* COSMOLOGICAL ARGUMENT

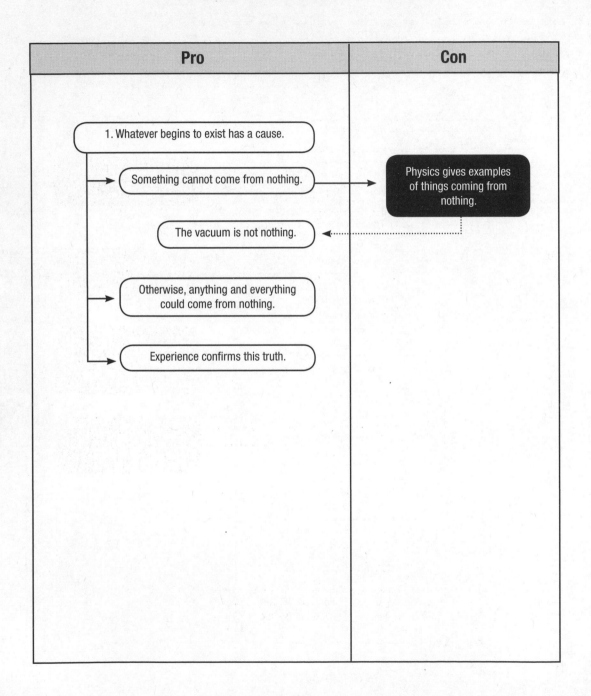

Pro	Con
1. Whatever begins to exist has a cause.	
Something cannot come from nothing.	Physics gives examples of things coming from nothing.
The vacuum is not nothing.	
Otherwise, anything and everything could come from nothing.	
Experience confirms this truth.	

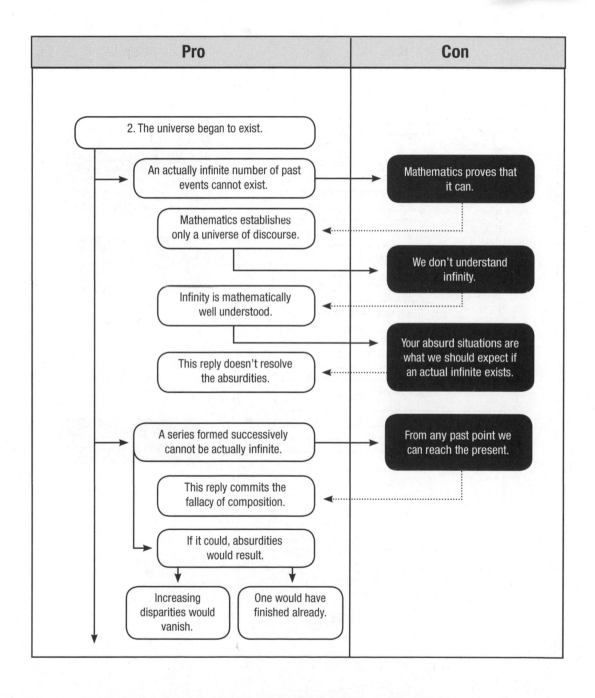

Pro	Con
2. The universe began to exist.	
An actually infinite number of past events cannot exist.	Mathematics proves that it can.
Mathematics establishes only a universe of discourse.	
	We don't understand infinity.
Infinity is mathematically well understood.	
	Your absurd situations are what we should expect if an actual infinite exists.
This reply doesn't resolve the absurdities.	
A series formed successively cannot be actually infinite.	From any past point we can reach the present.
This reply commits the fallacy of composition.	
If it could, absurdities would result.	
Increasing disparities would vanish.	One would have finished already.

THE *KALAM* COSMOLOGICAL ARGUMENT (cont.)

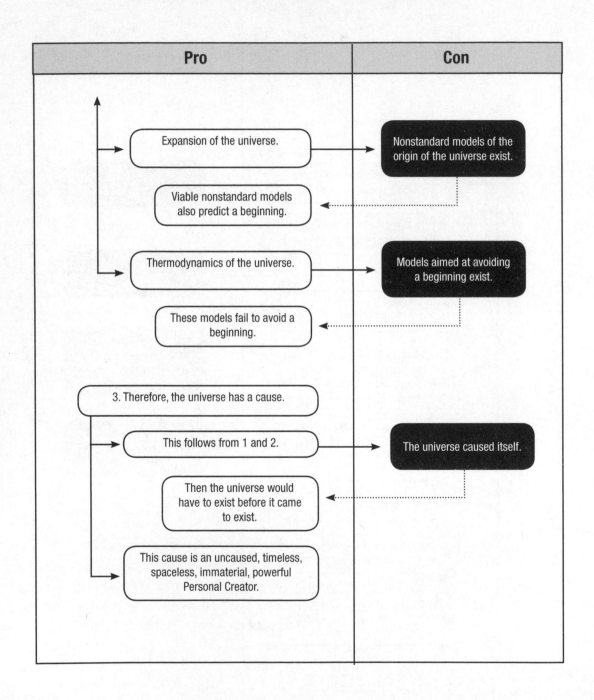

Pro	Con
Expansion of the universe.	Nonstandard models of the origin of the universe exist.
Viable nonstandard models also predict a beginning.	
Thermodynamics of the universe.	Models aimed at avoiding a beginning exist.
These models fail to avoid a beginning.	
3. Therefore, the universe has a cause.	
This follows from 1 and 2.	The universe caused itself.
Then the universe would have to exist before it came to exist.	
This cause is an uncaused, timeless, spaceless, immaterial, powerful Personal Creator.	

CHAPTER 5

WHY IS THE UNIVERSE FINE-TUNED FOR LIFE?

*Ever since the creation of the world his invisible nature, namely, his eternal power and
deity, has been clearly perceived in the things that have been made.* (Rom. 1:20 RSV)

The ancient Greek philosophers were struck with the order that pervades the cosmos. The stars and the planets in their constant revolution across the night sky were especially awesome to the ancients. Plato's Academy lavished extensive time and thought on the study of astronomy because, Plato believed, it was the science that would awaken man to his divine destiny.

According to Plato, there are two things that lead men to believe in God: the argument from the existence of the soul, and the argument "from the order of the motion of the stars, and of all things under the dominion of the Mind which ordered the universe" (*Laws* 12.966e). Plato employed these arguments to refute atheism and concluded that there must be a "best soul" who is the "Maker and Father of all," the "King," who ordered the primordial chaos into the rational cosmos that we observe today (*Laws* 10.893b–899c).

PLATO'S ACADEMY

Around 387 BC the Greek philosopher Plato purchased a house in a park known as Academeca just outside Athens, and there he opened a school that flourished for an astonishing nine hundred years, until it was shut down by the Byzantine emperor in AD 529. Plato's goal was the search for truth by means of rational inquiry. The Academy drew both senior thinkers and younger students, who explored together by means of dialogue profound questions concerning the ultimate nature of reality, the Good, the soul, logic, mathematics, and astronomy, as well as politics and society. Among the pupils who came to study at the Academy was an eighteen-year-old named Aristotle, who remained there until Plato's death. The influence of the Academy upon Western thought and history via those who passed through its gates is incalculable.

ARISTOTLE

An even more magnificent statement of divine design is to be found in a fragment from a lost work of Aristotle entitled *On Philosophy*. Aristotle, too, was filled with wonder at the majestic sweep of the glittering host across the night sky of ancient Greece. Anyone who has personally studied the heavens must lend a sympathetic ear to these men of antiquity who gazed up into the night sky, undimmed by pollution and the glare of city lights, and watched the slow but irresistible turn of the cosmos, replete with its planets, stars, and familiar constellations, across their view and wondered, *What is the cause of all this?*

Aristotle concluded that the cause was divine intelligence. He imagined the impact that the sight of the world would have upon a race of men who had lived underground and never beheld the sky:

> When thus they would suddenly gain sight of the earth, seas, and the sky; when they should come to know the grandeur of the clouds and the might of the winds; when they should behold the sun and should learn its grandeur and beauty as well as its power to cause the day by shedding light over the sky; and again, when the night had darkened the lands and they should behold the whole of the sky spangled and adorned with stars; and when they should see the changing lights of the moon as it waxes and wanes, and the risings and settings of all these celestial bodies, their courses fixed and changeless throughout all eternity—when they should behold all these things, most certainly they would have judged both that there exist gods and that all these marvelous works are the handiwork of the gods. (*On Philosophy*)

TALK ABOUT IT

Go outside at night and look up at the sky. How is what you see different from what Aristotle might have seen? How do you think this difference affects the way people today think and feel about the stars and planets?

In his *Metaphysics,* Aristotle went on to argue that there must be a First Uncaused Cause, which is God—a living, intelligent, immaterial, eternal, and most good being who is the source of order in the cosmos.

Reading the works of these ancient philosophers, one cannot help but think of Paul's words in his letter to the church in Rome: "Ever since the creation of the world his invisible nature, namely, his eternal power and deity, has been clearly perceived in the things that have been made" (Rom. 1:20 RSV). From earliest times men wholly ignorant of the Bible have concluded on the basis of the design in the universe that God must exist.

The Rebirth of Design

Today many astronomers, as a result of recent discoveries, are coming to a similar conclusion.

Scientists used to think that whatever the very early universe might have been like, given sufficient time and some luck, intelligent life forms like ourselves would eventually evolve somewhere. As a result of discoveries over the last forty years or so, we now know that that assumption was wrong. In fact, quite the opposite is true.

Astronomers have been stunned by the discovery of how complex and delicate a balance of initial conditions must be present in the big bang itself if the universe is to permit the existence of intelligent life anywhere at all in the cosmos. This delicate balance of initial conditions has come to be known as the "fine-tuning" of the universe for life. We've come to discover that the universe is fine-tuned for the existence of intelligent life with a complexity and delicacy that literally defy human comprehension.

Two Kinds of Fine-Tuning

There are two kinds of fine-tuning. The first involves the constants of nature and the second involves certain arbitrary physical quantities.

When the laws of nature are expressed as mathematical equations, certain constants feature prominently in them. Consider, for example, Newton's famous law of gravity. It states:

$F = Gm_1m_2/r^2$

According to this equation the force of gravity symbolized by F is equal to the value of the gravitational constant G multiplied by the masses of the two bodies that are being attracted to each other divided by the distance between them squared. The masses and the distance may vary depending on what objects you're talking about, but the value of G is constant.

TALK ABOUT IT

Imagine a universe in which the gravitational constant, G, was considerably stronger than in our universe. Do you think there could be galaxies in that universe? Why?

Nature's Constants

First, the constants of nature. What is a constant? When the laws of nature are expressed as mathematical equations, you find appearing in them certain symbols that stand for unchanging quantities, like the force of gravity, the electromagnetic force, and the subatomic "weak" force. These unchanging quantities are called constants. The laws of nature do not determine the value of these constants. There could be universes governed by the same laws of nature even though these constants had very different values. So the actual values of the various constants are not determined by nature's laws. Depending on the values of those constants, universes governed by the same laws of nature will look very different.

Arbitrary Quantities

In addition to the constants, there are certain arbitrary quantities that are just put in as initial conditions on which the laws of nature operate. Because these quantities are arbitrary, they're also not determined by the laws of nature. An example would be the amount of thermodynamic disorder (or entropy) in the early universe. It's just given in the big bang as an initial condition, and the laws of nature then take over and determine how the universe will develop from there. If the initial quantities had been different, then the laws would predict that a quite different universe would result.

Definition of "Fine-Tuning"

Now what scientists have been surprised to discover is that these constants and quantities must fall into an extraordinarily narrow range of values for the universe to be life-permitting. This is what is meant by the fine-tuning of the universe for life.

Examples of Fine-Tuning

Fine-tuning in this neutral sense is uncontroversial and well established. Physics abounds with examples of fine-tuning. Before I share a few, let me give you some numbers to give you a feel for the delicacy of the fine-tuning. The number of seconds in the entire history of the universe is around 10^{17} (that's 1 followed by seventeen zeroes: 100,000,000,000,000,000). The number of subatomic particles in the entire known universe is said to be around 10^{80} (1 followed by eighty zeroes). Such numbers are so huge that they're simply incomprehensible.

Now with those numbers in mind, consider the following examples of fine-tuning. The so-called *weak force*, one of the four fundamental forces of nature, which operates inside the nucleus of an atom, is so finely tuned that an alteration in its value by even one part out of 10^{100} would have prevented a life-permitting universe! Similarly, a change in the value of the so-called *cosmological constant*, which drives the acceleration of the universe's expansion, by as little as one part in 10^{120} would have rendered the universe life-prohibiting.

Remember the low-entropy state in which the universe began? (We talked about it in chapter 4 under "The Laws of Thermodynamics.") Roger Penrose of Oxford University has calculated that the odds of that low-entropy state's existing by chance alone is on the order of one chance out of $10^{10^{(123)}}$, a number that is so inconceivable that to call it astronomical would be a wild understatement.

The fine-tuning here is beyond comprehension. Having an accuracy of even one part out of 10^{60} is like firing a bullet toward the other side of the observable universe, twenty billion light-years away, and nailing a one-inch target!

The examples of fine-tuning are so many and so various that they aren't likely to disappear with the advance of science. Like it or not, fine-tuning is just a fact of life that is scientifically well established.

A KEY DISTINCTION

The term *fine-tuned* does *not* mean "designed." The expression is a neutral term that doesn't say anything about how the fine-tuning is best explained. *Fine-tuning* just means that the range of life-permitting values for the constants and quantities is extremely narrow. If the value of even one of these constants or quantities were to be altered by a hair's breadth, the delicate balance required for the existence of life would be upset and the universe would be life-prohibiting instead.

TALK ABOUT IT

How does it affect you to know that the universe is so precisely fine-tuned?

The philosopher John Leslie gives the following illustration to show why we needn't be concerned with universes governed by different laws of nature. Imagine a solitary fly, resting on a large, blank area of the wall. A single shot is fired, and the bullet strikes the fly. Now even if the rest of the wall outside the blank area is covered with flies, so that a randomly fired bullet would probably hit one, nevertheless it remains highly improbable that a single, randomly fired bullet would strike the solitary fly within the large, blank area. A life-permitting universe is like that solitary fly on the wall. When we consider universes governed by our laws of nature, almost all of them are life-prohibiting. So the odds that a universe selected randomly out of this lot would be life-permitting are practically nil.

A Possible Objection and Its Answer

Now some of you might be thinking, *But if the constants and quantities had had different values, then maybe different forms of life might have evolved.* But that underestimates the truly disastrous consequences of a change in the values of these constants and quantities.

When scientists say a universe is life-permitting, they're not talking about just present forms of life. By "life" scientists just mean the property of organisms to take in food, extract energy from it, grow, adapt to their environment, and reproduce. Anything that can fulfill those functions counts as life, whatever form it might take. And in order for life, so defined, to exist, the constants and quantities of the universe have to be unbelievably fine-tuned. In the absence of fine-tuning, not even matter, not even chemistry would exist, much less planets where life might evolve!

Another Objection and Its Answer

Sometimes people will object, "But maybe in a universe governed by *different* laws of nature, such disastrous consequences might not result." But this objection betrays a misunderstanding of the argument.

We're not concerned with universes governed by *different* laws of nature. We have no idea what such universes might be like! Rather we're concerned solely with universes governed by the *same* laws of nature but with *different* values of the constants and arbitrary quantities. Because the laws are the same, we can determine what would happen if the constants and quantities were to be altered. And the results turn out to be disastrous. Among universes governed by our laws of nature, there's almost no chance that a randomly chosen universe would be life-permitting.

An Argument for Design

The question we face, then, is this: What is the best explanation of the cosmic fine-tuning? Many people think that the reason the universe is finely tuned for life is because it was designed to be life-permitting by an intelligent Designer.

But design is not the only alternative. There are also physical necessity and chance. The key to inferring that design is the best explanation will be eliminating these other two alternatives.

Accordingly, we can present a very simple three-step argument:

1. The fine-tuning of the universe is due to either physical necessity, chance, or design.

2. It is not due to physical necessity or chance.

3. Therefore, it is due to design.

This is a logically valid argument whose conclusion follows necessarily from the two premises. So the only question is whether those premises are more plausibly true than false. So let's look at them.

PREMISE 1

The fine-tuning of the universe is due to either physical necessity, chance, or design.

The first premise, that *the fine-tuning of the universe is due to either physical necessity, chance, or design,* is unobjectionable because it just lists the three alternatives available for explaining the fine-tuning. If someone has a fourth alternative, he's welcome to add it to the list, and then we'll consider it when we come to premise 2. But there doesn't seem to be another alternative to the three listed here.

PREMISE 2

The fine-tuning is not due to physical necessity or chance.

So the crucial premise is the second premise: that *the fine-tuning is not due to physical necessity or chance.* Let's examine each of these alternatives in turn.

TALK ABOUT IT

In popular culture, where do you see chance promoted as an explanation for our world? What about necessity? What about design? Which of these ideas do you think gets the most airtime at the popular level?

Physical Necessity?

According to the first alternative, physical necessity, the universe *has* to be life-permitting. The constants and quantities must have the values they do, so that a life-prohibiting universe is physically impossible.

Implausibility of Physical Necessity

Now on the face of it, this alternative seems fantastically implausible. It would require us to say that a life-prohibiting universe is a physical impossibility. But why take such a radical view? The constants are not determined by the laws of nature. So why couldn't they be different? Moreover, the arbitrary quantities are just boundary conditions on which the laws of nature operate. Nothing seems to make them necessary. So the opponent of design is taking a radical line that requires some proof. But there is none. The alternative is put forward as a bare possibility.

Sometimes scientists do talk of a yet-to-be-discovered "theory of everything" (TOE), which certainly *sounds* like a physical explanation of everything, including the fine-tuning. But like so many of the colorful names given to scientific theories, this label is very misleading. A successful TOE would enable us to unify the four basic forces of nature (gravity, the weak force, the strong force, and electromagnetism) into a single force carried by a single kind of particle. It would result in a great simplification of physics. But it wouldn't even attempt to explain literally everything. For example, the most promising candidate for a TOE to date, so-called M-theory or superstring theory, only works if there are eleven dimensions. But the theory itself can't explain why just that particular number of dimensions should exist.

Moreover, M-theory doesn't predict uniquely a life-permitting universe. It permits a vast range of around 10^{500} different possible universes, all consistent with the same laws but varying in the values of the constants of nature. Almost all of these possible universes are life-prohibiting. So some explanation is needed why, out of all these possibilities, a life-permitting universe exists. We can't say

AN END RUN AROUND

EVOLUTION

Notice that by focusing on cosmic fine-tuning this argument does an end run around the whole emotionally charged issue of biological evolution. The argument from fine-tuning, if successful, will show that the evolution of intelligent life *anywhere* in the cosmos depends upon the design of the initial cosmic conditions. Any design arguments based on the origin of life, the origin of biological complexity, the origin of consciousness, and so on, will simply layer on more improbability, making it all the more unlikely that all this can be explained apart from a Designer.

that life-permitting universes are physically necessary, since based on M-theory, at least, that's clearly false.

So there's no evidence that a life-permitting universe is physically necessary. Quite the contrary, all the evidence indicates that life-prohibiting universes are not only possible but far, far more likely than any life-permitting universe.

Chance?

That leads to the second alternative: Could the fine-tuning be due simply to chance? According to this alternative, it's just an accident that all the constants and quantities fell into the life-permitting range. We basically just lucked out!

The fundamental problem here is that the chances that the universe that exists should happen to be life-permitting are so remote that this alternative becomes unreasonable.

Improbability of a Life-Permitting Universe

Sometimes people object that it's meaningless to speak of the probability of a fine-tuned universe's existing because there is, after all, only one universe. So you can't say that one out of every ten universes, for example, is life-permitting.

But the following illustration from the physicist John Barrow clarifies the sense in which a life-permitting universe is improbable. Take a sheet of paper and place upon it a red dot. That dot represents our universe.

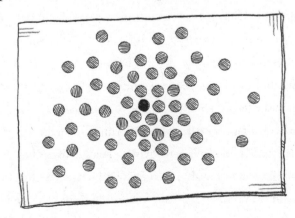

The so-called "cosmic landscape" of worlds permitted by M-theory has become something of a phenom lately. It's important to understand that the landscape is just a range of possibilities. Some people have misinterpreted it to mean that all these different universes actually exist. Some have thought it undermines the argument for design because the landscape must include life-permitting worlds like ours. But the cosmic landscape is not real; it's just a list of possibilities. It describes the range of universes that are consistent with M-theory.

Now alter slightly one or more of the finely tuned constants and physical quantities that we've been discussing. As a result we have a description of another universe, which we can represent as a new dot in the neighborhood of the first. If that new set of constants and quantities describes a life-permitting universe, make it a red dot; if it describes a universe that is life-prohibiting, make it a blue dot. Now repeat the procedure over and over again until the sheet is filled with dots. What you wind up with is a sea of blue with only a few pinpoints of red. That's the sense in which it is overwhelmingly improbable that the universe should be life-permitting. There are simply vastly more life-prohibiting universes in our local area of possible universes than there are life-permitting universes.

Lottery Illustrations

Sometimes people will appeal to the example of a lottery in order to justify the chance alternative. In a lottery where all the tickets are sold, it's fantastically improbable that any one person should win, yet *somebody* has to win! It would be unjustified for the winner, whoever he may be, to say, "The odds against my winning were twenty million to one. And yet I won! The lottery must have been rigged!"

In the same way, they say, *some* universe out of the range of possible universes has to exist. The winner of the universe lottery would also be unjustified to think that because his universe exists, this must have been the result of design, not chance. *All* the universes are equally improbable, but one of them, by chance, has to win.

This analogy is actually very helpful because it enables us to see clearly where the advocate of chance has misunderstood the argument for design and to offer a better, more accurate analogy in its place. Contrary to popular impression, the argument for design is not trying to explain why *this* particular universe exists. Rather it's trying to explain why a life-permitting universe exists. The lottery analogy was misconceived because it focused on why a particular person won.

The correct analogy would be a lottery in which billions and billions and

billions of white ping-pong balls were mixed together with just one black ping-pong ball, and you were told that one ball will be randomly selected out of the horde. If it's black, you'll be allowed to live; if it's white, you'll be shot.

Now notice that any particular ball that is randomly selected is equally improbable: No matter which ball rolls down the chute, the odds against that particular ball are fantastically improbable. But some ball must roll down the chute. This is the point illustrated by the first lottery analogy. That point, however, is irrelevant because we're not trying to explain why *this particular* ball was picked.

The crucial point is that whichever ball rolls down the chute, it is overwhelmingly more probable that *it will be white rather than black*. Getting the black ball is no more improbable than getting any *particular* white ball. But it is incomprehensibly more probable that you will get a white ball instead of a black one. So if the black ball rolls down the chute, you certainly should suspect that the lottery was rigged to let you live.

REINFORCING THE

LOTTERY STORY

If you're having difficulty seeing the point of the lottery analogy in the text, then imagine that in order for you to live, the black ball had to be randomly picked five times in a row. If the odds against getting the black ball even once are great enough, then getting it five times rather than once won't affect the probabilities significantly. But if you got the black ball five times in a row, everyone would recognize that it didn't happen by chance!

So in the correct analogy, we're not interested in why you got the particular ball you did. Rather we're puzzled by why, against overwhelming odds, you got a life-permitting ball rather than a life-prohibiting ball. That question is just not addressed by saying, "Well, some ball had to be picked!"

In the same way, some universe has to exist, but whichever universe exists, it is incomprehensibly more probable that it will be life-prohibiting rather than life-permitting. So we still need some explanation why a life-permitting universe exists.

THE ANTHROPIC PRINCIPLE

We can observe only those values of the fundamental constants and quantities that are compatible with our existence.

Is an Explanation Needed?

Some people have argued that no explanation is needed for why we observe a life-permitting universe because that's the only kind of universe we *can* observe! If the universe were not life-permitting, then we wouldn't be here to ask about it. (This is the so-called Anthropic Principle, which says that we can observe only properties of the universe that are compatible with our existence.)

This reasoning is fallacious. The fact that we can observe only a life-permitting universe does nothing to eliminate the need of an explanation for why a life-permitting universe exists.

Again, an illustration can help. Imagine you're traveling abroad and arrested on trumped-up drug charges. You're dragged in front of a firing squad of one hundred trained marksmen standing at point-blank range. You hear the command given: "Ready! Aim! Fire!" You hear the deafening sound of the guns. And then you observe that you're still alive! That all of the one hundred marksmen missed! Now what would you conclude?

"Well, I guess I shouldn't be surprised that they all missed! After all, if they hadn't all missed, I wouldn't be here to be surprised about it! Nothing more to be explained here!"

Of course not! It's true that you shouldn't be surprised that you don't observe that you're dead, since if you were dead, you wouldn't be able to observe it. But you should still be surprised that you do observe that you're alive, in light of the enormous improbability that all the marksmen would miss.

Indeed, you'd probably conclude that they all missed *on purpose*, that the whole thing was a set up, engineered for some reason by someone.

The Many Worlds Hypothesis

Theorists have therefore come to recognize that the Anthropic Principle cannot eliminate the need of an explanation of the fine-tuning *unless* it's conjoined with a many worlds hypothesis. According to that hypothesis, our universe is but one member of a world ensemble or "multiverse" of randomly ordered universes, preferably infinite in number. If all of these other universes really exist, then by chance alone life-permitting worlds will appear somewhere in the world ensemble. Since only finely tuned universes have observers in them, any observers existing in the world ensemble will naturally observe their worlds to be finely tuned. So no appeal to design is necessary to explain fine-tuning. It's pure chance.

First Response to the Many Worlds Hypothesis

One way to respond to the many worlds hypothesis would be to show that the multiverse itself also involves fine-tuning. For in order to be scientifically credible, some plausible mechanism must be suggested for generating the many worlds. But if the many worlds hypothesis is to be successful in attributing fine-tuning to chance alone, then the mechanism that generates the many worlds had better not be fine-tuned itself! For if it is, then the problem arises all over again: How do you explain the fine-tuning of the multiverse?

The proposed mechanisms for generating a world ensemble are so vague that it's far from clear that the physics governing the multiverse will not involve any fine-tuning. For example, if M-theory is the physics of the multiverse, then it remains unexplained, as we've seen, why exactly eleven dimensions exist. And the mechanism that actualizes all the possibilities in the cosmic landscape may involve fine-tuning. So the postulate of a world ensemble is by itself not enough to justify the alternative of chance.

Second Response to the Many Worlds Hypothesis

Moreover, many theorists are skeptical of the many worlds hypothesis itself. Why think that a world ensemble actually exists? We saw in chapter 4 that the Borde-Guth-Vilenkin theorem requires that even a multiverse of bubble universes must have a beginning. In that case the mechanism that generates the bubble universes has been chugging away for only a finite amount of time. So by now, there may well be only a finite number of bubbles in the world ensemble, which may not be enough to guarantee the appearance of

A BACKHANDED COMPLIMENT TO DESIGN

The current debate over fine-tuning has now become a debate over the many worlds hypothesis. In order to explain fine-tuning we're being asked to believe not merely that there are other unobservable universes, but that there is an infinite number of such worlds and that they randomly vary in their fundamental constants and quantities. All this is needed to guarantee that a life-permitting universe like ours will appear by chance in the ensemble. The many worlds hypothesis is really a sort of backhanded compliment to the design hypothesis. For otherwise sober scientists would not be flocking to adopt so speculative and extravagant a view as the many worlds hypothesis unless they felt absolutely compelled to. So if someone says to you, "The fine-tuning could have happened by chance!" or "The improbable happens!" or "It was just dumb luck!" ask him, "Then why do the detractors of design feel compelled to embrace an extravagance like the many worlds hypothesis in order to avoid design?"

a finely tuned universe by chance alone. There's no evidence that the sort of world ensemble required by the many worlds hypothesis actually exists.

By contrast, we have good, independent reasons for believing in a Designer of the cosmos, as Leibniz and al-Ghazali's arguments show.

Third Response to the Many Worlds Hypothesis

Moreover, the many worlds hypothesis faces what may be a devastating objection. Remember Boltzmann's many worlds hypothesis discussed in chapter 4? What sank Boltzmann's hypothesis was the fact that if our world is just a random member of a world ensemble, then it's vastly more probable that we should be observing a much smaller region of order. It turns out that a parallel problem faces the many worlds hypothesis as an explanation of cosmic fine-tuning.

TALK ABOUT IT

Given the flaws in the many worlds hypothesis, why do you think so many people prefer to believe in chance rather than in a Designer?

Roger Penrose has pressed this objection forcefully.[1] He points out that the odds of our universe's initial low-entropy condition's existing by chance alone are one chance out of $10^{10^{(123)}}$. By contrast the odds of our solar system's suddenly forming by the random collision of particles is one chance out of $10^{10^{(60)}}$. This number, says Penrose, is "utter chicken feed" in comparison with $10^{10^{(123)}}$. What that means is that it is *far* more likely that we should be observing an orderly universe no larger than our solar system, since a world of that size is unfathomably more probable than a fine-tuned universe like ours.

In fact, we wind up with the same sort of illusionism that saddled Boltzmann's hypothesis. A small world with the illusion of a wider, orderly universe is more probable than a fine-tuned, real universe. Carried to its logical extreme, this has led to what theorists have called "the invasion of the Boltzmann brains." For the most probable observable universe is one that consists of a single brain that pops into existence by a random fluctuation with illusory perceptions of the orderly cosmos! So if you accept the many worlds hypothesis, you're obligated to believe that you are all that exists and that this book, your body, the earth, and everything you perceive in the world are just illusions.

No sane person believes that he is a Boltzmann brain. Given atheism, therefore, it's highly improbable that there exists a randomly ordered world ensemble. Ironically, the best hope for partisans of the multiverse is to maintain that God created it and ordered its worlds, so that they're not randomly ordered. God could give preference to observable worlds that are cosmically fine-tuned. To be rationally acceptable, the many worlds hypothesis needs God.

With the failure of the many worlds hypothesis, the last ring of defense for the alternative of chance collapses. Neither physical necessity nor chance provides a good explanation of the fine-tuning of the universe.

Design: Dawkins' Objection

So what about design? Is this explanation better than physical necessity or chance, or is it equally implausible?

Detractors of design sometimes object that on this hypothesis the Cosmic Designer Himself remains unexplained. This objection is what Richard Dawkins calls "the central argument of my book" *The God Delusion*.[2] He summarizes his argument as follows:

1. One of the greatest challenges to the human intellect has been to explain how the complex, improbable appearance of design in the universe arises.

2. The natural temptation is to attribute the appearance of design to actual design itself.

3. The temptation is a false one because the designer hypothesis immediately raises the larger problem of who designed the designer.

4. The most ingenious and powerful explanation is Darwinian evolution by natural selection.

5. We don't have an equivalent explanation for physics.

6. We should not give up the hope of a better explanation arising in physics, something as powerful as Darwinism is for biology.

Therefore, God almost certainly does not exist.

Invalidity of Dawkins' Argument: The Conclusion Doesn't Follow

Dawkins' argument is jarring because the atheistic conclusion, "Therefore, God almost certainly does not exist," doesn't follow from the six previous statements even if we concede that each of them is true. There are no rules of logic that would permit such an inference. Dawkins' argument is plainly invalid.

At most, all that follows from Dawkins' argument is that we should not infer God's existence on the basis of the appearance of design in the universe. But that conclusion is quite compatible with God's existence and even with our justifiably believing in God's existence. Maybe we should believe in God on the basis of the cosmological argument or the moral argument. Maybe our belief in God isn't based on arguments at all but is grounded in religious experience or in divine revelation. The point is that rejecting design arguments for God's existence does nothing to prove that atheism is true or that belief in God is unjustified. Dawkins' lack of philosophical depth is plainly on display here.

Falsity of Dawkins' Premises

But does Dawkins' argument succeed even in undermining the argument for design? Not at all, for several of the steps of Dawkins' argument are plausibly false. Step 5 refers to the cosmic fine-tuning that has been the focus of our discussion. Dawkins has nothing by way of explanation for it, and therefore the hope expressed in step 6 represents nothing more than the faith of a naturalist.

Moreover, consider step 3. Dawkins' claim here is that we are not justified in inferring design as the best explanation of the complex order of the universe because then a new problem arises: Who designed the designer?

NATURALISM

Naturalism is the belief that only natural explanations (as opposed to supernatural ones) should be considered. Because a designer is defined as supernatural—beyond nature—naturalism rules out this explanation, regardless of evidence.

First Problem with Step 3: You Don't Need to Explain the Explanation

This claim is flawed on at least two counts. First, in order to recognize an explanation as the best, you don't need to have an explanation of the explanation. This is an elementary point in the philosophy of science. If archaeologists digging in the earth were to discover things looking like arrowheads and pottery shards, they would be justified in inferring that these artifacts are not the chance result of sedimentation and metamorphosis, but products of some unknown group of people, even though they had no explanation of who these people were or where they came from. Similarly, if astronauts were to come upon a pile of machinery on the back side of the moon, they would be justified in inferring that it was the product of intelligent agents, even if they had no idea whatsoever who these agents were or how they got there.

So in order to recognize an explanation as the best, you don't need to be able to explain the explanation. In fact, such a requirement would lead to an infinite regress of explanations, so that nothing could ever be explained and science would be destroyed! For before any explanation could be acceptable, you'd need an explanation of it, and then an explanation of the explanation of the explanation, and then…. Nothing could ever be explained.

So in the case at hand, in order to recognize that intelligent design is the best explanation of the appearance of design in the universe, one needn't be able to explain the Designer. Whether the Designer has an explanation can simply be left an open question for future inquiry.

Second Problem with Step 3: God Is Remarkably Simple

Second, Dawkins thinks that in the case of a divine Designer of the universe, the Designer is just as complex as the thing to be explained, so that no explanatory advance is made. This objection raises all sorts of questions about the role played by simplicity in assessing competing explanations. For example, there are many other factors besides simplicity that scientists weigh in determining which explanation is the best, such as explanatory power, explanatory scope, and so forth. An explanation that has broader explanatory scope may be less simple than a rival explanation but still be preferred because it explains more things. Simplicity is not the only, or even most important, criterion for assessing theories.

But leave those questions aside. Dawkins' fundamental mistake lies in his assumption that a divine Designer is just as complex as the universe. That is plainly false. As a pure mind without a body, God is a remarkably simple entity. A mind (or soul) is not a physical object composed of parts. In contrast to the contingent and variegated universe with all its inexplicable constants and quantities, a divine mind is startlingly simple. Certainly such a mind may have complex *ideas*—it may be thinking, for example, of the infinitesimal calculus—but the mind *itself* is a remarkably simple, spiritual entity. Dawkins has evidently confused a mind's ideas, which may, indeed, be complex, with a mind itself, which is an incredibly simple entity. Therefore, postulating a divine mind behind the universe most definitely does represent an advance in simplicity, for whatever that's worth.

TALK ABOUT IT

Given the flaws in Dawkins' reasoning, how do you account for the huge popularity of his book (more than 1.5 million copies sold)? What, other than logic, might explain its popular appeal?

Other steps in Dawkins' argument are also problematic, but I think enough has been said to show that his argument does nothing to undermine the fine-tuning argument for a cosmic Designer, not to speak of its serving as a justification of atheism. Several years ago the atheist philosopher Quentin Smith unceremoniously crowned Stephen Hawking's argument against God in *A Brief History of Time* as "the worst atheistic argument in the history of Western thought."[3] With the advent of *The God Delusion* the time has come, I think, to relieve Hawking of this weighty crown and to recognize Richard Dawkins' accession to the throne.

TALK ABOUT IT

If there really is a Designer who fine-tuned the universe, what can we learn about Him from the intricacy of the fine-tuning that is needed to create a world like ours?

Conclusion

Therefore it seems to me that of the three alternatives before us—physical necessity, chance, or design—the most plausible of the three is design. Plato and Aristotle would doubtless have been gratified by modern science's vindication of their views. We have, then, a third argument in our cumulative case for the existence of God.

1. Roger Penrose, *The Road to Reality* (New York: Alfred A. Knopf, 2005) 762–5.
2. Richard Dawkins, *The God Delusion* (New York: Houghton Mifflin, 2006), 157–8.
3. Quentin Smith, "The Wave Function of a Godless Universe," in *Theism, Atheism, and Big Bang Cosmology*, by William Lane Craig and Quentin Smith (Oxford: Clarendon Press, 1993), 322.

THE DESIGN ARGUMENT

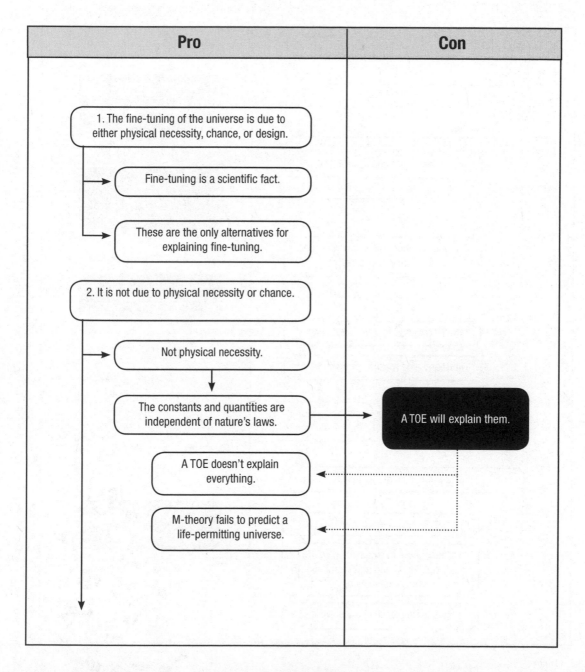

Pro	Con

1. The fine-tuning of the universe is due to either physical necessity, chance, or design.

→ Fine-tuning is a scientific fact.

→ These are the only alternatives for explaining fine-tuning.

2. It is not due to physical necessity or chance.

→ Not physical necessity.

The constants and quantities are independent of nature's laws.

A TOE will explain them.

A TOE doesn't explain everything.

M-theory fails to predict a life-permitting universe.

THE DESIGN ARGUMENT (cont.)

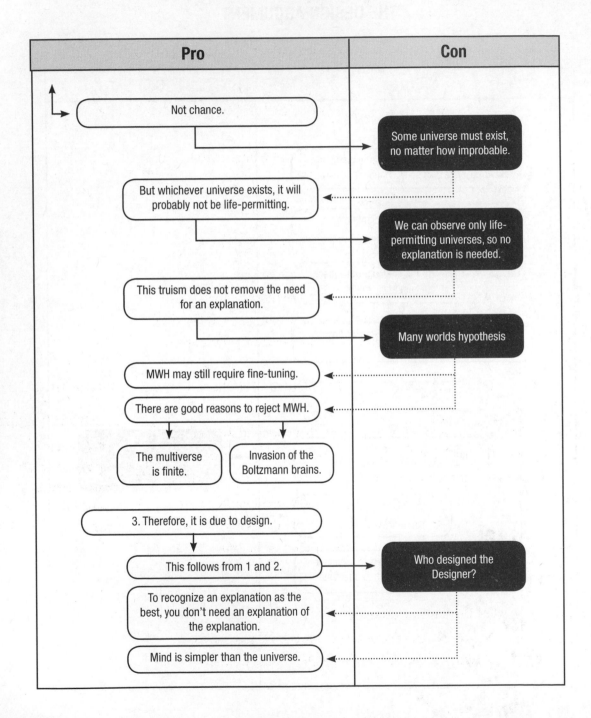

Pro	Con
Not chance.	
	Some universe must exist, no matter how improbable.
But whichever universe exists, it will probably not be life-permitting.	
	We can observe only life-permitting universes, so no explanation is needed.
This truism does not remove the need for an explanation.	
	Many worlds hypothesis
MWH may still require fine-tuning.	
There are good reasons to reject MWH.	
The multiverse is finite.	Invasion of the Boltzmann brains.
3. Therefore, it is due to design.	
This follows from 1 and 2.	Who designed the Designer?
To recognize an explanation as the best, you don't need an explanation of the explanation.	
Mind is simpler than the universe.	

CHAPTER 6

CAN WE BE GOOD WITHOUT GOD?

No one is good but God alone. (Mark 10:18 RSV)

Can we be good without God?

At first the answer to this question might seem so obvious that even to ask it is apt to make people angry. For while Christians find in God a source of moral strength that helps us to lead better lives than those we would have led without Him, still it would be arrogant and ignorant to claim that unbelievers don't often lead good moral lives—in fact, sometimes lives that put ours to shame.

But wait! While it would be arrogant and ignorant to claim that people cannot be good without *belief* in God, that wasn't the question. The question was: Can we be good *without God?* When we ask that question, we're posing a question about the nature of moral values. Are the values we hold dear and guide our lives by just social conventions, like driving on the right-hand versus left-hand side of the road? Or are they merely expressions of personal preference, like having a taste for certain foods? Or are they somehow valid and binding, independent of our opinion, and if they are objective in this way, what is their foundation?

A Moral Argument for God's Existence

Many philosophers have thought that morality provides a good argument for God's existence. One of the finest was William Sorley, who was a

WHAT IS THE BASIS OF
OUR VALUES?

Are they based on:
1. Social convention?
2. Personal preference?
3. Evolution?
4. God?

professor of moral philosophy at Cambridge University. In his *Moral Values and the Idea of God* (1918) Sorley argues that the best hope for a rational, unified view of reality is to postulate God as the ground of both the natural and the moral orders.

Sorley maintains that there is an objective moral order, which is as real and independent of us as is the natural order of things. He recognizes that in one sense we can't prove that objective moral values exist, but he points out that in this same sense we can't prove that the natural world of physical objects exists either! (You could be a body lying in the Matrix experiencing a virtual reality.) The moral order and the natural order are thus on a similar footing. Just as we assume the reality of the world of objects on the basis of our sense experience, so we assume the reality of the moral order on the basis of our moral experience.

TALK ABOUT IT

How do you respond to the idea that the objective moral order is just as real as the objective physical world? Why?

In Sorley's view both the natural order and the moral order are part of reality. The question, then, is: What worldview can combine these two orders into the most coherent explanatory form? Sorley argued that the best explanation is God. There must be an infinite, eternal Mind who is the architect of nature and whose moral purpose man and the universe are gradually fulfilling.

I myself stumbled into the moral argument while speaking on university campuses on the absurdity of life without God. I argued that if there is no God, then there is no foundation for objective moral values. Everything becomes relative. To my surprise the response of the students was to insist that objective moral values do exist. Certain things really are right or wrong.

Now what the students said didn't in any way refute my claim that without God there would be no objective values. Instead, they had unwittingly supplied the missing premise in a moral argument for God's existence! For now we can argue:

1. If God does not exist, objective moral values and duties do not exist.

2. Objective moral values and duties do exist.

3. Therefore, God exists.

This simple little argument is easy to memorize and is logically ironclad. I had argued for the truth of the first premise and the students had insisted on the second. Together the two premises imply the existence of God.

What makes this argument so powerful is that people generally believe both premises. In a pluralistic age, students are scared to death of imposing their values on someone else. So premise 1 seems correct to them because of its implicit relativism. At the same time, certain values have been deeply instilled into them, such as tolerance, open-mindedness, and love. They think it's objectively *wrong* to impose your values on someone else! So they're deeply committed to premise 2 as well.

This can lead to some very strange conversations. I remember talking with one student who would jump back and forth between the premises. When we'd talk about the first premise, he'd agree with it and deny the second premise. But when we'd move on to the second premise, he'd agree with it and deny the first. And so back and forth we went, with him unable to make up his mind! It would have been funny, had it not been so heartwrenching to see someone floundering in this way in a vain attempt to avoid God.

TALK ABOUT IT

Have you ever had a conversation with someone who said there are no objective moral values that apply to everyone? If so, how did that person deal with values like tolerance and love?

Let's examine more closely each of the argument's two premises in order to see what defense you can offer on their behalf and what objections the nonbeliever might raise against them.

PREMISE 1

If God does not exist, objective moral values and duties do not exist.

Two Important Distinctions

The first premise, that *if God does not exist, objective moral values and duties do not exist*, involves some important distinctions that must be grasped before we can look at reasons for thinking that premise to be true.

Values and Duties

First, notice that I distinguish *values* and *duties*. Values have to do with whether something is good or bad. Duties have to do with whether something is right or wrong. Now you might think at first that this is a distinction without a difference: "Good" and "right" mean the same thing, and the same goes for "bad" and "wrong." But if you think about it, you can see that this isn't the case.

Duty has to do with moral obligation, what you ought or ought not to do. But obviously you're not morally obligated to do something just because it would be good for you to do it. For example, it would be good for you to become a doctor, but you're not morally obligated to become a doctor. After all, it would also be good for you to become a homemaker or a farmer or a diplomat, but you can't do them all. Furthermore, sometimes all you have is bad choices (think of *Sophie's Choice*), but it's not wrong for you to choose one, since you must choose.

So there's a difference between good/bad and right/wrong. Good/bad has to do with something's *worth*, while right/wrong has to do with something's being *obligatory*.

Objective and Subjective

Second, there's the distinction between being *objective* or *subjective*. By *objective* I mean "independent of people's opinions." By *subjective* I mean "dependent on people's opinions." So to say that there are objective moral values is to say that something is good or bad no matter what people think about it.

Moral value refers to the worth of a person or action, whether it is good or bad. *Moral duty* refers to our obligation to act in a certain way, whether that action is right or wrong.

TALK ABOUT IT

Make a list of some *values*—some things you believe are good or bad. Then make a list of some *duties*—some things you believe are right or wrong. Compare your lists with someone else's to be sure you're clear about the distinction.

Similarly, to say that we have objective moral duties is to say that certain actions are right or wrong for us regardless of what people think.

So, for example, to say that the Holocaust was objectively wrong is to say that it was wrong even though the Nazis who carried it out thought that it was right, and it would still have been wrong even if the Nazis had won World War II and succeeded in exterminating or brainwashing everybody who disagreed with them, so that everyone believed the Holocaust was right.

Premise 1 asserts that if there is no God, then moral values and duties are not objective in that sense.

Defense of Premise 1

Objective Moral Values Require God

So consider, first, moral values. Traditionally moral values have been based in God, who is the highest Good. But if God does not exist, what is the basis of moral values? In particular, why think that human beings have moral worth? The most popular form of atheism is naturalism, which holds that the only things that exist are the things described by our best scientific theories. But science is morally neutral; you can't find moral values in a test tube. It follows immediately that moral values don't really exist; they're just illusions of human beings.

Even if the atheist is willing to go beyond the bounds of science, why think, given an atheistic worldview, that human beings are morally valuable? On a naturalistic view moral values are just the by-product of biological evolution and social conditioning. Just as a troop of baboons exhibit cooperative and even self-sacrificial behavior because natural selection has determined it to be advantageous in the struggle for survival, so their primate cousins *Homo sapiens* exhibit similar behavior for the same reason. As a result of sociobiological pressures there has evolved among *Homo sapiens* a sort of "herd morality," which functions well in the perpetuation of our species.

Objective means independent of human opinion. For example, the laws of nature hold whether we acknowledge them or not, so they are objective. *Subjective* means dependent on human opinion. For example, matters of taste, like whether coffee tastes good, are person-relative and so are subjective.

CHARLES DARWIN

SPECIESISM

Speciesism is "a prejudice or attitude of bias in favor of the interests of members of one's own species and against those of members of other species." British psychologist and philosopher Richard D. Ryder coined the term in 1970, and it was later picked up by many animal rights activists, including Peter Singer.

But on the atheistic view there doesn't seem to be anything about *Homo sapiens* that makes this morality objectively true. If we were to rewind the film of human evolution back to the beginning and start anew, people with a very different set of moral values might well have evolved.

As Darwin himself wrote in *The Descent of Man*,

> If … men were reared under precisely the same conditions as hive-bees, there can hardly be a doubt that our unmarried females would, like the worker-bees, think it a sacred duty to kill their brothers, and mothers would strive to kill their fertile daughters; and no one would think of interfering.[1]

For us to think that human beings are special and our morality objectively true is to succumb to the temptation to speciesism, an unjustified bias toward one's own species.

So if there is no God, any basis for regarding the herd morality evolved by *Homo sapiens* as objectively true seems to have been removed. Take God out of the picture, and all you're left with is an apelike creature on a speck of solar dust beset with delusions of moral grandeur.

Objective Moral Duties Require God

Second, now consider moral duties. Traditionally our moral duties were thought to spring from God's commandments, such as the Ten Commandments. But if there is no God, what basis remains for objective moral duties? On the atheistic view, human beings are just animals, and animals have no moral obligations to one another. When a lion kills a zebra, it kills the zebra, but it does not *murder* the zebra. When a great white shark forcibly copulates with a female, it forcibly copulates with her but it does not *rape* her—for there is no moral dimension to these actions. They are neither prohibited nor obligatory.

"I'm sorry, officer. I just don't like tofu."

So if God does not exist, why think that we have any moral obligations to do anything? Who or what imposes these moral duties upon us? Where do they come from? It's hard to see why they would be anything more than a subjective impression resulting from societal and parental conditioning.

Certain actions such as incest and rape may not be biologically and socially advantageous and so in the course of human development have become taboo. But that does absolutely nothing to show that rape or incest is really *wrong*. Such behavior goes on all the time in the animal kingdom. The rapist who goes against the herd morality is doing nothing more serious than acting unfashionably, like the man who belches loudly at the dinner table. If there is no moral lawgiver, then there is no objective moral law that we must obey.

TALK ABOUT IT

Try to come up with an atheist's argument to defend the idea that forcible copulation is morally wrong for humans but not for sharks. How would you reply?

Getting Clear about the Argument

Now it's extremely important that we clearly understand the issue before us. I can almost guarantee that if you share this moral argument with unbelievers, someone will say indignantly, "Are you saying that all atheists are bad people?" They'll think you are judgmental and intolerant. We need to help them see that this is a complete misunderstanding of the argument.

The question is *not:* Must we believe in God in order to live moral lives? There's no reason to think that nonbelievers cannot live what we'd normally call good and decent lives.

Again, the question is *not:* Can we recognize objective moral values and duties without believing in God? There's no reason to think that you have to believe in God in order to recognize that, for example, we ought to love our children.

Or again, the question is *not:* Can we formulate a system of ethics without referring to God? If the nonbeliever recognizes the intrinsic value of human beings, there's no reason to think he can't work out an ethical code of conduct that the believer will generally agree with. (Of course, he won't take into account any moral obligations we have toward God.)

Rather the question is: If God does not exist, do objective moral values and duties exist? The question is not about the necessity of *belief* in God for objective morality but about the necessity of the *existence* of God for objective morality.

I've been shocked at how often even professional philosophers, who should know better, confuse these two questions. For example, I participated in a debate at Franklin and Marshall College with the humanist philosopher Paul Kurtz on the topic "Goodness without God Is Good Enough." I argued that if God does not exist, there are no objective moral values, duties, or accountability for one's actions.

Prof. Kurtz, to my astonishment, completely missed the point. He replied,

> If God is essential, then how is it possible that millions
> of people who do not believe in God, nonetheless behave

morally? On your view, they should not. And so, your God is not essential…. Many people have been optimistic about life; they have lived a full life … and have found life exhilirating and … richly significant. Nor do they wring their hands about whether or not there is an afterlife. It's living life here and now that counts.[2]

Kurtz's point shows only that *belief* in God isn't essential to living a moral, optimistic life. It does nothing to refute my claim that if there is no God, then morality is just a human illusion.

To repeat: *Belief* in God is not necessary for objective morality; *God* is.

The Euthyphro Dilemma

The other response you can count on getting from unbelievers is the so-called Euthyphro dilemma, named after a character in one of Plato's dialogues. It basically goes like this: Is something good because God wills it? Or does God will something because it is good? If you say that something is good because God wills it, then what is good becomes arbitrary. God could have willed that hatred is good, and then we would have been morally obligated to hate one another. That seems crazy. Some moral values, at least, seem to be necessary. But if you say that God wills something because it is good, then what is good or bad is independent of God. In that case, moral values and duties exist independently of God, which contradicts premise 1.

Answer to the Euthyphro Dilemma

We don't need to refute either of the two horns of the Euthyphro dilemma, because the dilemma it presents is a false one: There's a third alternative, namely, God wills something because He is good. What do I mean by that? I mean that God's own nature is the standard of goodness, and His

THINK ABOUT IT

How would you explain the fact that atheists just know that harming an innocent human being is wrong, and can live good lives, without believing that God is the ultimate source of values and duties?

1. Is something good because God wills it? Then the good is arbitrary.
2. Does God will something because it is good? Then it is a moral value independent of God.

Solution: God wills something because He is good.

commandments to us are expressions of His nature. In short, our moral duties are determined by the commands of a just and loving God.

So moral values are not independent of God because God's own character defines what is good. God is essentially compassionate, fair, kind, impartial, and so on. His nature is the moral standard defining good and bad. His commands necessarily reflect His moral nature. Therefore, they're not arbitrary. When the atheist demands, "If God were to command child abuse, would we be obligated to abuse our children?" he's asking a question like "If there were a square circle, would its area be the square of one of its sides?" There is no answer because what it supposes is logically impossible.

So the Euthyphro dilemma presents us with a false choice, and we shouldn't be tricked by it. The morally good/bad is determined by God's nature, and the morally right/wrong is determined by His will. God wills something because He is good, and something is right because God wills it.

Atheistic Moral Platonism: Moral Values Simply Exist

The mention of Plato brings to mind another possible response to premise 1. Plato thought that the Good just exists on its own as a sort of self-existent Idea. (If you find this difficult to grasp, join the company!) Later Christian thinkers equated Plato's Good with God's moral nature; but Plato thought the Good just existed by itself. So some atheists might say that moral values like justice, mercy, love, and so on, just exist without any foundation. We can call this view atheistic moral platonism. It holds that objective moral values exist but are not grounded in God. What might we say about this view?

A STRAW MAN

The view of moral values and duties explained in the text has been eloquently defended in our day by such eminent philosophers as Robert Adams, William Alston, and Philip Quinn. Yet atheists continue to put forward the same old Euthyphro dilemma. In the recent *Cambridge Companion to Atheism* (2007), for example, the article on God and morality, written by a prominent ethicist, refers neither to the work of these scholars nor to the solution explained here, but attacks only the view that God arbitrarily made up moral values—a straw man that virtually nobody defends!

Answer to Atheistic Moral Platonism

First, atheistic moral platonism seems unintelligible. What does it mean to say, for example, that the moral value justice just exists? It's hard to make sense of this. It's easy to understand what it means to say that some person is just, but it's bewildering when someone says that in the absence of any people justice itself exists. Moral values seem to be properties of persons, and it's hard to understand how justice can exist as an abstraction.

Second, this view provides no basis for moral duties. Let's suppose for the sake of argument that moral values like justice, loyalty, mercy, forbearance, and the like just exist. How does that result in any moral obligations for me? Why would I have a moral duty to be, say, merciful? Who or what lays such an obligation on me? Notice that on this view moral vices like greed, hatred, lethargy, and selfishness also presumably exist on their own as abstractions. So why are we obligated to align our lives with one set of these abstractly existing objects rather than any other? Atheistic moral platonism, lacking a moral lawgiver, has no grounds for moral obligation.

Third, it's fantastically improbable that the blind evolutionary process should spit forth precisely that sort of creatures who correspond to the abstractly existing realm of moral values. This seems to be an utterly incredible coincidence when you think about it. It's almost as if the moral realm *knew* that we were coming. It's far more plausible, as Sorley contended, to think that both the natural realm and the moral realm are under the authority of a God who gave us both the laws of nature and the moral law than to think that these two independent realms just happened to mesh.

Stubborn Humanism: Whatever Contributes to Human Flourishing Is Good

So what's the atheist to do at this point? Most of them *want* to affirm the objective reality of moral values and duties. So they simply embrace some sort of humanism and stop there. Whatever contributes to human flourishing is good, and whatever detracts from it is bad, and that's the end of the story.

Answer to Stubborn Humanism

Just taking human flourishing as your ultimate stopping point seems, however, to be premature, because of the *arbitrariness* and *implausibility* of such a stopping point.

First, its arbitrariness. Given atheism, why think that what is conducive to human flourishing is any more valuable than what is conducive to the flourishing of ants or mice? Why think that inflicting harm on another member of our species is wrong? When I put this question to the Dartmouth ethicist Walter Sinnott-Armstrong in our debate on the existence of God, he replied, "It simply is. Objectively. Don't you agree?"[3] Of course, I agree that it *is* wrong to harm another human being, but I pointed out that this is not the question. The question is: Why *would it be* wrong if atheism were true? When I put this question to University of Massachusetts philosopher Louise Antony in our debate on "Is God Necessary for Morality?" she shot back, "I wonder if you have any friends!" I just smiled—but the point remains that, like it or

Humanism is the view that man is the measure of all things. In particular, man takes the place of God as the anchor of moral values, and moral duties are determined by what promotes human flourishing.

not, given an atheistic worldview, picking out human flourishing as morally special seems to be arbitrary.

Second, its implausibility. Atheists will sometimes say that moral properties like goodness and badness necessarily attach to certain natural states of affairs. For example, the property of badness necessarily attaches to a man's beating his wife. The property of goodness necessarily attaches to a mother's nursing her infant. Atheists will say that once all the purely natural properties are in place, then the moral properties necessarily come along with them. Now given atheism this seems extraordinarily implausible. Why think that these strange, nonnatural moral properties like "goodness" and "badness" even exist, much less somehow get necessarily attached to various natural states of affairs? I can't see any reason to think that, given an atheistic view of the world, a full description of the natural properties involved in some situation would determine or fix any moral properties of that situation.

These humanistic philosophers have simply taken a "shopping list" approach to ethical questions. Because they hold to humanism, they just help themselves to the moral properties they need to do the job. What's needed to make their view plausible is some sort of explanation for *why* moral properties attach to certain natural states of affairs. Again, it's inadequate for the humanist to assert that we do, in fact, see that human beings have intrinsic moral value, for that's not in dispute. Indeed, that's the second premise of the moral argument! What we want from the humanist is some reason to think that human beings would be morally significant if atheism were true. As it is, their humanism is just a stubborn moral faith.

By contrast God is a natural stopping point as a foundation for objective moral values and duties. For unless we are moral nihilists, we have to recognize some stopping point, and God as the ultimate reality is the natural place to stop. Moreover, God is by definition worthy of worship, so that He must be the embodiment of perfect moral goodness. Again, God, by definition, is the greatest conceivable being, and a being that is the ground and source of goodness is greater than one that merely shares in goodness. So theism isn't characterized by the sort of arbitrariness and implausibility that afflicts stubborn humanism.

PREMISE 2

Objective moral values and duties exist.

That brings us to our second premise, that *objective moral values and duties exist.* I initially thought that this would be the most controversial premise in the argument. In my debates with atheist philosophers, however, I find that almost nobody denies it. It might surprise you to learn that surveys taken at universities reveal, perhaps contrary to impression, that professors are more apt to believe in objective moral values than students, and that philosophy professors are more apt to believe in objective moral values than professors in general!

TALK ABOUT IT

What do you make of the fact that professors are more apt to believe in objective moral values than students, and that philosophy professors are more apt to believe in objective moral values than professors in general? What might this say about these three groups of people? How might age be a factor? Education? Popular culture?

Moral Experience

Philosophers who reflect on our moral experience see no more reason to distrust that experience than the experience of our five senses. I believe what my five senses tell me, namely, that there is a world of physical objects out there. My senses are not infallible, but that doesn't lead me to think that there is no external world around me. Similarly, in the absence of some reason to distrust my moral experience, I should accept what it tells me, namely, that some things are objectively good or evil, right or wrong.

Most of us would agree that in moral experience we do apprehend objective values and duties. When I was speaking several years ago on a Canadian university campus, I noticed a poster put up by the Sexual Assault and Information Center. It read: "Sexual Assault: No One Has the Right to Abuse a Child, Woman, or Man." Most of us recognize that sexual abuse of

another person is wrong. Actions like rape, torture, and child abuse aren't just socially unacceptable behavior—they're moral abominations. By the same token, love, generosity, and self-sacrifice are really good. People who fail to see this are just handicapped, the moral equivalent of someone who is physically blind, and there's no reason to let their impairment call into question what we see clearly.

I've found that although people give lip service to relativism, 95 percent can be very quickly convinced that objective moral values do exist after all. All you have to do is produce a few illustrations and let them decide for themselves. Ask what they think of the Hindu practice of *suttee* (burning widows alive on the funeral pyres of their husbands) or the ancient Chinese custom of crippling women for life by tightly binding their feet from childhood to resemble lotus blossoms. You can make the point especially effectively by using moral atrocities perpetrated in the name of religion. Ask them what they think of the Crusades or the Inquisition. Ask them if they think it's all right for Catholic priests to sexually abuse little boys and for the church to try to cover it up. If you're dealing with someone who's an honest inquirer, I can guarantee that almost every time that person will agree that there are objective moral values and duties.

Of course, sometimes you find hard-liners, but usually their position is seen to be so extreme that others are repulsed by it. For example, at a meeting of the Society of Biblical Literature a few years ago, I attended a panel discussion on "Biblical Authority and Homosexuality," in which all the panelists endorsed the legitimacy of homosexual activity. One panelist dismissed biblical prohibitions of such activity on the grounds that they reflect the cultural context in which they were written. Since this is the case for all of Scripture's commands (it wasn't written in a vacuum), he concluded that "there are no timeless, normative, moral truths in Scripture." In discussion from the floor, I pointed out that such a view leads to sociocultural relativism, which makes it impossible to criticize *any* society's moral values, *including* those of a society that persecutes homosexuals!

He responded with a fog of theological double-talk and claimed that there's no place outside Scripture where we can find timeless moral values either. "But that just *is* what we mean by moral relativism," I said. "In fact, on your view there's no content to the notion of the goodness of God. He might as well be dead. And Nietzsche recognized that the death of God leads to nihilism." At this point another panelist came in with that knock-down refutation: "Well, if you're going to get pejorative, we might as well not discuss it."

I sat down, but the point wasn't lost on the audience. The next man who stood up said, "Wait a minute. I'm rather confused. I'm a pastor and people are always coming to me, asking if something they've done is wrong and if they need forgiveness. For example, isn't it always wrong to abuse a child?" I couldn't believe the panelist's response. She replied: "What counts as abuse differs from society to society, so we can't really use the word *abuse* without tying it to a historical context."

"Call it whatever you like," the pastor insisted, "but child abuse is damaging to children. Isn't it wrong to damage children?" And still she wouldn't admit it! This sort of hardness of heart ultimately backfires on the moral relativist and exposes in the minds of most people the bankruptcy of such a worldview.

TALK ABOUT IT

What is it about humans that allows (and even encourages) them to live with logical inconsistency? Why, when faced with a logical argument like the one in this chapter, do they so easily say "Whatever" and go about their business unchanged?

Sociobiological Objections to Moral Experience

The question, then, is: Do we have any overriding reason to distrust our moral experience? Some people have claimed that the sociobiological account of the origins of morality undermines our moral experience. According to that account, you'll remember, our moral beliefs have been ingrained into us by evolution and social conditioning. Does that give us reason to distrust our moral experience?

Answer to Sociobiological Objections

The sociobiological account clearly does nothing to undermine the *truth* of our moral beliefs. For the truth of a belief is independent of *how you came to hold* that belief. You may have acquired your moral beliefs through a fortune cookie or by reading tea leaves, and they could still happen to be true. In particular, if God exists, then objective moral values and duties exist, regardless of how we come to learn about them. The sociobiological account at best proves that our *perception* of moral values and duties has evolved. But if moral values are gradually discovered, not invented, then our gradual and fallible perception of those values no more undermines their objective reality than our gradual, fallible perception of the physical world undermines its objective reality.

But perhaps the sociobiological account undermines, not the *truth* of our moral beliefs, but our *justification* for holding such beliefs. If your moral beliefs were based on reading tea leaves, they might accidentally turn out to be true, but you wouldn't have any justification for thinking that they are true. So you wouldn't know that they are true.

Similarly, the objection is that if our moral beliefs have been shaped by evolution, then we can't have any confidence in them because evolution aims, not at truth, but at survival. Our moral beliefs will be selected for their survival value, not for their truth. So we can't trust our moral experience and therefore don't know if premise 2 is true.

There are two problems with this objection to our knowledge of premise 2. First, it assumes that atheism is true. If there is no God, then our moral beliefs are selected by evolution solely for their survival value, not for their truth. I myself pressed this point in defending premise 1. If God does not exist, then the sociobiological account is true, and our moral beliefs are illusory. But, you see, that's no reason to think that the sociobiological account *is* true. Indeed, if God exists, then it's likely that He would want us to have fundamentally correct moral beliefs and so would either guide the evolutionary process to produce such beliefs or else instill them in us (Rom. 2:15). Apart from the

THE GENETIC

FALLACY

This informal fallacy attempts to invalidate a view by showing how a person came to believe that view. For example, "The only reason you believe in democracy is because you were raised in a democratic country. Therefore, your view that democracy is the best form of government is false." As an objection to the truth of moral judgments, the sociobiological account is guilty of the genetic fallacy.

Even Gentiles, who do not have God's written law, show that they know his law when they instinctively obey it, even without having heard it. They demonstrate that God's law is written in their hearts, for their own conscience and thoughts either accuse them or tell them they are doing right. (Rom. 2:14–15 NLT)

assumption of atheism, we have no reason to deny what our moral experience tells us.

Second, the objection is self-defeating. Given the truth of naturalism, *all* our beliefs, not just our moral beliefs, are the result of evolution and social conditioning. Thus, the evolutionary account leads to skepticism about knowledge in general. But this is self-defeating because then we should be skeptical of the evolutionary account itself, since it, too, is the product of evolution and social conditioning! The objection therefore undermines itself.

So given the warrant provided for premise 2 by our moral experience, we're justified in thinking that objective moral values and duties exist.

Conclusion

From the two premises, it follows that God exists. The moral argument complements the cosmological and design arguments by telling us about the moral nature of the Creator of the universe. It gives us a personal, necessarily existent being, who is not only perfectly good, but whose nature is the standard of goodness and whose commands constitute our moral duties.

In my experience, the moral argument is the most effective of all the arguments for the existence of God. I say this grudgingly because my favorite is the cosmological argument. But cosmological and teleological arguments don't touch people where they live. The moral argument cannot be so easily brushed aside. For every day you get up you answer the question of whether there are objective moral values and duties by how you live. It's unavoidable.

So, in answer to the question that opened this chapter: No, we cannot truly be good without God; but if we can in some measure be good, then it follows that God exists.

1. Charles Darwin, *The Descent of Man and Selection in Relation to Sex,* 2nd edition (New York: D. Appleton & Company, 1909), 100.
2. William Lane Craig and Paul Kurtz, "The Kurtz/Craig Debate," in *Goodness without God is Good Enough,* ed. Robert Garcia and Nathan King (Lanham, MD: Rowman & Littlefield, 2008), 34.
3. William Lane Craig and Walter Sinnott-Armstrong, *God?: A Debate between a Christian and an Atheist* (New York: Oxford University Press, 2003), 34.

THE MORAL ARGUMENT

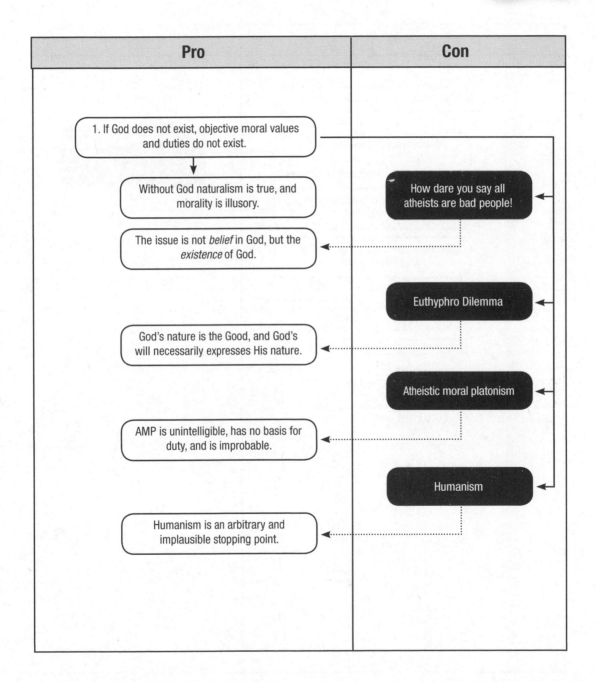

Pro	Con
1. If God does not exist, objective moral values and duties do not exist.	
Without God naturalism is true, and morality is illusory.	How dare you say all atheists are bad people!
The issue is not *belief* in God, but the *existence* of God.	
	Euthyphro Dilemma
God's nature is the Good, and God's will necessarily expresses His nature.	
	Atheistic moral platonism
AMP is unintelligible, has no basis for duty, and is improbable.	
	Humanism
Humanism is an arbitrary and implausible stopping point.	

THE MORAL ARGUMENT (cont.)

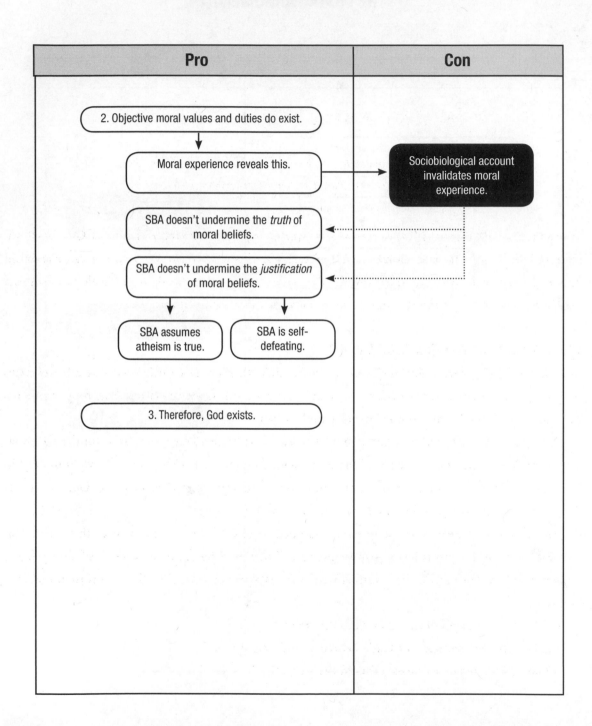

Pro	Con

2. Objective moral values and duties do exist.

Moral experience reveals this.

Sociobiological account invalidates moral experience.

SBA doesn't undermine the *truth* of moral beliefs.

SBA doesn't undermine the *justification* of moral beliefs.

SBA assumes atheism is true.

SBA is self-defeating.

3. Therefore, God exists.

CHAPTER 7

WHAT ABOUT SUFFERING?

*We also rejoice in our sufferings, because we know that suffering produces
perseverance; perseverance, character; and character, hope. (Rom. 5:3–4 NIV)*

In the previous four chapters we've seen four powerful arguments for the existence of God based on philosophical, scientific, and moral considerations. Together they make up a strong case for belief in God. But, of course, we need to consider the evidence on the other side of the scale too. Can the unbeliever offer equally powerful arguments to show that God does *not* exist?

"There's No Evidence That God Exists!"

As a matter of fact, there really aren't very many arguments against God's existence. The atheist's main complaint is that there isn't any evidence *for* God's existence. But if you've mastered the four arguments we've just run through, that complaint won't apply to you.

Nonbelievers aren't used to running into Christians who can actually give reasons for the hope that is in them. When the unbeliever says, "There's no evidence that God exists," you can stop him dead in his tracks by saying, "Gosh, I can think of at least four good arguments that show that God exists." At that point, he's got to say, "Like what?" and you're off and running!

You'll find nonbelievers are often so ill-equipped to discuss these issues that all they can do in response to the arguments is just repeat themselves, "That's no evidence that God exists!" One blogger characterized my debate with the British atheist Lewis Wolpert in Central Hall, Westminster, London, in this way:

Wolpert: "There's no evidence for God's existence!"

Craig: "There *is* evidence for God's existence, and here it is ..."

Wolpert: "There's no evidence for God's existence!"

Craig: "There *is* evidence for God's existence, and here it is …"

Wolpert: "There's no evidence for God's existence!"

Sadly, this characterization is not far from the truth! Sometimes it seems as if nonbelievers are deaf. They've been taught to repeat "There's no evidence for God's existence!" like a mantra, apparently believing that saying it again and again somehow makes it true. It's really a cover for intellectual laziness and lack of engagement. It's just a way of saying, "I'm not convinced by your arguments."

TALK ABOUT IT

Do you think it's ever helpful to engage with statements like, "I think religion is all just in your head," or, "Religion has done more harm to society than anything else"? If so, under what circumstances, and how? If not, why not?

So if the unbeliever responds to your arguments by saying, "That's no evidence that God exists!" just say politely, "Well, I guess you don't find my arguments convincing. So you must think some of my premises are false. Which premise do you reject, and why?"

One atheist I was talking with exclaimed at that point, "I reject all of them!" To which I replied, "Surely you don't reject *all* of them. Do you reject that 'The universe exists' or that 'The fine-tuning of the universe is due to physical necessity, chance, or design'?" He recognized that his remark had been careless. Try to get the unbeliever to engage with your specific premises.

TALK ABOUT IT

What are some of the emotional reasons why a person might reject God and have no interest in logical arguments?

All this underscores the importance of having these brief arguments memorized. Doing so will help you to stay on track. In response to your question "Which premise do you reject, and why?" the unbeliever is apt to say something like, "I think religion is all just in your head," or, "Religion has done more harm to society than anything else." Don't get distracted! Say, "I understand that's how you feel. But you said there's no evidence for God. So I want to know which premises in my argument you reject, and why." Try to get him to engage. Eventually you may get to the point where you can say to him, "You know, I don't think you really reject God because of the lack of evidence. I sense a deeper, emotional rejection of God going on here. What's the real reason you reject God?" At that point you've moved beyond apologetics into personal counseling.

My point is that having a few arguments in hand will completely invalidate the atheist's main reason for unbelief, that there's no evidence for God's existence.

Of course, even if there were no evidence for God's existence, that's no proof that God does *not* exist. An Australian forensic scientist I met while lecturing in Sydney told me that there's a saying beloved of criminologists: *Absence of evidence is not evidence of absence.* A suspect might still be the murderer even if there is no evidence that he is. To rule him out, you need an alibi, that is, positive evidence that he did not commit the crime. To rule out God's existence, the atheist needs more than just absence of evidence; he needs some positive evidence of absence.

Atheism Redefined as Absence of Belief

Very often atheists themselves admit that they have no evidence of God's absence, but they try to put a different spin on it. They'll tell you, "No one can prove a universal negative" (like "There is no God"). They think this somehow excuses them from needing evidence against God's existence.

But not only is it false that you can't prove a universal negative (all you have to do is show something is self-contradictory), but more importantly, this claim is really an admission that it's impossible to prove atheism! Atheism involves a universal negative, you can't prove a universal negative, therefore, atheism is unprovable. It turns out that it is the atheist who is believing a view for which there is and can be no evidence. This argument ought to be part of the Christian's apologetic arsenal!

What many atheists do at this point is to revise the definition of atheism, so that it's no longer the view that God does not exist but becomes merely the absence of belief in God. Anyone who lacks a belief in God counts as an atheist.

This is not only contrary to the traditional meaning of the word, but it is really hopeless as a definition. For on this new definition, atheism is no longer a viewpoint or position. Rather it's just a description of someone's psychological state, namely, the state of lacking a belief in God. As such, atheism is neither true nor false, and even babies turn out to be atheists! But can you imagine the following conversation between two young mothers?

Brooke: "Julie, I heard that you just had twins! Congratulations!"

Julie: "Yes, thank you! But, you know, it's so sad …"

Brooke: "What is?"

Julie: "Well, they're both atheists!"

On this redefinition even our cat Muff, who I'm sure has never even thought about the question, turns out to be an atheist!

Is Muff an atheist?

All of this still leaves us wondering whether or not God exists. Call it "atheism" or "shmatheism," what we want to know is if God exists, and

---

KEY TERMS

Theism: "God exists."

Atheism: "God does not exist."

Agnosticism: "God may or may not exist."

anyone who says that He does not needs to have some evidence or arguments for his position.

The Argument from Suffering

Thoughtful atheists do try to provide arguments against God's existence. Undoubtedly, the most important of these is the problem of suffering. When you consider the extent and depth of suffering in the world, whether due to natural disasters or to man's own inhumanity to man, then you have to admit that it's hard to believe in God. The horrible suffering in the world certainly seems to be evidence of God's absence.

In 1985, when Jan and I were living just outside Paris, the problem of suffering was brought home to me in a powerful way by two incidents shown on French television. In Mexico City a terrible earthquake had devastated blocks of high-rise apartment buildings. As rescue teams in the aftermath of the quake searched the rubble for survivors, they came across a ten-year-old boy who was trapped alive somewhere in the recesses of a collapsed building. During the next several days, the whole world watched in agony as the teams tried to remove the rubble to get to the boy. They could communicate with him, but could not reach him. His grandfather, who had been trapped with him, was already dead. "I'm scared!" he cried. After about eleven days, there was silence. Alone in the darkness, trapped without food and water, afraid, the little boy died before the rescue teams could free him.

That same year a mudslide swept over a village in Colombia. As rescuers came to help survivors, they came across a little girl who was pinned up to her chin in muddy water. For some reason or other, they could not free her or remove the water. All they could do was stand by helplessly and watch her die. Every night on the news we saw film of the little girl's decline. It was the most pathetic sight I have ever seen. She stood there, unable to move, spitting out the water that continually flowed into her mouth. As the days went by, she became more exhausted, and deep black circles formed under her eyes.

She was dying before our very eyes, as we watched on television. Finally, the evening newscaster reported that she was gone.

Those two incidents rent my heart. *Oh, God!* I thought. *How could You permit those children to die like that? If they had to die, so be it! But You could have let the boy be killed instantly by the collapse of the building or let the little girl drown suddenly. Why these tortuous, pointless, lingering deaths?* I'll be honest with you. When I see these sorts of things go on, it makes it hard to believe in God.

But as one colleague once wisely remarked to me, as a philosopher I'm called upon to say what I *think* about some question, not how I *feel* about it. And as difficult as the problem of suffering may be emotionally, that's no reason in and of itself to think that God does not exist.

Versions of the Problem of Suffering

So in dealing with this emotionally loaded topic, it's crucial that we make a number of distinctions to keep our thinking clear (Fig. 1).

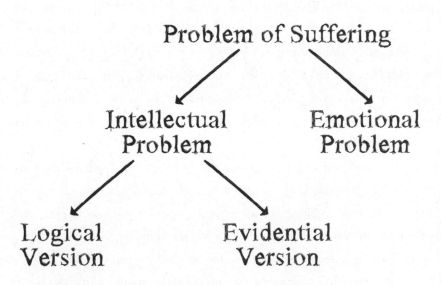

First and foremost, we must distinguish between the *intellectual* problem posed by suffering and the *emotional* problem posed by suffering. The intellectual problem concerns whether it's plausible to think that God and suffering can coexist. The emotional problem concerns people's dislike of a God who would permit suffering.

It's vital that we keep these problems distinct because the answer to the intellectual problem will doubtless seem dry and uncaring to the person who's struggling with the emotional problem, and the answer to the emotional problem will probably seem superficial and weak to anyone who's contemplating suffering as an abstract, philosophical question.

I'm convinced that for most people the terrible suffering in the world is really an emotional, not an intellectual, problem. Their unbelief is born, not out of *refutation,* but out of *rejection.* They just want nothing to do with a God who would allow them or others to suffer terribly. But in order to support my claim that suffering poses mainly an emotional problem, we need to examine in detail the intellectual problem to show that it fails as a proof of atheism.

Intellectual Problem of Suffering

Now in discussing the intellectual problem of suffering, it's important that we keep in mind who has the burden of proof here. In the previous chapters we were considering arguments for God, and so it was the believer who had to bear the burden of proof. But now it's the atheist's turn. We're considering arguments *for* atheism. We want to hear from the atheist some arguments against God. So now it's the atheist who must shoulder the burden of proof. It's up to him to give us an argument leading to the conclusion "Therefore, God does not exist."

Too often believers allow unbelievers to shift the burden of proof to the believer's shoulders. "Give me some good explanation for why God permits suffering," the unbeliever will demand, and then he sits back and plays the skeptic about all the believer's attempted explanations. The atheist winds up having to prove nothing. This may be clever debating strategy on the atheist's part, but it's philosophically illegitimate and intellectually dishonest.

Don't allow the atheist to shirk his intellectual responsibilities. He's the one who claims that the coexistence of God and suffering is impossible or improbable. So it's up to him to give us his argument and to support his premises. It's the Christian's turn to play the skeptic and question whether the atheist has shown that God cannot have or does not have a good reason for permitting the suffering in the world. Insist that the atheist bear his share of the burden of proof when it's his turn to present his case against God.

The intellectual problem of suffering comes in two versions. The *logical version* tries to show that the coexistence of God and suffering is logically impossible. The *evidential version* tries to show that the coexistence of God and suffering is highly improbable.

Now before you begin to talk to the unbeliever about the problem of suffering, you need to find out which version he's supporting. So just ask him, "Are you saying that it's *impossible* for God and the suffering in the world to both exist, or are you saying that it's merely *improbable* that God and suffering both exist?" If he's like most atheists, he's probably never thought about it and so doesn't have a clue. You may need to help him clarify what he himself believes by explaining the two versions to him. What he believes will then determine your response.

Logical Version: "It's Logically Impossible for God and Suffering to Coexist."

According to the logical version of the problem it's *logically impossible* for God and suffering to both exist. They're like the irresistible force and the immovable object. If one exists, then the other does not. Since suffering obviously exists, it follows that God does not exist.

The key to this argument is the atheist's claim that it's impossible that God and suffering both exist. The atheist is claiming that the following two statements are logically inconsistent:

1. An all-loving, all-powerful God exists.

2. Suffering exists.

Now the obvious question is, why think that these two statements are logically inconsistent? There's no *explicit* contradiction between them (one statement is not the opposite of the other). So if the atheist thinks there's some hidden, *implicit* contradiction between them, he must be making some hidden assumptions that would serve to bring out the contradiction and make it explicit. So the question is, what are those hidden assumptions?

There seem to be two hidden assumptions made by the atheist. They are:

3. If God is all-powerful, He can create any world that He wants.

4. If God is all-loving, He prefers a world without suffering.

The argument here is that God is all-loving and all-powerful. Therefore, He both *can* and *wants* to create a world without suffering. Therefore, it follows that the world has no suffering. But that contradicts 2, *Suffering exists.* Therefore, God must not exist.

In order for this argument to show a logical inconsistency between statements 1 and 2, both of the hidden assumptions made by the atheist have to be *necessarily true.* But are they?

Consider 3, that *If God is all-powerful, He can create any world that He wants.* Is that necessarily true? Well, not if it's possible that people have free will! It's logically impossible to *make* someone do something *freely.* That is as logically impossible as making a round square or a married bachelor. God's being all-powerful does not mean that He can bring about the logically impossible—indeed, there is no such "thing" as the logically impossible. It's just an inconsistent combination of words.

(If the unbeliever insists that an all-powerful being *can* do the logically impossible, then the problem of suffering evaporates immediately, for then God can bring it about that He and suffering both exist, even though this is logically impossible!)

Since it's possible that people have free will, it turns out that 3 is not necessarily true. For if people have free will, they may refuse to do what God

The notion of freedom under discussion here is called libertarian freedom. Some philosophers would say that the essence of libertarian freedom is the ability to choose between action A or not-A in the same circumstances. An arguably better analysis of libertarian freedom sees its essence in the absence of causal determination of a person's choice apart from the person's own causal activity. That is to say, causes other than the person himself do not determine how that person chooses in some set of circumstances; it is up to him how he chooses. This conception of freedom is very different from the voluntarist or compatibilist view, which defines freedom in terms of voluntary (or noncoerced) action, so that an action's being causally determined is compatible with its being "free." The notion of freedom operative in this chapter is libertarian freedom, which precludes God's determining how we shall freely choose.

desires. So there will be any number of possible worlds that God cannot create because the people in them wouldn't cooperate with God's desires. In fact, for all we know, it's possible that in any world of free persons with as much good as this world, there would also be as much suffering. This conjecture need not be true or even probable, but so long as it's even *logically possible*, it shows that it is not necessarily true that God can create any world that He wants. So assumption 3 is just not necessarily true. On this basis alone, the atheist's argument is logically fallacious.

But what about assumption 4, that *If God is all-loving, He prefers a world without suffering?* Is that necessarily true? It doesn't seem like it. For God could have overriding reasons for allowing the suffering in the world. We all know cases in which we permit suffering in order to bring about a greater good (like taking our child to the dentist). The atheist might insist that an all-powerful being would not be so limited. He could bring about the greater good directly, without allowing any suffering. But clearly, given freedom of the will, that may not be possible. Some goods, for example, moral virtues, can be achieved only through the free cooperation of people. It may well be the case that a world with suffering is, on balance, better overall than a world with no suffering. In any case, it is at least *possible*, and that is sufficient to defeat the atheist's claim that 4 is necessarily true.

The point is that the atheist, in asserting 3 and 4, has taken on a burden of proof so heavy that it's unsustainable. He would have to show that free will is impossible and

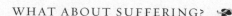

that it's impossible that a world with suffering would be better than a world with no suffering.

We can push the argument a notch further. We can make it plausible that God and suffering *are* logically consistent. All we have to do is come up with a statement that is consistent with God's existence and entails that suffering exists. Here is such a statement:

> 5. God could not have created another world with as much good as, but less suffering than, this world, and God has good reasons for permitting the suffering that exists.

The idea here is that given human freedom, God's options are restricted, and it may be that a world with as much good as the actual world, but with less suffering, wasn't an option. Nevertheless, God has good reasons for the suffering He allows. If statement 5 is even *possibly* true, it shows that it's possible that God and suffering both exist. And it surely is plausible that 5 is possibly true.

I'm therefore very pleased to report that after centuries of discussion, the books on the logical version of the problem of suffering have been closed. It's widely admitted by both atheist and Christian philosophers alike that the logical version of the problem of suffering has failed. The burden of proof it lays on the atheist's shoulders, namely, trying to show that the coexistence of God and suffering is impossible, is just too heavy to bear.

Evidential Version: "It's Improbable That God Could Have Good Reasons for Permitting Suffering."

But we're not out of the woods yet! For now we come to the evidential problem of suffering, which is still very much a live issue. The atheistic claim here is that the suffering in the world renders it *improbable* that God exists. In particular, it seems highly improbable that God could have good reasons for permitting the suffering in the world. So much of that suffering appears to be utterly pointless and unnecessary. Surely God could have reduced the suffering in the world without reducing the world's overall goodness. So the suffering in the world provides evidence that there is no God.

This is a much more powerful version of the argument than the logical version. Since its conclusion is more modest (namely, that it's improbable that God exists), the atheist's burden of proof is much lighter. So what can be said in response to this argument? I'll make three main points.

Human Limitations

First, *we're not in a position to say that it's improbable that God has good reasons for permitting the suffering in the world.*

The key to the evidential argument is the atheist's claim that God doesn't have good reasons for permitting the suffering that occurs. Now we all recognize that much of the suffering in the world looks unjustified. We see neither its point nor its necessity. The success of the atheist's argument will depend on whether we're warranted in inferring that because the suffering *looks* unjustified it really *is* unjustified. My first point is that we're just not in a position to make that kind of judgment with any confidence.

As finite persons, we're limited in space and time, in intelligence and insight. But God sees the end of history from its beginning and providentially orders history to His ends through people's free decisions and actions. In order to achieve His purposes God may have to allow a great deal of suffering along the way. Suffering that appears pointless within our limited framework may be seen to have been justly permitted by God within His wider framework.

I'll give two illustrations of this point, one from contemporary science and one from popular culture.

First illustration: In so-called chaos theory scientists have discovered that certain large-scale systems, for example, the weather or insect populations, are extraordinarily sensitive to the smallest disturbances. A butterfly fluttering on a twig in West Africa may set in motion forces that will eventually issue in a hurricane over the Atlantic Ocean. Yet it's impossible for anyone observing that butterfly fluttering on that branch to predict such an outcome. We have no way of knowing how the alteration of some seemingly insignificant event can radically alter the world.

❧ ON GUARD

Second illustration: The movie *Sliding Doors,* starring Gwyneth Paltrow, tells the story of a young woman who is rushing down the stairs to the subway to catch a train. As she nears the train, the movie splits into two paths her life might take. In the one life the doors to the train slide shut just before she can board. In the other life she makes it through the doors just before they close. Based on this seemingly trivial event, the two paths of her life increasingly diverge. In the one she's enormously successful, prosperous, and happy. In the other life she encounters failure, misery, and unhappiness. And all because of a split-second difference in getting through the subway doors!

Moreover, that difference is due to whether a little girl playing with her dolly on the stair railing is snatched away by her father or momentarily blocks the young woman's path as she hurries down the stairs to catch the train. We can't help but wonder about the innumerable other trivialities that led up to that event: whether the father and his daughter were delayed leaving the house that morning because she didn't like the cereal her mother gave her for breakfast, whether the man had been inattentive to his daughter because his thoughts were preoccupied with something he had read in the paper, and so on.

But the most interesting part is the film's ending: In the happy, successful life the young woman is suddenly killed in an accident, while the other life turns around, and the life of hardship and suffering turns out to be the truly good life after all! My point is obviously not that things always turn out for the best in this earthly life. No, my point is much more modest: Given the dizzying complexity of life, we are simply in no position at all to judge that God has no good reason for permitting some instance of suffering to afflict our lives.

Every event that occurs sends a ripple effect through history, such that God's reason for permitting it might not emerge until centuries later and perhaps in another country. Only an all-knowing God could grasp the complexities of directing a world of free people toward His envisioned goals. Just think of the innumerable, incalculable events involved in arriving at a single historical event, say, the Allied victory at D-day! We have no idea of what suffering might be involved in order for God to achieve some intended purpose through the freely chosen actions of human persons. Nor should we expect to discern God's reasons for permitting suffering. It's hardly surprising that much suffering seems pointless and unnecessary to us, for we are overwhelmed by such complexity.

This is not to appeal to mystery but rather to point to our inherent limitations, which make it impossible for us to say, when confronted with some example of suffering, that God probably has no good reason for permitting it to occur. Unbelievers themselves recognize these limitations in other contexts. For example, one of the decisive objections to utilitarianism (the theory of ethics that says that we should do whatever will bring about the greatest happiness for the greatest number of people) is that we have no idea of the ultimate outcome of our actions. Some short-term good might actually lead to untold misery, while some action that looks disastrous in the short term may bring about the greatest good. We don't have a clue.

Once we contemplate God's providence over the whole of human history,

TALK ABOUT IT

Is it helpful for you personally to understand that God may have good reasons for allowing some painful event that seems pointless? Please explain.

I think you can see how hopeless it is for finite, limited observers to speculate about the probability that God has a good reason for the suffering we observe. We're simply not in a position to assess such probabilities with any confidence.

The Full Scope of the Evidence

Second, *relative to the full scope of the evidence, God's existence is probable.*

Probabilities are always relative to some background information. For example, suppose we're given the information that Joe is a college student and that 90 percent of college students drink beer. Relative to that information it's highly probable that Joe drinks beer. But now suppose we're given the additional information that Joe is a student at Wheaton College, and that 90 percent of Wheaton students do not drink beer. Relative to this new information, it now becomes highly improbable that Joe is a beer drinker. To repeat: Probabilities are relative to background information.

Now the atheist says God's existence is improbable. You should immediately ask, "*Improbable relative to what?*" What is the background information? The suffering in the world? If that's all the background information you're considering, then it's no wonder God's existence looks improbable relative to that! (Though, as I've just argued, appearances can be deceiving!) But that's not the really interesting question. The interesting question is whether God's existence is probable relative to the *full* scope of the evidence. I'm convinced that whatever improbability suffering may cast upon God's existence, it's outweighed by the arguments for the existence of God.

Consider, in particular, the moral argument. Much of the suffering in the world consists of evil acts that people perpetrate upon one another. But then we may argue as follows:

1. If God does not exist, objective moral values do not exist.

2. Evil exists.

3. Therefore, objective moral values exist (some things are evil!).

4. Therefore, God exists.

 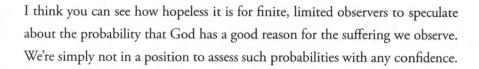

Although at a superficial level suffering calls into question God's existence, at a deeper level suffering actually *proves* God's existence. For apart from God, suffering is not really bad. If the atheist believes that suffering is bad or *ought not to be,* then he's making moral judgments that are possible only if God exists.

TALK ABOUT IT

If God doesn't exist, then suffering may be *painful,* but it isn't *bad* in a moral sense. Why, then, are even atheists aware that tragic events are bad? (Recall this subject from chapter 6.)

What you need to understand is that most people who write about the problem of suffering are tacitly assuming that there are no good arguments for the existence of God. So, for them, the question is whether suffering makes atheism probable given that *there's nothing on the other side of the scale.* But I think there are very weighty arguments for God on the other side of the scale. Therefore, I could concede that God's existence is improbable relative to the suffering in the world alone but point out that this is just outweighed by the arguments for God's existence.

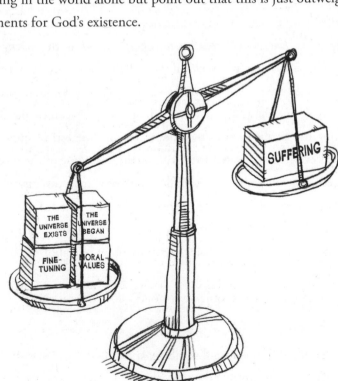

☙ ON GUARD

Suffering Makes More Sense under Christian Doctrine

Third, *Christianity entails doctrines that increase the probability of the coexistence of God and suffering.*

If the Christian God exists, then it's not so improbable that suffering should also exist. It actually turns out that the problem of suffering is *easier* to deal with given the Christian God rather than some bare-boned concept of God. For Christianity entails certain doctrines that increase the probability of suffering. What are these doctrines? Let me mention four:

1. *The chief purpose of life is not happiness, but the knowledge of God.* One reason that the problem of suffering seems so puzzling is that people naturally tend to assume that if God exists, then His purpose for human life is happiness in this life. God's role is to provide a comfortable environment for His human pets.

But on the Christian view, this is false. We are not God's pets, and the goal of human life is not happiness per se, but the knowledge of God—which in the end will bring true and everlasting human fulfillment. Much of the suffering in life may be utterly pointless with respect to the goal of producing human happiness; but it may *not* be pointless with respect to producing a deeper knowledge of God.

Innocent human suffering provides an occasion for deeper dependency and trust in God, either on the part of the sufferer or those around him. Of course, whether God's purpose is achieved through our suffering will depend on our response. Do we respond with anger and bitterness toward God, or do we turn to Him in faith for strength to endure?

Because God's ultimate goal for humanity is the knowledge of Himself—which alone can bring eternal happiness to people—history cannot be seen in its true perspective apart from the kingdom of God. The purpose of human history is the kingdom of God. God's desire is to draw freely as many people as He can into His everlasting kingdom. It may well be the

TALK ABOUT IT

Which do you tend to value more: temporal happiness or knowledge of God? How does that affect your actions and reactions?

HEALTH AND WEALTH?

The "health and wealth" gospel and the gospel of positive thinking that are being proclaimed in various megachurches and denominations are false gospels that are setting people up for a fall. That kind of gospel won't preach in Darfur or in Iraq or in a thousand other places. And if it won't preach there, it isn't the true gospel. We need to understand that God's plan for human history may involve terrible suffering for us, whose point or reason we can't expect to see. Our hope lies not in worldly happiness but in that day when God will wipe away every tear.

case that suffering is part of the means God uses to draw people freely into His kingdom.

A reading of a missions handbook such as Patrick Johnstone's *Operation World* reveals that it is precisely in countries that have endured severe hardship that Christianity is growing at its greatest rates, while growth curves in the indulgent West are nearly flat. Consider, for example, the following reports:[1]

China:

It is estimated that 20 million Chinese lost their lives during Mao's Cultural Revolution. Christians stood firm in what was probably the most widespread and harsh persecution the Church has ever experienced. The persecution purified and indigenized the Church. Since 1977 the growth of the Church in China has no parallels in history. Researchers estimate that there were 30–75 million Christians by 1990. Mao Zedong unwittingly became the greatest evangelist in history.

El Salvador:

The 12-year civil war, earthquakes, and the collapse of the price of coffee, the nation's main export, impoverished the nation. Over 80% live in dire poverty. An astonishing spiritual harvest has been gathered from all strata of society in the midst of the hate and bitterness of war. In 1960 evangelicals were 2.3% of the population, but today are around 20%.

Ethiopia:

Ethiopia is in a state of shock. Her population struggles with the trauma of millions of deaths through repression, famine, and war. Two great waves of violent persecution refined and purified the Church, but there were many martyrs. There have been millions coming to Christ. Protestants were fewer than 0.8% of the population in 1960, but by 1990 this may have become 13% of the population.

Examples like these could be multiplied. The history of mankind has been a history of suffering and war. Yet it has also been a history of the advance of the kingdom of God. Fig. 2 is a chart released in 1990 by the U.S. Center for World Mission documenting the growth in the number of committed Christians over the centuries.

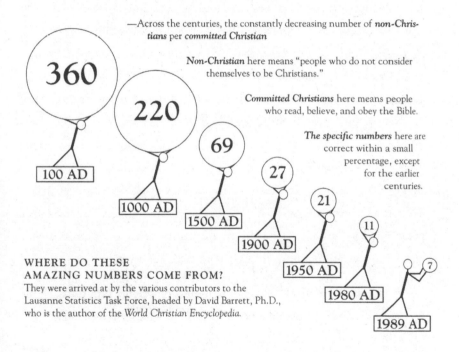

THE DIMINISHING TASK

—Across the centuries, the constantly decreasing number of *non-Christians* per *committed Christian*

Non-Christian here means "people who do not consider themselves to be Christians."

Committed Christians here means people who read, believe, and obey the Bible.

The specific numbers here are correct within a small percentage, except for the earlier centuries.

360 — 100 AD
220 — 1000 AD
69 — 1500 AD
27 — 1900 AD
21 — 1950 AD
11 — 1980 AD
7 — 1989 AD

WHERE DO THESE AMAZING NUMBERS COME FROM?
They were arrived at by the various contributors to the Lausanne Statistics Task Force, headed by David Barrett, Ph.D., who is the author of the *World Christian Encyclopedia.*

Fig. 2: Ratio of committed Christians to non-Christians over history. Neither category includes merely nominal Christians. Even if all of them were included with the non-Christians, there would still today be only about nine nonbelievers for every committed believer in the world.

According to Johnstone, "We are living in the time of the largest ingathering of people into the Kingdom of God that the world has ever seen."[2]

It's not at all improbable that this astonishing growth in God's kingdom is due in part to the presence of suffering in the world.

2. *Mankind is in a state of rebellion against God and His purpose.* Rather than submit to and worship God, people rebel against God and go their own way and so find themselves alienated from God, morally guilty before Him, groping in spiritual darkness, and pursuing false gods of their own making. The terrible human evils in the world are testimony to man's depravity in his state of spiritual alienation from God. The Christian isn't surprised at the moral evil in the world; on the contrary, he *expects* it. The Scriptures indicate that God has given mankind up to the sin it has freely chosen; He doesn't interfere to stop it but lets human depravity run its course (Rom. 1:24, 26, 28). This only serves to heighten mankind's moral responsibility before God, as well as our wickedness and our need of forgiveness and moral cleansing.

3. *God's purpose is not restricted to this life but spills over beyond the grave into eternal life.* According to Christianity, this life is but the cramped and narrow foyer opening up into the great hall of God's eternity. God promises eternal life to all who place their trust in Christ as Savior and Lord. When God asks His children to bear horrible suffering in this life, it is only with the prospect of a heavenly joy and recompense that is beyond all comprehension.

The apostle Paul underwent a life of incredible suffering. His life as an apostle was punctuated by "afflictions, hardships, calamities, beatings, imprisonments, tumults, labors, watching, hunger" (2 Cor. 6:4–5). Yet he wrote,

> We do not lose heart.… For this slight momentary affliction is preparing for us an eternal weight of glory beyond all comparison, because we look not to the things that are seen, but to the things that are unseen; for the things that are seen are transient, but the things that are unseen are eternal. (2 Cor. 4:16–18 RSV)

Paul lived this life in the perspective of eternity. He understood that the length of this life, being finite, is literally infinitesimal in comparison with the

So God abandoned them to do whatever shameful things their hearts desired. As a result, they did vile and degrading things with each other's bodies. They traded the truth about God for a lie. So they worshiped and served the things God created instead of the Creator himself, who is worthy of eternal praise! Amen. That is why God abandoned them to their shameful desires. . . . Since they thought it foolish to acknowledge God, he abandoned them to their foolish thinking and let them do things that should never be done. (Rom. 1:24–26, 28 NLT)

eternal life we'll spend with God. The longer we spend in eternity, the more the sufferings of this life will shrink by comparison toward an infinitesimal moment. That's why Paul called the sufferings of this life a "slight momentary affliction": He wasn't being insensitive to the plight of those who suffer horribly in this life—on the contrary, he was one of those people—but he saw that those sufferings were simply overwhelmed by the ocean of everlasting joy and glory that God will give to those who trust Him.

It may well be that there is suffering in the world that serves no earthly good at all, that is entirely pointless from a human point of view, but which God permits simply that He might overwhelmingly reward in the afterlife those who undergo such suffering in faith and confidence in God.

4. *The knowledge of God is an incommensurable good.* The passage cited from Paul also serves to make this point. Paul imagines, as it were, a scale in which all the suffering of this life is placed on one side, while on the other side is placed the glory that God will bestow upon His children in heaven. And the weight of glory is so great that it is beyond comparison with the suffering. For to know God, the locus of infinite goodness and love, is an incomparable good, the fulfillment of human existence. The sufferings of this life cannot even be compared to it. Thus, the person who knows God, no matter what he suffers, no matter how awful his pain, can still truly say, "God is good to me!" simply by virtue of the fact that he knows God, an incommensurable good.

These four Christian doctrines increase the probability of the coexistence of God and the suffering in the world. They in turn decrease any improbability that suffering might seem to cast upon the existence of God.

The atheist may respond at this point that we have no reason to think that these four Christian doctrines are true. Whoa! He's trying to shift the burden of proof again! It's the atheist who claims that suffering makes God's existence improbable. It's entirely legitimate for you to say, "Not the Christian God!" The atheist needs to show that the Christian God is improbable relative to the suffering in the world. So he needs to show either that these doctrines are probably false or else show that God's existence is improbable even given the

These four doctrines
increase the probability of
the coexistence of God and
suffering:
1. The chief purpose of life
is not happiness, but the
knowledge of God.
2. Mankind is in a state of
rebellion against God and His
purpose.
3. God's purpose is not
restricted to this life but spills
over beyond the grave into
eternal life.
4. The knowledge of God is
an incommensurable good.

truth of these doctrines. He has the burden of proof in either case. Don't let him foist it on you.

Let's return, then, to the two incidents that so powerfully portrayed to me the problem of suffering: the Mexican boy who slowly died from the collapse of a building and the Colombian girl who drowned in the aftermath of the mudslide. In the first place, both incidents concerned natural disasters intertwined with human moral sin. The whole of Latin America has been victimized by an unjust and uncaring upper class which has, in its lust for power and wealth, exploited the masses, leaving them poor and underprivileged. The suffering of those two children is indirectly attributable to this corrupt and unchristian system, for if the societies in which the children lived were following Christian principles, their families would not have been forced to live in unsafe housing that was improperly located or so poorly built that it disintegrated under the stress of earthquake or rain. In a world free from sin, it's possible that neither of these tragedies would have taken place. Hence, given a Christian doctrine of sin and mankind's fallen state, such tragedies are not surprising.

Why did God permit these children to suffer so? We're in no position to know. Perhaps through the tragic death of this boy, God knew Mexican authorities would be shocked into requiring new construction standards for earthquake-proof buildings, thereby saving many future lives. Maybe He let it happen because the authorities *should* be so shocked. Maybe He permitted it so that some other person, facing death or illness in a hospital and seeing the reports on television, would be inspired by the boy's courage to face his own challenge with faith and bravery. Maybe God permitted the Colombian girl to slowly drown because He knew that only then would her family—or somebody else—turn to Him in faith for eternal life. Or perhaps He knew that only through such a terrible incident would her family move away to another place where they, or even their descendants, might in turn come to be influenced or to influence someone else for Christ. Given our inherent limitations, we can only guess. Therefore, the atheist cannot prove

that it is either impossible or improbable that God had good reasons for permitting these events to occur.

The problem for the atheist becomes even more acute when we reflect that perhaps there wasn't any *earthly* reason at all why God permitted those catastrophes. Maybe they served no earthly good whatsoever. Perhaps the catastrophes were simply the unfortunate by-product of natural geological and meteorological laws and the children their unlucky victims. But when that little girl and boy finally left this life and stepped into the next, Jesus enfolded them in His loving arms, wiped away their tears, and filled them with a glorious happiness beyond all expression, saying, "Well done, My child; enter into the joy of your Master." In that eternity of joy, they will know a weight of glory beyond all comparison with what He asked them to suffer here.

In summary, the evidential version of the problem of suffering just can't be put through successfully. It requires probability judgments way beyond our ability, it fails to take into account the full scope of the evidence, and it is diminished in force when it comes to the Christian God. Since neither the logical nor the evidential version of the problem goes through, the intellectual problem of suffering fails as a disproof of God.

Emotional Problem of Suffering

But when I say "fails," I mean "fails intellectually." The anguish of the problem of suffering and the gnawing doubt may still remain. That brings us back to the emotional problem of suffering. I've already said that for most people suffering is not really an intellectual problem but an emotional problem.

You might be thinking, *Then why go through all this intellectual material if it's not really the problem?* Two reasons: First, people *think* their problem is intellectual, so by working through it we can respect their opinion and help them to see the real problem. Second, what I've shared can be of tremendous help to you when God calls upon you to go through suffering.

So what can be said to those who are struggling with the emotional

RESPONSE TO

THE EVIDENTIAL

ARGUMENT

1. We're not in a position to say that it's improbable that God lacks good reasons for permitting the suffering in the world.
2. Relative to the full scope of the evidence, God's existence is probable.
3. Christianity entails doctrines that increase the probability of the coexistence of God and suffering.

problem of suffering? In one sense, the most important thing may not be what one says at all. The most important thing may be just to be there as a loving friend and sympathetic listener. But some people may need counsel, and we ourselves may need to deal with this problem when we suffer. Does the Christian faith also have the resources to deal with this problem as well?

It certainly does! For it tells us that God is not a distant Creator or impersonal ground of being, but a loving Father who shares our sufferings and hurts with us.

On the cross Christ endured a suffering beyond all understanding: He bore the punishment for the sins of the whole world. None of us can comprehend that suffering. Though He was innocent, He voluntarily underwent incomprehensible suffering for us. And why?—because He loves us so much. How can we reject Him who gave up everything for us?

When God asks us to undergo suffering that seems unmerited, pointless, and unnecessary, meditation upon the cross of Christ can help to give us the strength and courage needed to bear the cross that we are asked to carry.

I mentioned earlier that knowing God is an incommensurable good to which our suffering cannot even be compared. Few of us really understand this truth. But a former colleague of mine got to know a woman who did. Tom used to make it his habit to visit shut-ins in nursing homes in an attempt to bring a bit of cheer and love into their lives. One day he met a woman whom he could never forget:

> As I neared the end of [the] hallway, I saw an old woman strapped up in a wheelchair. Her face was an absolute horror. The empty stare and white pupils of her eyes told me that she was blind. The large hearing aid over one ear told me that she was almost deaf. One side of her face was being eaten by cancer. There was a discolored and running sore covering part of one cheek, and it had pushed her nose to one side, dropped one eye, and distorted her jaw so that what should have been the corner of her mouth was the bottom of her

mouth. As a consequence, she drooled constantly.... I also learned later that this woman was eighty-nine years old and that she had been bedridden, blind, nearly deaf, and alone, for twenty-five years. This was Mabel.

I don't know why I spoke to her—she looked less likely to respond than most of the people I saw in that hallway. But I put a flower in her hand and said, "Here is a flower for you. Happy Mother's Day." She held the flower up to her face and tried to smell it, and then she spoke. And much to my surprise, her words, although somewhat garbled because of her deformity, were obviously produced by a clear mind. She said, "Thank you. It's lovely. But can I give it to someone else? I can't see it, you know, I'm blind."

I said, "Of course," and I pushed her in her chair back down the hallway to a place where I thought I could find some alert patients. I found one, and I stopped the chair. Mabel held out the flower and said, "Here, this is from Jesus."

Tom and Mabel became friends over the next few years, and Tom began to realize that he was no longer helping Mabel, but she was helping him. He began to take notes on what she said. After a stressful week, Tom went to Mabel and asked her, "Mabel, what do you think about as you lie here all day?" She replied,

"I think about my Jesus."

I sat there and thought for a moment about the difficulty, for me, to think about Jesus for even five minutes, and I asked, "*What* do you think about Jesus?" She replied slowly and deliberately as I wrote. And this is what she said:

I think how good He's been to me. He's been awfully good to me in my life, you know … I'm one of those kind who's mostly satisfied.… Lots of folks would think I'm kind of old-fashioned. But I don't care. I'd rather have Jesus. He's all the world to me."

And then Mabel began to sing an old hymn:

Jesus is all the world to me,
My life, my joy, my all.
He is my strength from day to day,
Without him I would fall.
When I am sad, to him I go,
No other one can cheer me so.
When I am sad, He makes me glad.
He's my friend.

This is not fiction. Incredible as it may seem, a human being really lived like this. I know. I knew her. *How could she do it?* Seconds ticked and minutes crawled, and so did days and weeks and months and years of pain without human company and without an explanation of why it was all happening—and she lay there and sang hymns. *How could she do it?*

The answer, I think, is that Mabel had something that you and I don't have much of. She had power. Lying there in that bed, unable to move, unable to see, unable to hear, unable to talk to anyone, she had incredible power.[3]

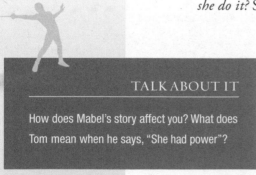

TALK ABOUT IT

How does Mabel's story affect you? What does Tom mean when he says, "She had power"?

Paradoxically, then, even though the problem of suffering is the greatest objection to the existence of God, at the end of the day God is the only solution to the problem of suffering. If God does not exist, then we are locked without hope in a world filled with pointless and unredeemed suffering. God is the final answer to the problem of suffering, for He redeems us from evil and takes us into the everlasting joy of an incommensurable good: fellowship with Himself.

1. Patrick Johnstone, *Operation World* (Grand Rapids, MI: Zondervan, 1993), 164, 207–8, 214.
2. Ibid., 25.
3. Thomas E. Schmidt, *Trying to Be Good: A Book on Doing for Thinking People* (Grand Rapids, MI: Zondervan, 1990).

THE PROBLEM OF SUFFERING

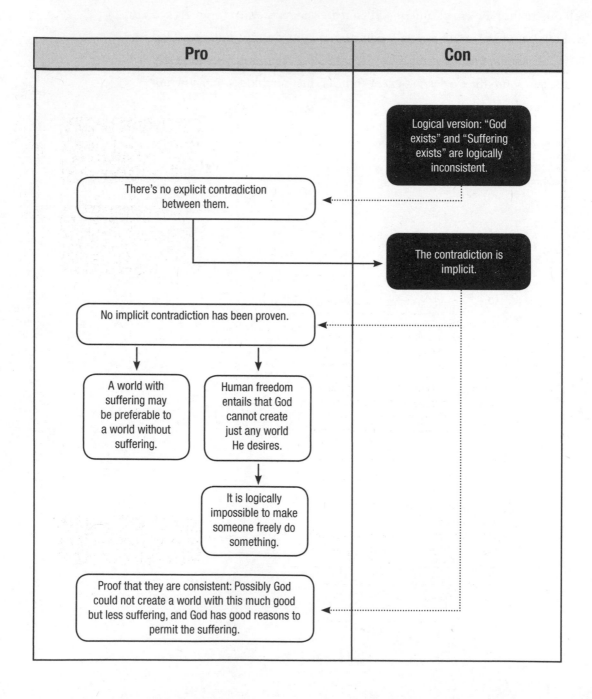

Pro	Con
	Logical version: "God exists" and "Suffering exists" are logically inconsistent.
There's no explicit contradiction between them.	
	The contradiction is implicit.
No implicit contradiction has been proven.	
A world with suffering may be preferable to a world without suffering.	Human freedom entails that God cannot create just any world He desires.
	It is logically impossible to make someone freely do something.
Proof that they are consistent: Possibly God could not create a world with this much good but less suffering, and God has good reasons to permit the suffering.	

THE PROBLEM OF SUFFERING (cont.)

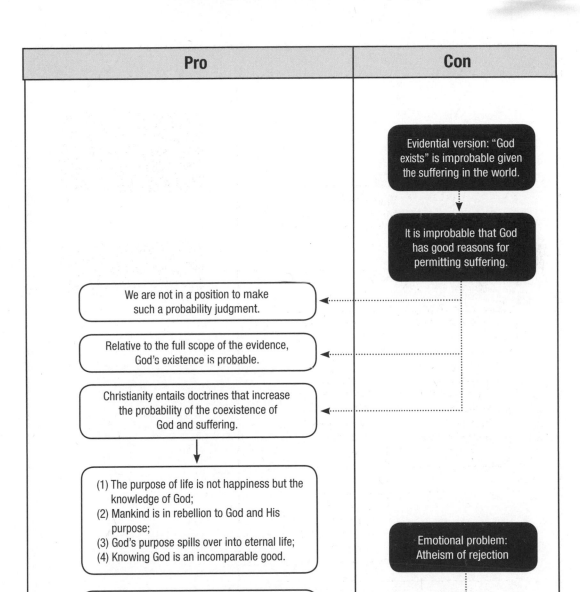

Pro	Con
	Evidential version: "God exists" is improbable given the suffering in the world.
	It is improbable that God has good reasons for permitting suffering.
We are not in a position to make such a probability judgment.	
Relative to the full scope of the evidence, God's existence is probable.	
Christianity entails doctrines that increase the probability of the coexistence of God and suffering.	
(1) The purpose of life is not happiness but the knowledge of God; (2) Mankind is in rebellion to God and His purpose; (3) God's purpose spills over into eternal life; (4) Knowing God is an incomparable good.	
	Emotional problem: Atheism of rejection
Meditate on the cross of Christ.	

A PHILOSOPHER'S JOURNEY OF FAITH,
PART TWO

As Jan and I were nearing the completion of my doctoral studies in philosophy at the University of Birmingham in England, our future path was again unclear to us. I had sent out a number of applications for teaching positions in philosophy at American universities but had received no bites. We didn't know what to do or where to go.

We were sitting one evening at the supper table in our little house in Birmingham, when Jan suddenly said to me, "Well, if money were no object, what would you really *like* to do next?"

I laughed because I remembered how the Lord had used her question to guide us in the past. I had no trouble responding. "If money were no object, what I'd really like to do is go to Germany and study under Wolfhart Pannenberg."

"Who's he?"

"Oh, he's this famous German theologian who's defended the resurrection of Christ historically," I explained. "If I could study with him, I could develop a historical apologetic for the resurrection of Jesus."

Well, that just lit a fire under her. The next day while I was away at the university, she slipped off to the library and began to research grants-in-aid for study at German universities. Most of the leads proved to be defunct or otherwise inapplicable to our situation. But she found two grants that were possibilities. You can imagine my surprise when she laid them out before me!

One was from a government agency called the Deutscher Akademischer Austausch Dienst (DAAD), which offered scholarships to study at German universities. Unfortunately, the grant amounts were small and not intended to cover all your expenses. The other was from a foundation called the

Alexander von Humboldt-Stiftung. This foundation was evidently an effort at *Kulturpolitik* (cultural politics) aimed at refurbishing Germany's image in the postwar era. It provided very generous fellowships to bring foreign scientists and other scholars to do research for a year or two at German laboratories and universities.

Reading the literature from the Humboldt-Stiftung just made my mouth water. They would pay for four months of a German refresher course at the Goethe Institute for the scholar and his spouse prior to beginning research, they would help find housing, they would pay for visits to another university if your research required it, they would pay for conferences, they would send pocket money from time to time, they would send you on a cruise down the Rhine—it was unbelievable! They even permitted recipients to submit the results of their research as a doctoral dissertation toward a degree from the German university at which they were working.

The literature sent by the Humboldt-Stiftung made it evident that the vast majority of their fellows were natural scientists—physicists, chemists, biologists, and so on. But it did say that applicants in any field were welcome. So we decided to apply in the field of theology and to propose as my research topic an examination of the historical evidence for the resurrection of Jesus! We decided to go for the doctoral degree in theology at the same time.

We then began to pray morning and night that God would give us this fellowship. Sometimes I could believe God for such a thing; but then I would think of this panel of eighty German scientists in Bonn evaluating the applications and coming to this proposal on the historical evidence for the resurrection of Jesus, and my heart would just sink!

It would take about nine months for the Humboldt-Stiftung to evaluate the applications, and in the meantime our lease was expiring, so we needed to move out of our house in Birmingham. So I said to Jan, "Honey, you've sacrificed a lot for me during my studies. Let's do something that you'd like to do. What would you really like to do?"

She said, "I've always wanted to learn French. I had to drop my French class in college because I got sick, and I've always felt bad I didn't get to learn French."

"Okay," I said, "let's go to France and enroll in a French language school!"

So we began to look into the possibilities. The obvious one was the Alliance Française, which is the official language school in France. But the far more interesting option was the Centre Missionnaire in Albertville, a Christian language school nestled in the French Alps for training foreign missionaries to French-speaking countries. They emphasized learning to really speak French, with as little foreign accent as possible, as well as to read and write it, along with all the biblical and theological vocabulary only a Christian school would provide.

So we wrote to the Centre Missionnaire, asking if we could study there. To our dismay, they wrote back informing us that applicants have to be missionaries officially with a mission board and, moreover, the course would cost several thousand dollars. Well, we didn't have that kind of money. We had spent just about all of the money given to us by the businessman to do our doctoral studies in Birmingham.

So I wrote back to the Centre Missionnaire explaining our financial situation. I also explained that while we weren't officially missionaries, we did want to serve the Lord, and I included a letter of commendation from one of the elders at the Brethren church we were attending in Birmingham. Then I basically forgot about it.

Time passed, and none of my other efforts to find a job had materialized. We had shipped all of our belongings back to my parents' home in Illinois. In one week we had to move out of our house in Birmingham, and we had nowhere to go.

I remember walking despondently out to the mailbox that day and finding there a letter from the Centre Missionnaire. I opened it halfheartedly and began to read. And then—my eyes suddenly grew wide, as I read the words: "It doesn't really matter to us whether you are missionaries as long as you want to serve the Lord. And as for the money, you just pay what you can, and we'll trust God for the rest." Unbelievable!

Once again we felt as though God had just miraculously plucked us up and transported us to another country to do His will. We later learned that the Centre had actually turned down paying missionaries and accepted us instead. We went to France with a deep sense of divine commissioning and so threw ourselves into our language studies. It was unbelievably rigorous, with drills and constant repetition and not a few tears, but by the end of our six months I was preaching in French at our small church, and Jan had the joy of leading our French neighbors to faith in Christ.

✣

Our French language training was to end in August, and as of July we still hadn't heard a decision from the Humboldt-Stiftung. We were getting nervous. (Jan has since formulated a saying that aptly describes our lives: "The Lord is always almost late!") Then one day we received a letter from the Humboldt-Stiftung. The only problem was: It was in German, and my rusty high school German wasn't up to the task of figuring it out!

So we grabbed the letter and rushed into the village to a small bookstore, where we found a French-German dictionary. As we stood there slowly translating the letter into French, hoping against hope, we could scarcely contain our excitement. "We are pleased to inform you that you have been granted a fellowship from the Alexander von Humboldt Foundation to study the historicity of the resurrection of Jesus under the direction of Professor Dr. Wolfhart Pannenberg at the University of Munich." So for the next two years the German government *paid me* to study the historical evidence for the resurrection of Jesus! Incredible! Absolutely incredible!

Jan and I arrived in Germany on a cold January day to begin our language studies at the Goethe Institute in Göttingen, a small university town near the East German border. We had chosen Göttingen because "high German" is spoken by the ordinary people in that region, as opposed to a local dialect. It's amazing how much you can learn in four months when you're immersed

in the language. With my postdoctoral studies in Munich looming, we were supermotivated to learn German. We hired a university student named Heidi to help us with our pronunciation. After a couple of months we determined to speak only German with each other until 8:00 p.m., when we'd revert to English. It's funny, but even when you know the meaning of the words, "Ich liebe dich" just doesn't convey the same feeling as "I love you" to a native English speaker!

By the end of our four months I had finished the advanced class with the highest grade of "1," and Jan, whose knowledge of German when we started didn't extend beyond "eins, zwei, drei," was able to converse freely with the shopkeepers and people in our town. One evening during dinner at the Goethe Institute she astonished me. There's a German proverb, "Ohne Fleiss, kein Preis!" ("Without effort, no reward!") So during the meal Jan asked the Turkish fellow next to her (in German) to pass the meat. But he showed her the empty serving dish and offered her the bowl of rice instead. To which she instantly retorted, "Danke, nein! Ohne Fleisch, kein Reis!" ("No thanks! Without meat, no rice!") I about split! Here she was already punning in German!

I must confess that it had seemed a little nutty to spend nine months learning French just before going off to do postdoctoral studies in Germany. But the Lord's providence is amazing. The first day I showed up at the theology department at the University of Munich to confer with Prof. Dr. Pannenberg, he took me into the departmental library and pulled three books off the shelf and said, "Why don't you get started with these?" To my amazement, two of the three were in French! I thought to myself, *Praise You, Lord!* I could never have said to Pannenberg that I didn't read French. That would have been equivalent to saying that I wasn't qualified to do the research! God knew what He was doing.

Doing my doctorate in theology under Prof. Dr. Pannenberg was the most difficult thing I've ever done in my life. I even had to pass a Latin qualifying exam to get the degree, which necessitated my taking Latin in

German! But by the end of our time in Munich I'd learned so much about the resurrection of Jesus that I was worlds away from where I'd been when we first came. As a Christian, I of course believed in Jesus' resurrection, and I was familiar with popular apologetics for it, but I was quite surprised to discover as a result of my research how solid a historical case can be made for the resurrection. Three books came out of that research, one of which served as the dissertation for my second doctorate, this time in theology from the University of Munich.[1]

Since that time I've had the opportunity to debate some of the world's leading skeptical New Testament scholars, like John Dominic Crossan, Marcus Borg, Gerd Lüdemann, and Bart Ehrman, as well as best-selling popularizers like John Shelby Spong, on the historicity of Jesus' resurrection. In all objectivity, I have to say I've been shocked at how impotent these eminent scholars are when it comes to refuting the evidence for Jesus' resurrection. (You can read or listen to these debates yourself and form your own opinion—just go to www.reasonablefaith.org.)

Very often, and I mean, *very* often, it will be philosophical considerations, *not* historical considerations, that lie at the root of their skepticism. But, of course, these men aren't trained in philosophy and so make amateurish blunders which a trained philosopher can easily spot. I'm so thankful that the Lord in His providence led us first to do doctoral work in philosophy before turning to a study of Jesus' resurrection, for it is really philosophy and not history that undergirds the skepticism of radical critics.

In the next three chapters I want to show you how you can extend your apologetic case beyond mere belief in God to belief in the biblical God revealed by Jesus. That will require immersing ourselves in the quest of the historical Jesus.

---

1. For the rest of the story, see my chapter "Failure" in *Hard Questions, Real Answers* (Wheaton, IL: Crossway, 2003).

CHAPTER 8

WHO WAS JESUS?

And he asked them, "But who do you say that I am?" (Mark 8:29 RSV)

When I was a student at Trinity during the midseventies I saw an article posted on a bulletin board about a forthcoming book entitled *The Myth of God Incarnate*. It described how Professor John Hick at the University of Birmingham had assembled a team of seven scholars who claimed that the divine Christ we read about in the gospels is a myth. In reality, they argued, Jesus of Nazareth never claimed to be the Son of God or the Lord or any sort of divine figure. Of course, an event like Jesus' resurrection was out of the question as a literal, historical event. Accordingly, we need to jettison these false and outmoded beliefs.

I remember feeling irritated and frustrated by the article. *Why don't our New Testament scholars answer this stuff?* I thought. *Why does it go unchallenged in the press?* Little did I realize that a veritable revolution in New Testament scholarship was transpiring that would soon reverse such skepticism and establish the gospels as historically credible sources for the life and claims of Jesus. Radical critics still get a free pass from the press today for their sensational assertions, but they are being increasingly marginalized within the academy, as scholarship has come to a new appreciation of the historical reliability of the New Testament documents. In the next two chapters we want to look at some of the evidence that will enable you to make a case for the radical personal claims and resurrection of Jesus and so for faith in Him.

Setting the Stage

An event without a context is inherently ambiguous. That's especially true for an alleged miracle. Considered in isolation, an alleged miracle might be nothing more than a scientific aberration, a freak of nature. Thus, an event like Jesus' resurrection must be explored in its historical context if we're to understand it correctly.

So what is the proper context for understanding Jesus' resurrection? It is Jesus' own unparalleled life and claims. The resurrection comes as the climax to Jesus' extraordinary life and ministry. So before we look at the historical credibility of Jesus' resurrection, let's set the stage by asking who Jesus thought Himself to be.

Primacy of the New Testament Documents

Now immediately we confront a problem. Since Jesus Himself didn't leave behind any writings of His own, we're dependent upon the records of others for knowing what Jesus said and did. Now this situation isn't unusual for figures of antiquity. For example, the famous Greek philosopher Socrates also left behind no writings of his own. We're dependent upon his disciple Plato for most of our knowledge of Socrates' life and teaching. In the same way, we're dependent upon the records of Jesus' followers for His life and teaching.

But while this situation isn't unusual, it does raise the question, how do we know that these records are accurate? Maybe Jesus' followers *said* that He said and did certain things that He really didn't. In particular, since the early Christians believed that Jesus was God, maybe they made up sayings and stories about how Jesus claimed to be divine. So we shouldn't be surprised that Jesus in the gospels makes claims and does things implying His divinity. Maybe the historical Jesus who really lived was very different from the divine figure we read about in the gospels. How can we tell if these records are historically accurate?

Well, up until the modern era these sorts of questions were basically unanswerable. But with the rise of textual criticism and the modern study of history, historians began to develop the tools to unlock these questions. Today Jesus is no longer just a figure in a stained-glass window, but a real, flesh-and-blood person of history, just like Julius Caesar or Alexander the Great, whose life can be investigated by the standard methods of history. The

writings contained in the New Testament can be scrutinized using the same historical criteria that we use in investigating other sources of ancient history like Thucydides' *Peloponnesian War* or the *Annals* of Tacitus.

Now the first thing we need to do in order to conduct a historical investigation of Jesus is to assemble our sources. Jesus of Nazareth is referred to in a range of ancient sources inside and outside the New Testament, including Christian, Roman, and Jewish sources.[1] This is really quite extraordinary when you reflect on how obscure a figure Jesus was. He had at most a three-year public life as an itinerant Galilean preacher. Yet we have far more information about Jesus than we do for most *major* figures of antiquity.

The most important of these historical sources have been collected into the New Testament. References to Jesus outside the New Testament tend to *confirm* what we read in the gospels, but they don't really tell us anything *new*. Therefore, the focus of our investigation must be upon the documents found in the New Testament.

Now I find that many laymen don't understand this procedure. They think that if you examine the New Testament writings themselves rather than look at sources outside the New Testament, then somehow you're reasoning in a circle, using the Bible to prove the Bible. If you even quote a passage out of the New Testament, they think you're somehow begging the question, presupposing that the New Testament is reliable.

But that's not at all what historians are doing when they examine the New Testament. They're not treating the Bible as a holy, inspired book and trying to prove it's true by quoting it. Rather they're treating the New Testament just like any other collection of ancient documents and investigating whether these documents are historically reliable.

It's important to understand that originally there wasn't any such book called "The New Testament." There were just these separate documents handed down from the first century, things like the Gospel of Luke, the Gospel of John, the Acts of the Apostles, Paul's letter to the church in Corinth, Greece, and so on. It wasn't until a couple centuries later that the church officially collected all these documents under one cover, which came to be known as the New Testament.

The church chose only the earliest sources, which were closest to Jesus and the original disciples, to include in the New Testament and left out the later, secondary accounts like the forged apocryphal gospels, which everyone knew were fakes. So from the very nature of the case, the best historical sources were included in the New Testament. People who insist on evidence taken only from writings *outside* the New Testament don't understand what they're asking us to do. They're demanding that we ignore the earliest, primary sources about Jesus in favor of sources that are later, secondary, and less reliable, which is just crazy as historical methodology.

This is important because all of the radical reconstructions of the historical Jesus in the news today are based on later writings outside the New Testament, in particular the so-called apocryphal gospels. What are the apocryphal gospels? They're gospels forged under the apostles' names, like the Gospel of Thomas, the Gospel of Peter, the Gospel of Philip, and so forth. They

first began to appear in the second half of the second century after Christ. Revisionists claim that these extrabiblical writings are the key to correctly reconstructing the historical Jesus.

Professor Luke Johnson, a distinguished New Testament scholar at Emory University, points out that all of the recent spate of books claiming to uncover the real Jesus follow the same predictable pattern:

1. The book begins by trumpeting the scholarly credentials of the author and his prodigious research.

2. The author claims to offer some new, and maybe even suppressed, interpretation of who Jesus *really* was.

3. The truth about Jesus is said to be discovered by means of sources outside the Bible that enable us to read the gospels in a new way that is at odds with their face-value meaning.

4. This new interpretation is provocative and even titillating, for example, that Jesus married Mary Magdalene or was the leader of a hallucinogenic cult or a peasant cynic philosopher.

5. It is implied that traditional Christian beliefs are therefore undermined and need to be revised.[2]

If you hear of books following this familiar pattern, your critical antennae should automatically go up! You are about to be duped. For the fact is that there is no historically credible source outside the New Testament that calls into question the portrait of Jesus painted in the gospels. The apocryphal gospels are later, derivative writings shaped by the theology of the second century and beyond. What this means is that despite all the hoopla, the documents contained in the New Testament are our primary sources for the life of Jesus.

So try not to think of the New Testament as a single book; think of it as what it originally was: a bunch of separate documents coming to us out of the first century telling this remarkable story about Jesus of Nazareth. The question then must be: How historically reliable are these documents?

APOCRYPHAL GOSPELS

The so-called apocryphal gospels are gospels forged under the apostles' names during the centuries after Christ. None is earlier than the second half of the second century after Christ. While not very valuable as sources for the life of Jesus, they are significant to the church historian who wants to learn about the various competing movements, often deeply influenced by pagan gnostic philosophy, that the Christian church contended with during the first few centuries after Christ. Some of the apocryphal gospels include:

Gospel of Peter

Gospel of Thomas

Gospel of the Hebrews

Infancy Gospel of Thomas

Gospel of Judas

Gospel of Philip

Burden of Proof

Here we confront the very crucial question of the burden of proof. Should we assume that the gospels are reliable unless they are proven to be unreliable? Or should we assume that the gospels are unreliable unless they are proven to be reliable? Are they innocent until proven guilty or guilty until proven innocent? Skeptical scholars almost always assume that the gospels are guilty until proven innocent, that is, they assume that the gospels are unreliable unless and until they are proven to be correct concerning some particular fact. I'm not exaggerating here: This really is the procedure of skeptical critics.

I want to list, however, five reasons why I think this skeptical assumption is wrong.

1. *There was insufficient time for legendary influences to erase the core historical facts.* Sometimes laymen say, "How can you know anything that happened two thousand years ago?" What they fail to understand is that the crucial time gap is not the gap between the evidence and today; rather what's important is the gap between the evidence and the original events that the evidence is about. If the gap between the events and the evidence is short, then it doesn't matter how far the event and the evidence have receded into the past. Good evidence doesn't become poor evidence just because of the passage of time! So long as the time gap between the event and the evidence for that event is short, it's just irrelevant how long it has been to the present day.

The question then is how close the sources for Jesus' life are to the time He lived. I'll say something about that in a minute.

Fig. 1. Our primary sources for Jesus' life all come from the first century AD, most of them within 60 years of Jesus' crucifixion. By contrast, the apocryphal gospels were written at least over 100 years after the crucifixion.

2. *The gospels are not analogous to folk tales or contemporary "urban legends."* Tales like those of Paul Bunyan and Pecos Bill or contemporary urban legends like the "vanishing hitchhiker" rarely concern actual historical individuals and are thus not like the gospel narratives, which are about real people who actually lived, real events that actually occurred, and real places that actually existed. Did you know that you can read about people like Pontius Pilate, Joseph Caiaphas, and even John the Baptist in the writings of the Jewish historian Josephus?

3. *The Jewish transmission of sacred traditions was highly developed and reliable.* In an oral culture like that of first-century Israel, the ability to memorize and retain large tracts of oral tradition was a highly prized and highly developed skill. From the earliest age children in the home, elementary school, and the synagogue were taught to memorize faithfully sacred tradition. The disciples would have exercised similar care with the teachings of Jesus. To compare the Jewish transmission of traditions to the child's game of "telephone" is a gross misrepresentation.

4. *There were significant restraints on the embellishment of traditions about Jesus, such as the presence of eyewitnesses and the apostles' supervision.* Those who had seen and heard Jesus were still on the scene and could be asked about what Jesus had said and done. Moreover, the traditions about Jesus remained under the supervision of the original apostles. These factors would act as a natural check on tendencies to elaborate the facts in a direction contrary to the one preserved by those who had known Jesus. In fact, in the case of the gospels, it would be more accurate to speak of "oral history" rather than "oral tradition," since the living eyewitnesses and apostles were still around.

5. *The gospel writers have a proven track record of historical reliability.* Where the gospel writers can be checked, discrepancies are the exception, not the norm. The typical result of such a check is that the gospels are shown to be reliable.

Now I don't have space to discuss all five of these points. So let me say something about the first and the fifth points.[3]

First, *there was insufficient time for legendary influences to erase the core historical facts.* No modern scholar thinks of the gospels as bald-faced lies, the result of a massive conspiracy. The only places you find such conspiracy theories are on atheist Web sites and in sensationalist books and movies. When you read the pages of the New Testament, there's no doubt that these people sincerely believed in the truth of what they proclaimed. Rather ever since the nineteenth century, skeptical scholars have explained away the gospels as *legends.* Like stories of Robin Hood or King Arthur and the Knights of the Round Table, as the stories about Jesus were passed on over the decades, they got muddled and exaggerated and mythologized until the original facts were all but lost. The Jewish teacher was transformed into the divine Son of God.

One of the major problems with the legend hypothesis, however, which is almost never addressed by skeptical critics, is that the time gap between Jesus' death and the writing of the gospels is just too short for this to have happened.

This point has been well explained by A. N. Sherwin-White in his book *Roman Society and Roman Law in the New Testament.* Professor Sherwin-White is *not* a theologian; he's a professional Greco-Roman historian of times prior to and contemporaneous with Jesus. According to Sherwin-White, the sources for Roman and Greek history are usually biased and removed one or two generations or even centuries from the events they record. Yet, he says, historians reconstruct with confidence the course of Roman and Greek history. For example, the two earliest biographies of Alexander the Great were written by Arrian and Plutarch more than four hundred years after Alexander's death, and yet classical historians still consider them to be trustworthy. The fabulous legends about Alexander the Great did not develop until the centuries *after* these two writers. According to Sherwin-White, the writings of Herodotus enable us to determine the rate at which legend accumulates, and the tests show that even two generations is too short a time span to allow legendary tendencies to wipe out the hard core of historical facts.

HERODOTUS

Herodotus (fifth century BC) was a Greek who wrote a long work he called *Istoriai*. This Greek word meant "Inquiries" or "Researches," but we generally call it *The Histories*, and our word *history* comes from this title. He was the first writer who tried to collect historical information systematically—information about the war between the Greeks and Persians that was fought in his parents' day. He claimed to have traveled and interviewed eyewitnesses from Babylon to Sicily, although he also liked to include stories that are more colorful than credible, and we don't know if he really went to all the places he described. While far from 100 percent reliable, Herodotus's work is full of clues for the careful modern historian. Legendary influences did not erase the core historical facts of the Greco-Persian war.

When Professor Sherwin-White turns to the gospels, he finds the skepticism of the radical critics to be quite unjustified. All historians agree that the gospels were written down and circulated during the first generation after the events, while the eyewitnesses were still alive. In order for the gospels to be legendary at their core, more generations would be needed between the events they record and the date of their composition.

In fact, adding a time gap of two generations to Jesus' death in AD 30 lands you in the second century, when the apocryphal gospels first begin to appear. These do contain all sorts of fabulous stories about Jesus, trying to fill in the years between his boyhood and the beginning of his ministry, for example. These are better candidates for the legends sought by the critics, not the biblical gospels.

This point becomes even more devastating for skepticism when we realize that the gospels themselves use *sources* that go back even closer to events of Jesus' life. For example, the story of Jesus' suffering and death, commonly called the passion story, was probably not originally written by Mark. Rather Mark used a source for this narrative. Mark is the earliest gospel, and his source must be even earlier still. In fact, Rudolf Pesch, a German expert on Mark, says the passion source must go back to at least AD 37. That's just seven years after Jesus' death.

Or again, Paul in his letters passes on information concerning Jesus about His teaching, the Last Supper, His betrayal, crucifixion, burial, and resurrection appearances. Paul's letters were written even before the gospels, and some of his information, for example, what he passes on in his first letter to the Corinthian church about Jesus' resurrection appearances, has been dated to within five years after Jesus' death. It just becomes irresponsible to speak of legends in such cases.

The Gospel Writers' Reliability

Now to my fifth point: *The gospel writers have a proven track record of historical reliability.* Again let's look at just one example: Luke. Luke was the author of a two-part work: the Gospel of Luke and the Acts of the Apostles. These are really one work and are separated in our Bibles only because the church grouped the gospels together in the New Testament.

Luke is the gospel author who writes most self-consciously as a historian. In the preface to his work he writes:

> Inasmuch as many have undertaken to compile a narrative of the things which have been accomplished among us, just as they were delivered to us by those who from the beginning were eyewitnesses and ministers of the word, it seemed good to me also, having followed all things closely for some time past, to write an orderly account for you, most excellent Theophilus, that you may know the truth concerning the things of which you have been informed. (Luke 1:1–4 RSV)

This preface is written in classical Greek such as the great Greek historians used; after this Luke switches to a more common Greek. But he has put his reader on alert that he can write, if he wants to, like the learned historian. He speaks of his lengthy investigation of the story he's about to tell and assures us that it's based on eyewitness information and is accordingly the truth.

Now who was this author we call Luke? He was clearly not himself an eyewitness to Jesus' life. But we discover an important fact about him from the book of Acts. Beginning in the sixteenth chapter of Acts, when Paul reaches Troas in modern-day Turkey, the author suddenly starts using the first-person plural: "*We* set sail from Troas to Samothrace," "*We* remained in Philippi some days," "As *we* were going to the place of prayer," etc. The most obvious explanation is that the author had joined Paul on his evangelistic tour of the Mediterranean cities. Eventually he accompanies Paul back to Israel and finally to Jerusalem. What this means is that the author of Luke-Acts was, in fact, in firsthand contact with the eyewitnesses of Jesus' life and ministry in Jerusalem.

Skeptical critics have done backflips to try to avoid this conclusion. They say that the use of the first-person plural in Acts should not be taken literally; it was just a literary device that was common in ancient sea voyage stories. Never mind that many of the passages in Acts are not about Paul's sea voyage but take place on land! The more important point is that this theory, when you check it out, turns out to be sheer fantasy. There just was no literary device in the ancient world of sea voyages in the first-person plural—the whole thing has been shown to be a scholarly fiction! There's no avoiding the conclusion that Luke-Acts was written by a traveling companion of Paul who had the opportunity to interview eyewitnesses to Jesus' life while in Jerusalem.

So who were some of these eyewitnesses? Perhaps we can get some clue by subtracting from the Gospel of Luke everything found in the other gospels and seeing what is unique to Luke. When you do this, what you discover is that many of Luke's unique narratives are connected to *women* who followed Jesus: people like Joanna and Susanna, and, significantly, Mary, Jesus' mother.

Was the author reliable in getting the facts straight? The book of Acts enables us to answer that question decisively. The book of Acts overlaps significantly with the secular history of the ancient world, and the historical accuracy of Acts is indisputable. This has recently been demonstrated anew by Colin Hemer, a classical scholar who turned to New Testament studies, in his book *The Book of Acts in the Setting of Hellenistic History.*[4] Hemer goes through the book of Acts with a fine-tooth comb, pulling out a wealth of historical detail, ranging from what would have been common knowledge down to details that only a local person would know. Again and again Luke's accuracy is demonstrated: From the sailings of the Alexandrian corn fleet to the coastal terrain of the Mediterranean islands to the peculiar titles of local officials, Luke gets it right.

LUKE'S UNIQUE NARRATIVES

A few of the narratives that are unique to Luke are:

The birth narratives that focus on Mary and her cousins (Luke 1:5—2:40)

The account of Jesus as a boy (Luke 2:41–52)

Jesus' rejection in his hometown, Nazareth (Luke 4:14–30)

The account of the women who traveled with Jesus and funded his ministry (Luke 8:1–3)

TALK ABOUT IT

Does it make sense to assume that sources are untrustworthy except where they can be proven accurate? As a thought experiment, consider what you know about your parents' lives before you were born. Rule out everything they or any other family member has told you, as they are all biased. You can be sure of only what you can verify through evidence such as bank statements, legal deeds, letters, and the testimony of impartial witnesses. What, then, do you really know about your parents?

According to Professor Sherwin-White, "The confirmation of historicity in Acts is overwhelming. Any attempt to reject its historicity even in matters of detail must now appear absurd."[5] The judgment of Sir William Ramsey, a world-famous archaeologist, still stands: "Luke is a historian of the first rank.... This author should be placed along with the very greatest of historians."[6]

Given Luke's care and demonstrated reliability, as well as his contact with eyewitnesses within the first generation after the events, this author is trustworthy.

On the basis of the five reasons I listed, I personally think that we should assume the historical reliability of what the gospels say about Jesus unless they are proven to be wrong. But in any case, at the very least, we cannot assume they are wrong until proven right. We should at least adopt a position of neutrality.

Criteria of Authenticity

Now if we do adopt a position of neutrality when approaching the gospels, how do we move beyond neutrality to the affirmation that some event is actually historical? Scholars have developed a number of so-called "criteria of authenticity" to enable us to do that.

It's vital that these criteria be properly stated and understood, for they've often been grossly misused. The criteria are really signs of historical credibility. A story in the gospels exhibiting one of these signs is, all things being equal, more likely to be historical than it would have been without it. In other words, the presence of one of these signs increases the probability that the recorded incident is historical.

What are some of these signs of historical authenticity? Here's a list of some of the most important:

1. *Historical fit*: The incident fits in with known historical facts of the time and place.

2. *Independent, early sources*: The incident is related in multiple

sources, which are near to the time when the incident is said to have occurred and which don't rely on each other or on a common source.

3. *Embarrassment*: The incident is awkward or counterproductive for the early Christian church.

4. *Dissimilarity*: The incident is unlike earlier Jewish ideas and/or unlike later Christian ideas.

5. *Semitisms*: Traces of Hebrew or Aramaic language (spoken by Jesus' countrymen) appear in the story.

6. *Coherence*: The incident fits in with facts already established about Jesus.

TALK ABOUT IT

Why would embarrassment be a sign of historical authenticity? Can you think of any passages in the gospels that an editor would have left out if he were interested in making the gospels' heroes look as good as possible?

Notice a couple of things about these "criteria." First, they're all *positive* signs of historical credibility. Therefore, they can only be used to *establish* the historicity of some incident, not to *deny* it. If a story is *not* embarrassing or dissimilar or found in independent early sources, that obviously doesn't mean that the incident isn't historical.

The only way you could justifiably use the criteria to deny historical credibility would be by presupposing that the gospels are unreliable until they are proven to be reliable. We're right back to the burden of proof issue again! If we adopt a position of neutrality in approaching the gospels, then the failure to prove an incident is historical just leaves you in a position of neutrality. You just don't know whether it's historical or not.

Second, the criteria don't presuppose the general reliability of the gospels. The criteria apply to specific incidents, not to a whole book. So they can be used to detect historical nuggets of information in any source, even the apocryphal gospels or the Qur'an. That means that in order to defend the historical credibility of some event in the life of Jesus, say, His burial, you don't need to defend the historical credibility of other events like His birth in Bethlehem,

His feeding the five thousand, His triumphal entry into Jerusalem, and so on. Specific incidents can be evaluated on their own by these criteria.

So if you're arguing on the basis of the criteria that Jesus made a specific radical claim, and the unbeliever points to *other* sayings that he thinks are not authentic, that doesn't matter. You're not trying to prove biblical inerrancy at this point. You're just trying to show that Jesus made this specific radical claim, and it's simply irrelevant whether or not he made some *other* claim.

Before we apply these criteria to events and sayings of Jesus in the gospels, it's worth noting a general problem facing critics who deny that Jesus made any radical claims at all. We know from Paul's letters that within twenty years of Jesus' death Jesus was regarded and worshipped by his contemporaries as God incarnate (Phil. 2:5–7). It's inexplicable how monotheistic Jews could have attributed divinity to a man they had accompanied during his lifetime if he never claimed any such things himself. Monotheism is the heart of the Jewish religion, and it would have been blasphemous to say that a human being was God. Yet this is precisely what the earliest Christians did proclaim and believe about Jesus! Such a claim must have been rooted in Jesus' own teaching. And, in fact, we do find in Jesus' teachings and activities both *explicit* and *implicit* personal claims that imply His divinity.

Explicit Claims

In the gospels there are a number of explicit self-descriptions used by Jesus that provide insight into His self-understanding. Until recently, critical scholars have been quite skeptical of the authenticity of such claims. In *The Myth of God Incarnate* the seven British theologians headed by Professor Hick asserted that the majority of New Testament scholars at that time agreed that Jesus never claimed to be the Messiah or the Son of God or claimed any of the divine titles that are attributed to Him in the gospels. Today no such skeptical consensus exists. On the contrary, the balance of scholarly opinion on Jesus' use of personal titles may have actually tipped in the opposite direction.

Let's take a look at the authenticity of three of Jesus' explicit claims: His

Your attitude should be the same as that of Christ Jesus:
Who, being in very nature God,
  did not consider equality with God something to be grasped,
but made himself nothing,
  taking the very nature of a servant,
  being made in human likeness.
—Philippians 2:5–7 NIV

claims to be the Messiah, the unique Son of God, and the Son of Man. As we look at each title, I'll first show by means of the criteria of authenticity that Jesus did make such a claim, and then, second, I'll discuss the significance of that claim for who Jesus held Himself to be.

Messiah

Israel's ancient hope for a Messiah or Anointed One sent from God had revived during the century prior to Jesus' birth. The most important messianic concept was the idea of a descendant of King David who would become king over Israel and the nations. More than just a warrior king, He would also be a spiritual shepherd of Israel.

The Greek word for Messiah is "*Christos,*" or Christ. Early Christians connected this title so closely to Jesus that it became practically a proper name: "Jesus Christ." The very term used to describe His followers, "Christians," shows how central their belief was that Jesus was the promised Messiah.

What Did Jesus Claim?

The question is: Where did they come up with this idea? If Jesus Himself never claimed to be the Messiah, what would prompt His followers to call Him that? He did not, in fact, reestablish David's throne in Jerusalem; instead, He was crucified by His enemies. Even the belief that God had raised Him from the dead would not have led His followers to see Him as the Messiah, for there just was no connection between resurrection and messiahship. Only if Jesus' crucifixion was the direct result of His claim to be the Messiah would His resurrection lead His followers to see Him as the risen Messiah.

Moreover, there's good evidence that Jesus did, in fact, think that he was the Messiah. For example, there's the story of Peter's famous confession:

> Jesus went on with his disciples to the villages of Caesarea
> Philippi; and on the way he asked his disciples, "Who
> do people say that I am?" And they answered him, "John
> the Baptist; and others, Elijah; and still others, one of the

prophets." He asked them, "But who do you say that I am?"
Peter answered him, "You are the Messiah." (Mark 8:27–30)

Is this a historical incident? Well, it would be natural for people of that time to be interested in who Jesus claimed to be. Independent accounts tell us that John the Baptist was confronted with a similar question (Luke 3:15–16; John 1:19–27). No doubt the disciples, who had left their families and jobs to follow Jesus, would have asked themselves whom they were following! Peter's reply to Jesus' question is independently confirmed in John 6:69, where Peter says, "We have come to believe and know that you are the Holy One of God."

"You're a Cynic philosopher with political ambitions! . . . No, wait! You're . . ."

Another story illustrating Jesus' messianic self-consciousness is the story of Jesus' answer to John the Baptist in prison (Matt. 11:2–6; Luke 7:19–23). Many scholars think this story comes from a very old source shared by Matthew and Luke. John asks Jesus, "Are you the one who is to come, or are we to wait for another?" The criterion of embarrassment supports the historicity of this incident, since John the Baptist seems to be doubting Jesus. The phrase "the

one who is to come" harks back to John's prophecy of "the one who is coming after me," which is independently recorded in Mark and John (Mark 1:7; John 1:27). Jesus' answer to John is a blend of prophecies from Isaiah 35:5–6; 26:19; 61:1, the last of which explicitly mentions being God's Anointed One. "Go and tell John what you have seen and heard: the blind receive their sight, the lame walk, the lepers are cleansed, the deaf hear, the dead are raised, the poor have good news brought to them. And blessed is anyone who takes no offense at me." Perhaps most remarkably of all, these very signs are listed as signs of the Messiah's coming in one of the Dead Sea Scrolls from the Jewish sect that lived at Qumran at the time of Jesus (4Q521).

In sum, the criteria of embarrassment, historical fit, and coherence with other authentic material, coupled with its presence in a very early source, give good grounds for seeing this incident as historical.

But even more convincing than Jesus' *words* are Jesus' *actions,* which disclose His sense of being the Messiah. His triumphal entry into Jerusalem seated on a donkey was a dramatic, provocative assertion of His messianic status. The story is independently told by Mark and John (Mark 11:1–11; John 12:12–19). They agree on the core of the story: One week before His death Jesus rode into Jerusalem seated on a colt and was hailed by the Passover festival crowds with shouts of "Hosanna! Blessed is He who comes in the name of the Lord!" in anticipation of the coming of David's kingdom.

In mounting a colt and riding into Jerusalem, Jesus is deliberately fulfilling the prophecy of Zechariah 9:9:

ENTRY INTO JERUSALEM

As they approached Jerusalem and came to Bethphage and Bethany at the Mount of Olives, Jesus sent two of his disciples, saying to them, "Go to the village ahead of you, and just as you enter it, you will find a colt tied there, which no one has ever ridden. Untie it and bring it here. If anyone asks you, 'Why are you doing this?' tell him, 'The Lord needs it and will send it back here shortly.'"

They went and found a colt outside in the street, tied at a doorway. As they untied it, some people standing there asked, "What are you doing, untying that colt?" They answered as Jesus had told them to, and the people let them go. When they brought the colt to Jesus and threw their cloaks over it, he sat on it. Many people spread their cloaks on the road, while others spread branches they had cut in the fields. Those who went ahead and those who followed shouted, "Hosanna!"

"Blessed is he who comes in the name of the Lord!"

"Blessed is the coming kingdom of our father David!"

"Hosanna in the highest!"

Jesus entered Jerusalem and went to the temple. He looked around at everything, but since it was already late, he went out to Bethany with the Twelve.

—Mark 11:1–11 NIV

Rejoice greatly, O daughter Zion!
Shout aloud, O daughter Jerusalem!
Lo, your king comes to you;
triumphant and victorious is he,
humble and riding on a donkey,
on a colt, the foal of a donkey.

Jesus is deliberately and provocatively claiming to be the promised king of Israel.

Skeptical scholars have sometimes questioned the historicity of Jesus' triumphal entry because such a public demonstration would have led to Jesus' immediate arrest by the Romans. But this is a very weak objection. A man on a slowly moving donkey with no show of arms would hardly have looked menacing. His triumphal entry was not something the Romans were expecting or would have understood, and His procession probably just melted into the crowd once it got to Jerusalem. According to Mark 11:11, upon His arrival Jesus just looks around and then leaves. He does nothing to provoke arrest by the Roman authorities.

Virtually all critics acknowledge that during the following week Jesus did cause some sort of disruption in the Jerusalem temple, which resulted in a temporary halt to commercial activities there. The last sentence of Zechariah's prophecy is "And there shall no longer be traders in the house of the LORD of hosts on that day" (Zech. 14:21). Jesus is deliberately fulfilling these prophecies, asserting His authority in the holiest precincts of Judaism.

The temple comes up again at Jesus' trial. We have independent reports that Jesus had made a prophecy about the temple's destruction (Mark 14:58; John 2:19), which the Jewish authorities sought to turn against Him. In Jewish literature of Jesus' day God is identified as the one who built the temple and who threatens to destroy it. In the Dead Sea Scrolls the Messiah is called the Son of God, who will build the temple (4Q174). At the trial Jesus is accused of claiming to do the same thing. His refusal to answer these charges provokes the high priest to demand, "Are you the Messiah, the Son of the Blessed One?" (Mark 14:61). This accusation shows that Jesus was on trial for His messianic claims.

The Roman authorities at that time reserved for themselves the right to administer capital punishment, so the Jewish authorities could not execute Jesus. But Jesus' claim to be the Messiah could be represented to the Roman authorities as treasonous, so that they would execute Jesus. Independent sources testify that the plaque nailed to the cross over Jesus' head recording the charge against Him read, "The King of the Jews" (Mark 15:26; John 19:19). The criterion of dissimilarity also supports the authenticity of the charge, for "the King of the Jews" was never a title used for Jesus by the early church. Historical scholars see this charge against Jesus as so firmly established that it is historical bedrock.

The overlapping of so many factors, each ratified by criteria such as independent sources, historical fit, dissimilarity, and so on, makes for a powerful cumulative case that Jesus did, indeed, see Himself as the Jewish Messiah.

What Did Jesus Mean?

In claiming to be the Messiah, Jesus has not necessarily said anything superhuman. Scholars typically take the Messiah to be just a human figure. But it must be said that the picture of the Messiah in several pre-Christian Jewish documents is of an extraordinarily exalted figure. In the extrabiblical Psalms of Solomon he is called "the Lord Messiah," who "will strike the earth with the word of his mouth forever.... And he himself [will be] free from sin ... and he will not weaken in his days" (17:32–37). In Isaiah we read,

> For to us a child is born,
> to us a son is given;
> and the government will be upon his
> shoulder,
> and his name will be called
> "Wonderful Counselor, Mighty God,
> Everlasting Father, Prince of Peace." (Isa.
> 9:6 RSV)

TALK ABOUT IT

What are you learning about Jesus from this chapter that is helpful for you personally? What have you learned that you could share with a non-Christian whom you know?

Here the title "Mighty God" is given to the Messiah, whose reign, Isaiah goes on to say, will be without end. In the first-century extrabiblical Similitudes of Enoch the Messiah is portrayed as a godlike figure who has existed with the Lord "prior to the creation of the world and for eternity" (1 Enoch 48:6). So the idea of Messiah as a heavenly, divine figure was afoot in Jesus' day.

When we come to Jesus' self-understanding, notice that John the Baptist is described as the fulfillment of Malachi's and Isaiah's prophecies of a messenger crying in the wilderness:

> Behold, I send my messenger to prepare the way before me, and the Lord whom you seek will suddenly come to his temple. (Mal. 3:1 RSV)

> A voice cries: "In the wilderness prepare the way of the LORD, make straight in the desert a highway for our God." (Isa. 40:3 RSV)

In Matthew 11:10 and Luke 7:27 Jesus Himself identifies John the Baptist as the messenger of Malachi 3:1. So who is to come after the messenger, according to these prophecies? It is the Lord, God Himself! Jesus goes on to speak of Himself as the Son of Man who has come after John the Baptist (Matt. 11:19; Luke 7:34). As we'll see, the Son of Man is a divine-human figure who could fulfill both the divine and human aspects of John's prediction. So Jesus' claim to be the Messiah could very well be fraught with divine significance, if such a self-understanding is consistent with the rest of the evidence we'll examine.

The Son of God

What Did Jesus Claim?

We've already seen that at Jesus' trial the high priest challenged Him about being the Son of God. This is a claim that Jesus often makes in the gospels. We'll look at just three examples.

First, consider Jesus' parable of the wicked tenants of the vineyard (Mark 12:1–9). In this parable, the vineyard symbolizes Israel (Isa. 5:1–7), the owner is God, the tenants are the Jewish religious leaders, and the servants are prophets sent by God. The tenants beat and reject the owner's servants. Finally, the owner decides that he has one left to send: his only, beloved son. "They will respect my son," he says. But instead, the tenants kill the son because he is the heir to the vineyard.

Even skeptical scholars recognize the authenticity of this parable, since it's also found in one of their favorite sources, the Gospel of Thomas (65), and so is by their reckoning independently confirmed. Moreover, the parable not only reflects the actual experience of absentee landowners in the ancient world but also employs typical images and themes found in Jewish parables: Israel as a vineyard, God as the owner, unworthy rebellious tenants, the figure of a son, and so on, so that it fits well within a Jewish context. The parable also contains interpretative nuances rooted in the Aramaic paraphrases of Isaiah 5, which were in use in Jesus' day. There are, furthermore, aspects of the parable that make it unlikely that the parable originated later in the Christian church. For example, the concern in the parable over who should possess the vineyard after it's taken away from the present tenants was a nonissue for the early Christians, since Rome destroyed Jerusalem in AD 70. And the absence of the resurrection of the slain son in the parable doesn't fit well with the early Christians' belief in Jesus' resurrection.

Now what does this parable tell us about Jesus' self-understanding? It tells us that He thought of Himself as

Then he began to speak to them in parables. "A man planted a vineyard, put a fence around it, dug a pit for the wine press, and built a watchtower; then he leased it to tenants and went to another country. When the season came, he sent a slave to the tenants to collect from them his share of the produce of the vineyard. But they seized him, and beat him, and sent him away empty-handed. And again he sent another slave to them; this one they beat over the head and insulted. Then he sent another, and that one they killed. And so it was with many others; some they beat, and others they killed. He had still one other, a beloved son. Finally he sent him to them, saying, 'They will respect my son.' But those tenants said to one another, 'This is the heir; come, let us kill him, and the inheritance will be ours.' So they seized him, killed him, and threw him out of the vineyard. What then will the owner of the vineyard do? He will come and destroy the tenants and give the vineyard to others." (Mark 12:1–9)

God's only Son, distinct from all the prophets, God's final messenger, and even the heir of Israel itself! Notice that you can't delete the figure of the son from the parable as an inauthentic, later addition, for then the parable lacks any climax and point. Moreover, the uniqueness of the son is not only explicitly stated in the parable but is inherently implied by the tenants' plan to murder the heir in order to claim possession of the vineyard. So this parable discloses to us that Jesus believed and taught that He was the only Son of God.

Jesus explicitly claims to be God's Son in Matthew 11:27 (compare Luke 10:22): "All things have been handed over to me by my Father; and no one knows the Son except the Father, and no one knows the Father except the Son and anyone to whom the Son chooses to reveal him." Again there's good reason to regard this as an authentic saying of Jesus. It's a saying of Jesus from a source shared by Matthew and Luke and is therefore very early. The saying has also been shown to go back to an original Aramaic version, which counts in favor of its authenticity. Moreover, it's unlikely that early Christians invented this saying because it says that the Son is unknowable—"no one knows the Son except the Father"—which would exclude even Jesus' followers from knowing him. But the conviction of the post-Easter church is that we *can* know the Son (Phil. 3:8–11). So this saying is unlikely to be the product of later church theology.

So what does this saying tell us about Jesus' self-concept? It tells us that He thought of Himself as the exclusive Son of God and the *only* revelation of God the Father to mankind! Think of it! Jesus thought of Himself as God's Son in an absolute and unique sense and as having the exclusive authority to reveal His Father God to men.

Finally, another fascinating saying revealing Jesus' sense of being God's Son is His claim concerning the date of His return: "But about that day or hour no one knows, neither the angels in heaven, nor the Son, but only the Father" (Mark 13:32). It seems highly unlikely that this saying could be the later product of Christian theology, because it ascribes ignorance to the Son. The criterion of embarrassment requires the authenticity of the reference to the Son's ignorance. Just how embarrassing the saying was is evident in the

More than that, I regard everything as loss because of the surpassing value of knowing Christ Jesus my Lord. For his sake I have suffered the loss of all things, and I regard them as rubbish, in order that I may gain Christ and be found in him, not having a righteousness of my own that comes from the law, but one that comes through faith in Christ, the righteousness from God based on faith. I want to know Christ and the power of his resurrection and the sharing of his sufferings by becoming like him in his death, if somehow I may attain the resurrection from the dead. (Phil. 3:8–11)

❧ ON GUARD

fact that although Matthew reproduces it (Matt. 24:36), Luke omits it, and most copyists of Matthew's gospel also chose to drop the verse (though it is preserved in the best manuscripts). That Mark preserves this saying, despite his emphasis on Jesus' predictive power and foreknowledge, is testimony to his faithfulness in handing on the traditions about Jesus. Here once more we see Jesus' consciousness of being God's unique Son.

What Did Jesus Mean?

On the basis of these three sayings of Jesus, we have good evidence that Jesus thought of Himself as the unique Son of God. Once again, however, we mustn't jump the gun. For although Gentile readers of the gospels would be apt to interpret the expression "Son of God" in terms of divine status, in a Jewish context this wasn't the customary sense of the title. Jewish kings were referred to as God's sons, and in Jewish literature a righteous man could be characterized as God's child, having God as his father.

Still, given the *uniqueness* and *exclusivity* of Jesus' claim, such generic usage is really irrelevant. We've seen that Jesus thought of Himself as God's Son in a singular sense that set Him apart from even the prophets who had gone before. But what was that sense?

The answer may be, once more, that Jesus thought of Himself as God's unique Son merely in the sense that He was the promised Messiah. The nonbiblical book 4 Ezra 7:28–29 speaks of Messiah as God's Son but nonetheless as mortal: "My son the Messiah shall be revealed … and those who remain shall rejoice four hundred years. And after these years my son the Messiah shall die, and all who have human breath." The Dead Sea Scrolls also show that the Messiah was thought to be God's Son. The uniqueness of Jesus' sonship could be a function of the uniqueness of the Messiah.

On the other hand, it must be said in all honesty that these Jewish texts do not even approach the sort of absoluteness and exclusivity claimed by Jesus in the sayings we've examined. There's nothing in the Dead Sea Scrolls to suggest that the Messiah is the *only* Son of God. Being the Messiah might set

JEWISH
PSEUDEPIGRAPHA

There are a number of Jewish writings that date from just before or around the time of Christ, and that were written under the names of famous prophets and kings. These works are not included in the Old Testament but are valuable to the historian for the glimpse they provide into Jewish religious life and thinking at the time of Christ. Some of the pseudepigrapha are:

Testament of the Twelve Patriarchs: second century BC

1 Enoch: second century BC

Psalms of Solomon: first century BC

4 Ezra: first century AD

2 Baruch: second century AD

Jesus apart from all the prophets who had come before Him and make Him the heir of Israel, as claimed in His parable of the vineyard, but being a merely human Messiah would not give Him exclusive knowledge of the Father or make Him the absolute revelation of God, as claimed in Matthew 11:27. Moreover, the saying in Mark 13:32 not only discloses Jesus' sense of unique sonship but also presents us with an ascending scale from men to angels to the Son to the Father. Jesus' sense of being God's Son involved a sense of proximity to the Father that transcended that of any human being (such as a king or prophet) or even any angelic being.

Such an exalted conception of God's Son is not foreign to first-century Judaism. The New Testament itself bears witness to this fact (Col. 1:13–20; Heb. 1:1–12). Similarly, in 4 Ezra 13 Ezra sees a vision of a man arising out of the sea who is identified by God as "my Son" (13:32, 37). The Son is portrayed in this book as a preexistent, heavenly figure who is revealed on earth at the proper time and who proceeds to subdue all the nations.

So we have here the same ambiguity with the title "the Son of God" that we encountered in considering the title "Messiah." These titles have many different meanings and are therefore ambiguous when taken out of context. In order to understand the meaning that Jesus invested in such self-descriptions we need to look at Jesus' teaching and actions. But before we do so, there's one more title, the most significant of all, that demands our attention.

The Son of Man

What Did Jesus Claim?

It's very likely that Jesus claimed to be the Son of Man. This was Jesus' favorite self-description and is the title found most frequently in the gospels (over eighty times). Yet remarkably, this title is found only once outside the gospels in the rest of the New Testament (Acts 7:56). That shows that the designation of Jesus as "the Son of Man" was not a title that arose in later Christianity and was then written back into the traditions about Jesus. On the basis of the criteria of independent sources and of dissimilarity, we can say with confidence that Jesus called Himself "the Son of Man."

What Did Jesus Mean?

The key question then becomes the *meaning* of the phrase. Some critics maintain that in calling himself "Son of Man" Jesus merely meant "a human person," just as the Old Testament prophet Ezekiel referred to himself as "a son of man." But with Jesus there's a crucial difference. For Jesus did not refer to Himself as "a son of man," but as "*the* Son of Man." Jesus' use of the phrase with the definite article "the" is consistent throughout the gospels.

By using the definite article, Jesus was directing attention to the divine-human figure prophesied in Daniel 7:13–14 (RSV). Daniel describes his vision in the following way:

> I saw in the night visions,
> and behold, with the clouds of heaven
> there came one like a son of man,
> and he came to the Ancient of Days
> and was presented before him.
> And to him was given dominion
> and glory and kingdom,
> that all peoples, nations, and languages
> should serve him;
> his dominion is an everlasting dominion,
> which shall not pass away,
> and his kingdom one
> that shall not be destroyed.

That Jesus believed in the appearance of the figure described in Daniel's vision is reported in independent sources (Mark 8:38; 13:26–27; Matt. 10:32–33/Luke 12:8–9; Matt. 24:27, 37, 39/Luke 17:24, 26, 30). In Daniel's vision the figure looks like a human being (a son of man), but He comes on the clouds of heaven, and to Him is given a dominion and glory that belong properly to God alone.

Other Jewish writings outside the Bible speak similarly of the Son of Man. The Similitudes of Enoch describe the preexistent Son of Man (1 Enoch 48:3–6; compare 62:7) who "shall depose the kings from their thrones and kingdoms" (1 Enoch 46:5) and shall sit "upon the throne of his glory" (1 Enoch 69:29). I've also mentioned the similar vision of 4 Ezra 13, in which Ezra sees "something like the figure of a man come up out of the heart of the sea," whom the Most High identifies as "my son" (4 Ezra 13:37) and who preexists with the Most High.

The point in mentioning these passages is not that people of that time listening to Jesus would have recognized His allusions to such works or ideas—they evidently didn't—but rather that the understanding of Daniel's Son of Man as a divine-human figure fits with first-century Jewish ideas and therefore could have been in Jesus' mind. By using the indirect expression "the Son of Man" to refer to Himself, Jesus prevented a premature revelation of His superhuman and messianic status.

Some scholars recognize that Jesus believed in a coming, end-time figure called the Son of Man, but they claim that Jesus was talking about somebody else! Such an interpretation is sheer fancy. It would require us to say that all of the Son of Man sayings used by Jesus to refer either to Himself or to an earthly, suffering figure are inauthentic. If even one of these sayings is authentic, then this interpretation is invalid. For example, Matthew 8:20, "Foxes have holes, and birds of the air have nests; but the Son of Man has nowhere to lay his head," is generally taken to be authentic, but it obviously doesn't refer to some end-time, cosmic figure.

Moreover, this interpretation can't make sense of Jesus' claim to ultimate authority. There's something of a scholarly consensus, as we'll see, that Jesus had a sense of unsurpassed authority. He put Himself in God's place by His words and actions. But then it makes no sense to suppose that He thought someone *else* was coming to judge the world, someone who would, in fact, judge Jesus Himself. Jesus' consciousness of unsurpassed authority is

incompatible with the view that He thought someone else was the coming Son of Man.

All three of the titles we've examined so far come together in a remarkable way at Jesus' trial. Mark records,

> Then the high priest stood up before them and asked Jesus, "Have you no answer? What is it that they testify against you?" But he was silent and did not answer. Again the high priest asked him, "Are you the Messiah, the Son of the Blessed One?" Jesus said, "I am; and you will see the Son of Man seated at the right hand of the Power, and coming with the clouds of heaven." Then the high priest tore his clothes and said, "Why do we still need witnesses? You have heard his blasphemy! What is your decision?" All of them condemned him as deserving death. (Mark 14:60–64)

Here in one fell swoop Jesus affirms that He is the Messiah, the Son of God, and the coming Son of Man. He compounds His crime by adding that He is to be seated at God's right hand, a claim that is truly blasphemous in Jewish ears. The trial scene beautifully illustrates how in Jesus' self-understanding all the diverse claims blend together, thereby taking on connotations that outstrip any single title taken out of context.

Implicit Claims

So the skepticism of earlier scholars concerning Jesus' explicit claims has greatly receded as we've gained insight into first-century Palestinian Judaism. Moreover, we can gain additional insight into Jesus' self-understanding by examining His teaching and behavior.

Most scholars believe that Jesus, in what He taught and by the way He acted, made claims that imply the same thing as the titles "Messiah," "the Son of God," and "the Son of Man." In other words, the titles only serve to express *explicitly* what Jesus in His teaching and behavior had already expressed about

Himself *implicitly*. Let's therefore review some of the implicit personal claims of Jesus widely accepted in New Testament scholarship, wholly apart from the question of the titles.

Jesus' Preaching of the Kingdom

One of the undisputed facts about Jesus is that the centerpiece of His preaching was the coming of the kingdom of God. As we'll see, Jesus carried out a ministry of miraculous healings and exorcisms as signs to the people of the inbreaking of God's kingdom.

The question then arises as to Jesus' role in that kingdom. Was He merely a herald of that kingdom or did He have a more significant role to play? Here we encounter the very interesting saying of Jesus concerning His twelve disciples' role in the coming kingdom: "Truly, I say to you, in the new world … you who have followed me will also sit on twelve thrones, judging the twelve tribes of Israel" (Matt. 19:28 RSV; compare Luke 22:28–30). The saying is likely to be authentic, not only because it seems to envision an earthly kingdom that did not immediately materialize, but also because of the awkwardness of envisioning a throne for Judas Iscariot, who was known to have fallen away. Jesus' calling *twelve* disciples is no accident: The number twelve corresponds to the twelve tribes of Israel.

Now if the twelve disciples are to sit on thrones judging the twelve tribes of Israel, who will be the king over all of Israel? The clear answer is, Jesus Himself. He will certainly not be beneath one of the disciples or outside of Israel, but He will be over the disciples as the King of Israel. In short, Jesus thought of Himself as Israel's royal Messiah. Thus Jesus' messianic self-understanding is implicit in His proclamation of the inbreaking of God's kingdom in His person and ministry, wholly apart from His explicit claims.

Jesus' Authority

Jesus' personal sense of acting and speaking with divine authority is evident in a number of ways.

His Teaching

First, His authority comes to expression in the *content* and *style* of His teaching. These two aspects of His teaching are especially evident in the Sermon on the Mount. A Jewish rabbi's typical style of teaching was to quote extensively from other learned teachers, who provided the basis of authority for his own teaching. But Jesus did exactly the opposite. He began, "You have heard that it was said to the men of old …" and quoted the law of Moses. Then he continued, "But I say to you …" and gave His own teaching. Jesus thus equated His own authority with that of the divinely given law. It's no wonder that Matthew comments, "When Jesus finished these sayings, the crowds were astonished at his teaching, for he taught them as one who had authority, and not as their scribes" (Matt. 7:28–29 RSV).

But it's not just that Jesus placed His personal authority on a par with that of the divine law. More than that, He *adjusted* the law on His own authority. Although modern Jewish scholars have tried to assimilate Jesus' teachings to the tradition of Judaism, Jesus' placing His own personal authority over the divine law given through Moses is the rock upon which all such attempts are finally broken. Take, for example, Jesus' teaching on divorce in Matthew 5:31–32 (compare Mark 10:2–12). Here Jesus explicitly quotes the teaching of the law (Deut. 24:1–4) and opposes to it, on the basis of His own authority, His teaching on the matter. In Mark's gospel, He declares that Moses does not represent the perfect will of God on this matter and presumes to correct the law on His own authority as to what is really the will of God. But no human being, no prophet or teacher or charismatic, has that kind of authority.

His Use of "Truly, I Say to You"

Second, Jesus' use of the words "Truly, I say to you" expresses His authority. This expression is historically unique and is recognized on all hands to have been the way Jesus marked off His authoritative word on some subject. The Jewish writer Ahad Ha'am protests, "Israel cannot accept with religious enthusiasm, as the word of God, the utterances of a man who speaks in his

> You have heard the law that says, "A man can divorce his wife by merely giving her a written notice of divorce." But I say that a man who divorces his wife, unless she has been unfaithful, causes her to commit adultery. And anyone who marries a divorced woman also commits adultery. (Matt. 5:31–32 NLT)

own name—not 'thus saith the Lord,' but '*I* say unto you.' This 'I' is in itself sufficient to drive Judaism away from the Gentiles forever."[7]

His Exorcisms

Third, Jesus' authority is especially evident in His role as an exorcist. Embarrassing as it may be to many modern theologians, it's historically certain that Jesus believed He had the power to cast out demons. This was a sign to people of His divine authority. He declared, "But if it is by the finger of God that I cast out the demons, then the kingdom of God has come to you" (Luke 11:20). This saying, which is recognized by New Testament scholars as authentic, is remarkable for two reasons. First, it shows that Jesus claimed divine authority over the spiritual forces of evil. Second, it shows that Jesus believed that in Himself the kingdom of God had come. Jesus is saying, "My ability to rule the spiritual forces of darkness shows that in me the kingdom of God is already present among you." In claiming that in Himself the kingdom of God had already arrived, as visibly demonstrated by His exorcisms, Jesus was, in effect, putting Himself in God's place.

His Claim to Forgive Sins

Finally, Jesus' sense of divine authority comes clearly to expression in His claim to forgive sins. Several of Jesus' parables, which are acknowledged on all hands to have been uttered by the historical Jesus, show that He assumed the prerogative to forgive sins. In parables like the prodigal son, the lost sheep, and so forth, Jesus describes persons who have wandered away from God and are lost in sin. In Jewish thought such a person was irretrievably lost and therefore given up as dead. But Jesus extended forgiveness to such persons and welcomed them back into the fold. The problem is that no one but God had the authority to make such a proclamation. No mere prophet could presume to speak for God on this matter. Jesus "is consciously speaking as the voice of God on matters that belong only to God."[8]

What Jesus taught in His parables, He acted out in real life. One of the most radical features of the historical Jesus was His practice of inviting prostitutes, tax collectors, and other outcasts into fellowship with Him around the dinner table. This was a living illustration of God's forgiveness of them and His invitation to them to fellowship in the kingdom of God. In table fellowship with the immoral and unclean, Jesus is acting in the place of God to welcome them into God's kingdom. It's no wonder that the religious authorities saw this presumptuous activity as blasphemous! (Compare the reaction to Jesus' claim in Mark 2:1–12 that He has authority as the Son of Man to forgive sins.)

Thus, most New Testament critics acknowledge that the historical Jesus acted and spoke with a self-consciousness of divine authority and that, furthermore, He saw in His own person the coming of the long-awaited kingdom of God and invited people into its fellowship.

"This guy acts like he thinks he's a god."

Jesus' Miracles

Jesus believed Himself to be not only an exorcist but a miracle worker. Recall His reply to the disciples of John the Baptist, "Go and tell John what you hear and see: the blind receive their sight, the lame walk, the lepers are cleansed, the deaf hear, the dead are raised, and the poor have good news brought to them. And blessed is anyone who takes no offense at me" (Matt. 11:4–5–6). Jesus evidently believed that He had the power to heal people and even to raise the dead.

Moreover, the miracle stories are so widely represented in all the gospel sources that it would be implausible to think that they're not rooted in the life of Jesus. Therefore, the consensus of New Testament scholarship today is that Jesus did perform "miracles"—however you might want to explain these. At the end of his long and detailed study of Jesus' miracles, the preeminent historical Jesus scholar John Meier concludes that Jesus' role as a miracle healer "has as much historical corroboration as almost any other statement we can make about the Jesus of history."[9]

The miracles of Jesus take on a deeper significance in that they, like His exorcisms, were taken to be signs of the inbreaking of the kingdom of God. As such, Jesus' miracles were fundamentally different from the wonders performed by pagan magicians or Jewish holy men. Moreover, Jesus' miracles differed from those of Jewish holy men in that Jesus never prays for a miracle to be done. He may first express thanks to God the Father, but then He does the miracle Himself. And He does so in His own name, not God's. Moreover, none of the other Jewish miracle-workers carried out a prophetic ministry, made messianic claims, or brought any new teaching in conjunction with their miracles. Thus, Jesus' self-understanding cannot be reduced simply to that of another charismatic Jewish holy man.

Jesus' Role as Judge

Jesus held that people's attitudes toward Himself would be the determining factor in how God will judge them on the judgment day. He proclaimed, "I tell you, everyone who acknowledges me before others, the Son of Man also will acknowledge before the angels of God; but whoever denies me before others will be denied before the angels of God" (Luke 12:8–9). I have no doubt that

Jesus is referring here to Himself as the Son of Man, not to somebody else. But be that as it may, the point is that whoever the Son of Man may be, Jesus is claiming that people will be judged before Him on the basis of their response to Jesus. Think of it: People's eternal destiny is fixed by how they respond to Jesus! Make no mistake: If Jesus were *not* divine, then this claim could only be regarded as the most narrow and objectionable dogmatism. For Jesus is saying that people's salvation depends on their confession to Jesus Himself.

Conclusion

A discussion of Jesus' personal claims could go on and on. But I think enough has been said to indicate the radical self-concept of Jesus. Here is a man who thought of Himself as the promised Messiah, God's only Son, Daniel's Son of Man to whom all dominion and authority would be given, who claimed to act and speak with divine authority, who held Himself to be a worker of miracles, and who believed that people's eternal destiny hinged on whether or not they believed in Him. Today there is virtually a consensus that Jesus came on the scene with an unheard-of authority, namely with the authority of God, with the claim of the authority to stand in God's place.

Jesus' radical personal claims and activities, culminating in His trial and crucifixion, constitute the proper historical context for evaluating the evidence for Jesus' resurrection. Historians are unanimous that Jesus of Nazareth, having been condemned by the Jewish authorities for blasphemy and delivered to the Roman authorities on the pretext of treason, met His death by crucifixion. But what happened next?

1. For a readable survey, see Richard France, *The Evidence for Jesus* (London: Hodder & Stoughton, 1986); see also Robert E. Van Voorst, *Jesus Outside the New Testament* (Grand Rapids, MI: Wm. B. Eerdmans, 2000).
2. Luke Timothy Johnson, *The Real Jesus* (San Francisco: HarperSanFrancisco, 1996).
3. For further discussion see Craig Blomberg, *The Historical Reliability of the Gospels* (Downers Grove, IL: IVP, 2009); more advanced readers may wish to profit from Paul Eddy and Gregory Boyd, *The Jesus Legend* (Grand Rapids, MI: Baker, 2007).
4. Colin J. Hemer, *The Book of Acts in the Setting of Hellenistic History*. Edited by Conrad H. Gempf (Tübingen: J.C.B. Mohr, 1989).
5. A. N. Sherwin-White, *Roman Society and Roman Law in the New Testament* (Oxford: Clarendon Press, 1963), 189.

6. William M. Ramsay, *The Bearing of Recent Discovery on the Trustworthiness of the New Testament* (London: Hodder & Stoughton, 1915), 222.

7. Ahad Ha'am, "Judaism and the Gospels," in *Nationalism and the Jewish Ethic,* ed. H. Kohn (New York: Schocken Books, 1962), 298.

8. Royce Gordon Gruenler, *New Approaches to Jesus and the Gospels* (Grand Rapids, MI: Baker, 1982), 46.

9. John P. Meier, *A Marginal Jew,* vol. 2, *Mentor, Message, and Miracles* (New York: Doubleday, 1994), 969-70.

I. Jesus had a divine-human self-understanding.

    A. The worship of Jesus by monotheistic Jews as God incarnate within twenty years of His death requires an adequate cause to be found in Jesus' own claims.

    B. Explicit claims

        1. Messiah

            a. The belief in the early church that Jesus was the Messiah requires an adequate cause.

            b. Peter's confession (Mark 8:27–30)

            c. Jesus' answer to John the Baptist (Matt. 11:2-6; Luke 7:19–23)

            d. Jesus' triumphal entry (Mark 11:1–11; John 12:12–19)

            e. Jesus' action in the temple (Mark 11:15–17)

            f. Jesus' condemnation by the Sanhedrin (Mark 14:61–65)

            g. Jesus' crucifixion as "King of the Jews" (Mark 15:26)

        2. The Son of God

            a. Parable of the vineyard (Mark 12:1–9)

            b. "No one knows the Father but the Son" (Matthew 11:27)

            c. "No one knows … not even the Son" (Mark 13:32)

            d. Jesus' trial confession (Mark 14:60–64)

        3. The Son of Man

            a. Jesus' favorite title

            b. Reference to the divine-human figure of Daniel 7 (Dan. 7:13–14)

            c. Jesus' trial confession (Mark 14:60–64)

    C. Implicit claims

        1. Jesus' preaching of the kingdom of God (Matt. 19:28)

        2. Jesus' authority

            a. The content and style of Jesus' teaching (Matt. 5:31–32)

            b. "Truly, I say to you" (Mark 8:12; 9:1; etc.)

   c. Jesus' role as an exorcist (Luke 11:20)

   d. Jesus' claim to forgive sins (Mark 2:1–12)

  3. Jesus' miracles (Matt. 11:4–5)

  4. Jesus' role as Judge (Luke 12:8–9)

CHAPTER 9

DID JESUS RISE FROM THE DEAD?

Why seek ye the living among the dead? (Luke 24:5 KJV)

As a part of my doctoral studies in Munich I sat in on various lectures and seminars given by Prof. Dr. Pannenberg. One morning he surprised us by announcing that we had a guest lecturer, a Canadian Jewish scholar named Pinchas Lapide, who now taught in Tel Aviv. When Pannenberg announced that Professor Lapide's topic that morning was to be the resurrection of Jesus, a feeling of resignation swept over me. I figured we were about to be served up the same old *Quatsch* that is tirelessly repeated by liberal theologians in Germany: The story of the empty tomb is a late legend, Paul didn't believe in a physical resurrection body, the resurrection appearance stories in the gospels are the product of an anti-docetic apologetic, blah, blah, blah. But as Lapide lectured, to my growing astonishment, he was not toeing the party line but defending historically Jesus' messianic claims, the credibility of the empty tomb narrative, and so on. When at the end of his lecture he announced that he therefore concluded that the best explanation of the evidence was that the God of Israel raised Jesus from the dead, I nearly fell off my chair! Nothing so illustrates the historical credibility of Jesus' resurrection as the fact that this Jewish scholar was convinced on the basis of the evidence that his God, the God of Israel whom he worshipped, had raised Jesus of Nazareth from the dead.

In this chapter I want to summarize the crucial elements in a historical case for Jesus' resurrection, so that you can share it with anyone who asks you why you believe in the biblical God. A historical case for Jesus' resurrection will involve two steps: *first*, determining what is the evidence to be explained and, *second*, inferring which explanation of the evidence is the best explanation.

It seems to me that the evidence can be summed up in three independently established facts: (1) Jesus' empty tomb, (2) Jesus' appearances alive after His death, and (3) the origin of the disciples' belief in His resurrection. Furthermore, I think that the best explanation of these three facts is "God raised Jesus from the dead." I'll call this the resurrection hypothesis. The significance or meaning of Jesus' resurrection will be given by the context in which it occurs: It comes as God's vindication of Jesus' radical personal claims for which He was condemned as a blasphemer.

Let's look first at the evidence to be explained and then at the best explanation of that evidence.

The Evidence for Jesus' Resurrection

If the three facts mentioned above—the empty tomb, the postmortem appearances, and the origin of the belief in Jesus' resurrection—can be established, and if no plausible, natural explanation can account for them as well as the resurrection hypothesis, then we're justified in inferring Jesus' resurrection as the best explanation of the facts. So let's examine the evidence supporting each of these three facts.

The Fact of Jesus' Empty Tomb

Here I'll summarize five lines of evidence supporting the fact that the tomb of Jesus was found empty by a group of His women followers on the Sunday after His crucifixion.

RESURRECTION

In Jesus' day it was clear what the various Greek, Aramaic, etc. words for resurrection did *not* mean. Resurrection did *not* mean life after death in some disembodied form, it did *not* mean the immortality of the soul in either torment or paradise, and it did *not* mean reincarnation. It meant the reversal of death, restoration to some kind of bodily immortality. Many pagans believed in disembodied life after death, but they considered resurrection impossible. Some (not all) Jews expected resurrection for the righteous at the end of days—but not for anybody before then. A resurrected body might differ from our bodies, but it had to be a body. Neither a ghost nor a disembodied soul nor a spirit on a higher plane of consciousness would have been called "resurrected."

The Evidence of Jesus' Burial

First, *the historical reliability of the story of Jesus' burial supports the empty tomb.* Now you might ask, how does the fact of Jesus' burial prove that His tomb was found empty? The answer is this: If the burial story is basically accurate, then the location of Jesus' tomb was known in Jerusalem to both Jew and Christian alike, since both were present when Jesus was laid in the tomb. But in that case, the tomb must have been empty when the disciples began to preach that Jesus was risen.

Why? *First,* the disciples could not have believed in Jesus' resurrection if His corpse still lay in the tomb. It would have been wholly un-Jewish, not to say stupid, to believe that a man was raised from the dead when his body was known to be still in the grave. *Second,* even if the disciples had preached Jesus' resurrection despite His occupied tomb, scarcely anybody else would have believed them. One of the most remarkable facts about the early Christian belief in Jesus' resurrection was that it flourished in the very city where Jesus had been publicly crucified. So long as the people of Jerusalem thought that Jesus' body was in the tomb, few would have been prepared to believe such nonsense as that Jesus had been raised from the dead. And *third,* even if they had so believed, the Jewish authorities would have exposed the whole affair simply by pointing to Jesus' tomb or perhaps even exhuming the body as decisive proof that Jesus had not been raised.

To suggest, as some critics have said, that the Jewish authorities didn't take this business about Jesus' being risen as anything more than a minor nuisance not worth dealing with is fantastic and contrary to the evidence. They were deeply concerned about squelching the budding Christian movement (think of their hiring Saul of Tarsus to persecute Jewish Christians!). They would certainly have checked out the tomb.

Even if the remains in the tomb were no longer recognizable, the burden of proof would have been upon anyone who said that these were *not* Jesus' remains. But no such dispute over the identification of Jesus' corpse ever seems to have taken place. As we'll see, the dispute between Jewish non-Christians and Jewish Christians lay elsewhere.

Thus, if the story of Jesus' burial is historical, then it's a very short inference to the fact of the empty tomb. For that reason, critics who deny the empty tomb feel compelled to argue against the burial. Unfortunately for them, Jesus' burial in the tomb is one of the best-established facts about Jesus. Space doesn't permit me to go into all the details of the evidence for the burial. But let me just mention a couple of points:

1. *Jesus' burial is reported in extremely early, independent sources.* The account of Jesus' burial in a tomb by Joseph of Arimathea is part of Mark's source material for the passion story (the story of Jesus' suffering and death). Mark is the earliest of the four gospels, so this is a very early source, which most scholars think is based on eyewitness testimony.

Moreover, Paul in 1 Corinthians 15:3–5 quotes an old Christian tradition that he had received from the earliest disciples. Paul probably received this tradition no later than his visit to Jerusalem in AD 36 (Gal. 1:18), if not earlier in Damascus. It therefore goes back to within the first five years after Jesus' death in AD 30. The tradition is a summary of the early Christian preaching and may have been used in Christian instruction. Its form would have made it suitable for memorization. Here's what it says:

> that Christ died for our sins in accordance with the scriptures,
> and that he was buried,
> and that he was raised on the third day in accordance with the scriptures,
> and that he appeared to Cephas, then to the Twelve.

Notice that the second line of this tradition refers to Jesus' burial.

But, we might wonder, was the burial mentioned in Paul's tradition the same event as the burial by Joseph of Arimathea? The answer to that question is made clear by a comparison of the four-line formula passed on by Paul with the gospel narratives on the one hand and the sermons in the Acts of the Apostles on the other:

1 Cor. 15:3–5	Acts 13:28–31	Mark 15:37—16:7
Christ died …	Though they found no cause for a sentence of death, they asked Pilate to have him killed.	And Jesus gave a loud cry and breathed his last.
he was buried …	They took him down from the tree and laid him in a tomb.	Joseph bought a linen cloth, and taking down the body, wrapped it in the linen cloth and laid it in a tomb.
he was raised …	But God raised him from the dead …	"He has been raised, he is not here. Look, there is the place they laid him."
he appeared …	… and for many days he appeared to those who came up with him from Galilee to Jerusalem, and they are now his witnesses to the people.	"But go, tell his disciples and Peter that he is going ahead of you to Galilee; there you will see him."

This remarkable correspondence of independent traditions is convincing proof that Paul's four-line formula is a summary or outline of the basic events of Jesus' passion and resurrection, including His burial in the tomb. We thus have evidence from some of the earliest, independent sources in the New Testament for the burial of Jesus in the tomb.

But that's not all! Further independent testimony to Jesus' burial by Joseph is also found in the sources behind Matthew and Luke and the Gospel of John. The differences between Mark's account of the burial and those of Matthew and Luke suggest that they had sources other than Mark alone.

The gospel writers used sources for the life of Jesus, as they themselves tell us. Much of New Testament studies is devoted to detecting those sources, for they will drive you back very close to the events themselves, thereby reducing the probability of legend or alteration. Mark, for example, was likely one of the sources used by Matthew and Luke. Mark evidently had a source for the passion story, since it stands out in his gospel as a connected narrative. Matthew and Luke also had other sources than Mark; some think they had a collection of Jesus' sayings to which scholars have assigned the arbitrary name "Q." By contrast John is usually thought to be independent of the other three gospels. Paul says explicitly that in 1 Corinthians 15:3–5 he is handing on prior tradition about Jesus, a fact confirmed by the many non-Pauline traits in the writing. Many scholars think that behind the sermons in Acts lie sources for early Christian preaching that Luke used. These are just a few of the principal sources that lie behind the New Testament documents.

Moreover, we have another independent source for the burial in John's gospel. Finally, we have the early sermons in the book of Acts, which probably preserve the early preaching of the apostles. These sermons also mention Jesus' interment in a tomb. Thus, we have the remarkable number of at least five independent sources for Jesus' burial, some of which are extraordinarily early.

2. *As a member of the Jewish Sanhedrin that condemned Jesus, Joseph of Arimathea is unlikely to be a Christian invention.* Joseph is described as a rich man, a member of the Jewish Sanhedrin. The Sanhedrin was a sort of Jewish high court, made up of seventy of the leading men of Judaism, which presided in Jerusalem. There was an understandable hostility in the early church toward the Jewish Sanhedrists. In Christian eyes, they had engineered a judicial murder of Jesus. The sermons in Acts, for example, go so far as to say that the Jewish leaders crucified Jesus (Acts 2:23, 36; 4:10)! Given his status as a Sanhedrist, Joseph is the last person you'd expect to care properly for Jesus. Thus, Jesus' burial by Joseph is very probable, since it would be almost inexplicable why Christians would make up a story about a Jewish Sanhedrist who does what is right by Jesus.

For these and other reasons, most New Testament critics agree that Jesus was buried by Joseph of Arimathea in a tomb. According to the late John A. T. Robinson of Cambridge University, the burial of Jesus in the tomb is "one of the earliest and best-attested facts about Jesus."[1] But if this conclusion is correct, then, as I've explained, it's very difficult to deny the fact of the empty tomb.

The Independent Reports of the Empty Tomb

The second line of evidence regarding the empty tomb is this: *The discovery of Jesus' empty tomb is independently reported in very early sources.* Mark's passion source probably didn't end with Jesus' burial but with the women's discovery of Jesus' empty tomb. For the burial story and the empty tomb story are really one story, forming a smooth, continuous narrative. They're linked by grammatical and linguistic ties. Furthermore, it seems unlikely that the early Christians would have circulated a story of Jesus' passion ending in His burial. The passion story is incomplete without victory at the end. Hence, Mark's source probably included and may have ended with the discovery of the empty tomb.

We've seen that in 1 Corinthians 15:3–5 Paul quotes from an extremely early tradition that refers to Christ's burial and resurrection. Although the empty tomb is not explicitly mentioned, a comparison of the four-line formula with the gospel narratives on the one hand and the sermons in Acts on the other reveals that the third line is, in fact, a summary of the empty tomb story.

Moreover, two further features of Paul's tradition imply the empty tomb. First, the expression "he was buried," followed by the expression "he was raised" implies the empty tomb. The idea that a man could be buried and then be raised from the dead and yet his body still remain in the grave is a peculiarly modern notion! For first-century Jews there would have been no question but that the tomb of Jesus would have been empty. Therefore, when the tradition states that Christ "was buried and he was raised," it automatically implies that an empty tomb was left behind. Given the early date and origin of this tradition, its drafters could not have believed such a thing were the tomb not empty.

Second, the expression "on the third day" implies the empty tomb. Very briefly summarized, since no one actually saw Jesus rise from the dead, why did the early disciples proclaim that He had been raised "on the third day"? Why not the seventh day? The most likely answer is that it was on the third

MARK'S BURIAL

ACCOUNT

It was Preparation Day (that is, the day before the Sabbath). So as evening approached, Joseph of Arimathea, a prominent member of the Council, who was himself waiting for the kingdom of God, went boldly to Pilate and asked for Jesus' body. Pilate was surprised to hear that he was already dead. Summoning the centurion, he asked him if Jesus had already died. When he learned from the centurion that it was so, he gave the body to Joseph. So Joseph bought some linen cloth, took down the body, wrapped it in the linen, and placed it in a tomb cut out of rock. Then he rolled a stone against the entrance of the tomb. Mary Magdalene and Mary the mother of Jesus saw where he was laid. (Mark 15:42–47 NIV)

Mark's Empty Tomb Account

When the Sabbath was over, Mary Magdalene, Mary the mother of James, and Salome bought spices so that they might go to anoint Jesus' body. Very early on the first day of the week, just after sunrise, they were on their way to the tomb and they asked each other, "Who will roll the stone away from the entrance of the tomb?"
But when they looked up, they saw that the stone, which was very large, had been rolled away. As they entered the tomb, they saw a young man dressed in a white robe sitting on the right side, and they were alarmed.
"Don't be alarmed," he said. "You are looking for Jesus the Nazarene, who was crucified. He has risen! He is not here. See the place where they laid him. But go, tell his disciples and Peter, 'He is going ahead of you into Galilee. There you will see him, just as he told you.'"
Trembling and bewildered, the women went out and fled from the tomb. They said nothing to anyone, because they were afraid. (Mark 16:1–8 NIV)

day that the women discovered the tomb of Jesus empty; and so naturally, the resurrection itself came to be dated on that day.

We have, then, extraordinarily early, independent evidence for the fact of Jesus' empty tomb. The discovery of Jesus' empty tomb cannot be written off as a later, legendary development.

But there's more! For once again there are good reasons to discern independent sources for the empty tomb in the other gospels and Acts. Matthew is clearly working with an independent source, for he includes the story of the guard at the tomb, which is unique to his gospel. Moreover, his comment about how the rumor that the disciples had stolen Jesus' body "is still told among Jews to this day" (Matt. 28:15) shows that Matthew is responding to prior tradition. Luke also has an independent source, for he tells the story, not found in Mark, of two disciples visiting the tomb to verify the women's report that the tomb was vacant. The story can't be regarded as Luke's creation, since the incident is independently reported in John. And, again, given John's independence of the other three gospels, we have yet another independent report of the empty tomb. Finally, in the sermons in the book of Acts, we again have indirect references to the empty tomb. For example, Peter draws the sharp contrast, David "died and was buried, and his tomb is with us to this day," but "this Jesus God raised up" (Acts 2:29–32; compare 13:36–37).

Historians think they've hit historical pay dirt when they have two independent accounts of the same event. But in the case of the empty tomb we have no less than

six, and some of these are among the earliest materials to be found in the New Testament.

The Simplicity of Mark's Account

The third line of evidence for the empty tomb is that *Mark's story is simple and lacks legendary development.* Like the burial account, Mark's account of the empty tomb is remarkably simple and unembellished by theological motifs likely to characterize a later legendary account. For example, the resurrection itself is not witnessed or described, and there's no reflection on Jesus' triumph over sin and death, no use of divine titles, no quotation of fulfilled prophecy, no description of the risen Lord. It's very different from a Christian fictional creation—just compare how the resurrection is portrayed in modern passion plays!

To appreciate how restrained Mark's narrative is, you only have to read the account in the apocryphal Gospel of Peter, which describes Jesus' triumphant exit from the tomb as a gigantic figure whose head reaches above the clouds, supported by giant angels, followed by a talking cross, heralded by a voice from heaven, and all witnessed by a Roman guard, the Jewish leaders, and a multitude of spectators! This is how real legends look: They're colored by theological and apologetical developments. By contrast, Mark's account is stark in its simplicity.

The Women's Discovery

Fourth, *the tomb was probably discovered empty by women.* In order to grasp this point, we need to understand two things about the place of women in Jewish society.

THE GOSPEL OF PETER'S ACCOUNT OF THE RESURRECTION

Early in the morning, as the Sabbath dawned, there came a large crowd from Jerusalem and the surrounding areas to see the sealed tomb. But during the night before the Lord's day dawned, as the soldiers were keeping guard two by two in every watch, there came a great sound in the sky, and they saw the heavens opened and two men descend shining with a great light, and they drew near to the tomb. The stone which had been set on the door rolled away by itself and moved to one side, and the tomb was opened and both of the young men went in.

Now when these soldiers saw that, they woke up the centurion and the elders (for they also were there keeping watch). While they were yet telling them the things which they had seen, they saw three men come out of the tomb, two of them sustaining the other one, and a cross following after them. The heads of the two they saw had heads that reached up to heaven, but the head of him that was led by them went beyond heaven. And they heard a voice out of the heavens saying, "Have you preached unto them that sleep?" The answer that was heard from the cross was, "Yes!" (Gospel of Peter 9:1—10:5)

Flavius Josephus (AD 37–100) was born into a Jewish priestly family as Joseph ben Mattathias. He became a military commander of Jewish forces in Galilee during the Jewish Revolt of AD 66, which ended in the destruction of Jerusalem in AD 70. Trapped in a cave by Roman forces, Josephus persuaded his men that they draw lots and kill each other successively, the last man committing suicide. But as the last one left alive, Josephus promptly surrendered to the Romans and joined their cause. After the war he became a Roman citizen and adopted his Roman name. His principal works are a history of the Jewish Revolt and a history of the Jewish people entitled *Antiquities of the Jews*. In this latter work he mentions Jesus of Nazareth twice, as well as Jesus' brother James, John the Baptist, Caiaphas, Pilate, and other persons mentioned in the gospels.

First, women were not regarded as credible witnesses. This attitude toward the testimony of women is evident in the Jewish historian Josephus's description of the rules for admissible testimony: "Let not the testimony of women be admitted, on account of the levity and boldness of their sex" (*Antiquities* IV.8.15). No such regulation is to be found in the Bible. It is rather a reflection of the patriarchal society of first-century Judaism.

Second, women occupied a low rung on the Jewish social ladder. Compared to men, women were second-class citizens. Consider these rabbinical texts: "Sooner let the words of the Law be burnt than delivered to women!" (Sotah 19a) and again: "Happy is he whose children are male, but unhappy is he whose children are female!" (Kiddushin 82b). The daily prayer of every Jewish man included the blessing, "Blessed are you, Lord our God, ruler of the universe, who has not created me a Gentile, a slave, or a woman" (Berachos 60b).

So, given their low social status and inability to serve as legal witnesses, it's quite amazing that it is *women* who are the discoverers of and principal witnesses to the empty tomb! If the empty tomb story were a legend, then the male disciples would have been made to be the ones who discover the empty tomb. The fact that women, whose testimony was deemed worthless, were the chief witnesses to the fact of the empty tomb can only be plausibly explained if, like it or not, they actually *were* the discoverers of the empty tomb, and the gospels faithfully record what for them was a very embarrassing fact.

The Earliest Jewish Response

Finally, *the earliest Jewish response to the proclamation of Jesus' resurrection presupposes the empty tomb.* In Matthew's gospel we find an attempt to refute the earliest Jewish response to the Christian proclamation of the resurrection:

> While they were going, behold, some of the guard went into the city and told the chief priests all that had taken place. And when they had assembled with the elders and taken counsel, they gave a sum of money to the soldiers and said, "Tell people, 'His disciples came by night and stole him away while we were asleep.' And if this comes to the governor's ears, we will satisfy him and keep you out of trouble." So they took the money and did as they were directed; and this story has been spread among the Jews to this day. (Matt. 28:11–15 RSV)

Now our interest isn't so much in Matthew's story of the guard at the tomb as in his incidental remark at the end, "This story has been spread among the Jews to this day." This remark reveals that the author was concerned to refute a widespread Jewish explanation of the resurrection.

Now what were unbelieving Jews saying in response to the disciples' proclamation that Jesus was risen? That these men were full of new wine? That Jesus' body still lay in the tomb in the garden? No. They were saying, "The disciples stole away His body." Think about that. "*The disciples stole away His body.*" The Jewish authorities did not deny the empty tomb but instead entangled themselves in a hopeless series of absurdities trying to explain it away. In other words, the Jewish claim that the disciples had stolen the body presupposes that the body was missing.

TALK ABOUT IT

If you were to talk with a non-Christian friend about this evidence for the empty tomb, how do you think he or she would respond?

Taken together, these five lines of evidence constitute a powerful case that Jesus' tomb was, indeed, found empty on the first day of the week by a group of His women followers. As a historical fact, this seems to be well established. According to Jacob Kremer, a New Testament critic who has specialized in the study of the resurrection: "By far most scholars hold firmly to the reliability of the biblical statements about the empty tomb."[2] In fact, in a survey of over 2,200 publications on the resurrection in English, French, and German since 1975, Gary Habermas found that 75 percent of scholars accepted the historicity of the discovery of Jesus' empty tomb.[3] The evidence is so compelling that even a number of Jewish scholars, such as Pinchas Lapide and Geza Vermes, have declared themselves convinced on the basis of the evidence that Jesus' tomb was found empty. But there is even more to come.

The Fact of Jesus' Postmortem Appearances

In 1 Corinthians 15:3–8, Paul writes:

> For I delivered to you what I also received:

> … that Christ died for our sins in accordance with the Scriptures,
> and that he was buried,
> and that he was raised on the third day in accordance with the Scriptures,
> and that he appeared to Cephas, then to the Twelve.

> Then he appeared to more than five hundred brethren at one time, most of whom are still alive, though some have fallen asleep. Then he appeared to James, then to all the apostles. Last of all, as to one untimely born, he appeared also to me. (author's translation)

This is a truly remarkable claim. We have here an indisputably authentic letter of a man personally acquainted with the first disciples, and he reports that they actually saw Jesus alive after His death. More than that, he says that he

himself also saw an appearance of Jesus. What are we to make of this claim? Did Jesus really appear to people alive after His death?

To answer this question, let's first consider the evidence for the resurrection appearances of Jesus. Once again, space won't allow me to examine in detail all the evidence for Jesus' postmortem appearances. But I'd like to look at three main lines of evidence.

Paul's List of Eyewitnesses

First, *Paul's list of eyewitnesses to Jesus' resurrection appearances guarantees that such appearances occurred.* In 1 Corinthians 15, Paul gives a list of witnesses to Jesus' resurrection appearances. Let's look briefly at each appearance to see whether it's plausible that such an event actually took place.

1. *Appearance to Peter.* We have no story in the gospels telling of Jesus' appearance to Peter. But the appearance is mentioned here in the old Christian tradition quoted by Paul, which originated in the Jerusalem church, and it's vouched for by the apostle Paul himself. As we know from Galatians 1:18, Paul spent about two weeks with Peter in Jerusalem three years after his conversion on the Damascus road. So Paul knew personally whether Peter claimed to have had such an experience or not. In addition to this, the appearance to Peter is mentioned in another old Christian tradition found in Luke 24:34: "The Lord has risen indeed, and he has appeared to Simon!" That Luke is passing on a prior tradition here is evident from the awkward way in which it is inserted into his story of the appearance to the Emmaus disciples. So although we have no story of the appearance to Peter, it is quite well founded historically. As a result, virtually all New Testament critics agree that Peter saw an appearance of Jesus alive from the dead.

2. *Appearance to the Twelve.* Undoubtedly, the group referred to here is that original group of twelve disciples who had been chosen by Jesus during His ministry—minus, of course, Judas, whose absence didn't affect the formal title of the group. This is the best-attested resurrection appearance of Jesus. It, too, is included in the very early traditional formula that Paul cites, and

Paul himself had contact with members of the Twelve. Moreover, we have independent stories of this appearance in Luke 24:36–42 and John 20:19–20. Undoubtedly, the most notable feature of these appearance stories is the physical demonstrations of Jesus' showing His wounds and eating before the disciples. The purpose of the physical demonstrations is to show two things: first, that Jesus was raised *physically*; and second, that He was the *same Jesus* who had been crucified. There can be little doubt that such an appearance occurred, for it is attested in the old Christian tradition, vouched for by Paul, who had personal contact with the Twelve, and is independently described by both Luke and John.

3. *Appearance to five hundred brethren.* The third appearance comes as somewhat of a shock: "Then he appeared to more than five hundred brethren at one time"! This is surprising, since we have no mention whatsoever of this appearance elsewhere in the New Testament. This might make us rather skeptical about this appearance, but Paul himself apparently had personal contact with these people, since he knew that some had died. This is seen in Paul's parenthetical comment, "most of whom are still alive, though some have fallen asleep." Why does Paul add this remark? The great New Testament scholar of Cambridge University, C. H. Dodd, replies, "There can hardly be any purpose in mentioning the fact that most of the 500 are still alive, unless Paul is saying, in effect, 'The witnesses are there to be questioned.'"[4] Notice, Paul could never have said this if the event had not occurred. He could not have challenged people to talk to the witnesses if the event had never taken place and there were no witnesses. But evidently there were witnesses to this event, and Paul knew that some of them had died in the meantime. Therefore, the event must have taken place.

I think that this appearance is not related in the gospels because it probably took place in Galilee. As one pieces together the various resurrection appearances in the gospels, it seems that they occurred first in Jerusalem, then in Galilee, and then in Jerusalem again. The appearance to the five hundred would have to be out of doors, perhaps on a hillside near a Galilean village.

In Galilee thousands had gathered to hear Jesus teach during His ministry. Since the gospels focus their attention on the appearances in Jerusalem, we don't have any story of this appearance to the five hundred. An intriguing possibility is that this was the appearance predicted by the angel at the tomb and described by Matthew (28:16–17).

4. *Appearance to James.* The next appearance is one of the most amazing of all: Jesus appeared to James, His younger brother. What makes this amazing is that apparently neither James nor any of Jesus' younger brothers believed in Jesus during His lifetime (Mark 3:21, 31–35; John 7:1–10). They didn't believe He was the Messiah, or a prophet, or even anybody special. By the criterion of embarrassment, this is doubtless a historical fact of Jesus' life and ministry.

But after the resurrection, Jesus' brothers show up in the Christian fellowship in the upper room in Jerusalem (Acts 1:14). There's no further mention of them until Acts 12:17, the story of Peter's deliverance from prison by the angel. What are Peter's first words? "Report this to *James.*" In Galatians 1:19 Paul tells of his two-week visit to Jerusalem about three years after his Damascus Road experience. He says that besides Peter, he saw none of the other apostles *except James* the Lord's brother. Paul at least implies that James was now being reckoned as an apostle. When Paul visited Jerusalem again fourteen years later, he says there were three "pillars" of the church in Jerusalem: Peter, John, and *James* (Gal. 2:9). Finally, in Acts 21:18 James is the sole head of the Jerusalem church and of the council of elders. We hear no more about James in the New Testament; but from Josephus, the Jewish historian, we learn that James was stoned to death illegally by the Sanhedrin sometime after AD 60 (*Antiquities* 20.200).

Not only James but also Jesus' other brothers became believers and were active in Christian preaching, as we see from 1 Corinthians 9:5: "Do we not have the right to be accompanied by a believing wife, as do the other apostles and *the brothers of the Lord* and Cephas?"

Now, how is this to be explained? On the one hand, it seems certain that Jesus' brothers did not believe in Him during His lifetime. Jesus' crucifixion would only confirm in James' mind that his elder brother's messianic pretensions were delusory, just as he had thought. On the other hand, it's equally certain that Jesus' brothers became ardent Christians, active in ministry. Many of us have brothers. What would it take to make you believe that your brother is the Lord, so that you would die for this belief, as James did? Can there be any doubt that the reason for this remarkable transformation is to be found in the fact that "then he appeared to James"? Even the skeptical New Testament critic Hans Grass admits that the conversion of James is one of the surest proofs of the resurrection of Jesus Christ.[5]

Jesus appears to James.

5. *Appearance to "all the apostles."* This appearance was probably to a limited circle of Christian missionaries somewhat wider than the Twelve. For such a group, see Acts 1:21–22. Once again, the fact of this appearance is guaranteed by Paul's personal contact with the apostles themselves.

6. *Appearance to Saul of Tarsus.* The final appearance is just as amazing as the appearance to James: "Last of all," says Paul, "he appeared to me also." The story of Jesus' appearance to Saul of Tarsus (or Paul) just outside Damascus is related in Acts 9:1–9 and is later told again twice. That this event actually occurred is established beyond doubt by Paul's references to it in his own letters.

This event changed Saul's whole life. He was a rabbi, a Pharisee, a respected Jewish leader. He hated the Christian heresy and did everything in his power to stamp it out. He tells us that he was even responsible for the *execution* of Christian believers. Then suddenly he gave up everything. He left his position as a respected Jewish leader and became a Christian missionary: He entered a life of poverty, labor, and suffering. He was whipped, beaten, stoned and left for dead, shipwrecked three times, in constant danger, deprivation, and anxiety. Finally, he made the ultimate sacrifice and was martyred for his faith at Rome. And it was all because on that day outside Damascus, he saw "Jesus our Lord" (1 Cor. 9:1).

In summary, Paul's testimony makes it historically certain that various individuals and groups of people experienced appearances of Jesus after His death and burial.

The Independent Gospel Accounts

Further, *the gospel accounts provide multiple, independent reports of postmortem appearances of Jesus*, even some of the same appearances found in Paul's list. The appearance to Peter is independently mentioned by Paul and Luke (1 Cor. 15:5; Luke 24:34) and is universally acknowledged by critics. The appearance to the Twelve is independently reported by Paul, Luke, and John (1 Cor. 15:5; Luke 24:36–53; John 20:19–31) and is again not in dispute. The appearance to the women disciples is independently reported by Matthew and John (Matt. 28:9–10; John 20:11–17) and enjoys, as well, ratification by the criterion of embarrassment, given the low credibility accorded to the testimony of women. It's generally agreed that the absence of this appearance from the list of appearances in the tradition quoted by Paul is a reflection of the discomfort in citing female witnesses. Finally, that Jesus appeared to the disciples in Galilee is independently reported by Mark, Matthew, and John (Mark 16; Matt. 28:16-20; John 21).

Taken sequentially, the appearances follow the pattern of Jerusalem, then Galilee, then Jerusalem again, matching the pilgrimages of the disciples as they returned to Galilee following the Passover/Feast of Unleavened Bread and then traveled again to Jerusalem two months later for Pentecost.

From this evidence what should we conclude? We can call these appearances hallucinations if we want to, but we cannot deny that they occurred. Even the skeptical critic Gerd Lüdemann is emphatic: "It may be taken as historically certain that Peter and the disciples had experiences after Jesus' death in which Jesus appeared to them as the risen Christ."[6] The evidence makes it certain that on separate occasions different individuals and groups had experiences of seeing Jesus alive from the dead. This conclusion is virtually indisputable.

The Bodily Nature of the Appearances

Thirdly, *the resurrection appearances were physical, bodily appearances.* So far the evidence I've presented doesn't depend on the *nature* of the postmortem appearances of Jesus. I've left it open whether they were visionary or physical in nature. It remains to be seen whether even visionary experiences of the risen Jesus can be plausibly explained on purely psychological grounds. But if the appearances were physical and bodily in nature, then a purely psychological explanation becomes next to impossible. So it's worth examining what we can know about the nature of these appearances.

1. *Paul implies that the appearances were physical.* He does this in two ways.

First, he conceives of the resurrection body as physical. Everyone recognizes that Paul does not teach the immortality of the soul alone but the resurrection of the body. In 1 Corinthians 15:42–44 Paul describes the differences between the present, earthly body and our future, resurrection body, which will be like Christ's. He draws four essential contrasts between the earthly body and the resurrection body:

The earthly body is:	*But the resurrection body is*:
mortal	immortal
dishonorable	glorious
weak	powerful
natural	spiritual

Now only the last contrast could possibly make us think that Paul did not believe in a physical resurrection body. But what does he mean by the words translated here as "natural/spiritual"?

The word translated "natural" literally means "soul-ish." Now obviously, Paul doesn't mean that our present body is made out of soul. Rather by this word he means "dominated by or pertaining to human nature." Similarly, when he says the resurrection body will be "spiritual," he doesn't mean "made out of spirit." Rather, he means "dominated by or oriented toward the Spirit." It's the same sense of the word "spiritual" used when we say that someone is a spiritual person.

In fact, look at the way Paul uses exactly those same words in 1 Corinthians 2:14–15 (ESV):

> The natural person does not accept the things of the Spirit of God, for they are folly to him, and he is not able to understand them because they are spiritually discerned. The spiritual person judges all things, but is himself to be judged by no one.

Natural person does not mean "physical person," but "person oriented toward human nature." And *spiritual person* does not mean "intangible, invisible person" but "person oriented toward the Spirit." The contrast is the same in 1 Corinthians 15. The present, earthly body will be freed from its slavery to sinful human nature and become instead fully empowered and directed by God's Spirit. Thus, Paul's doctrine of the resurrection body implies a physical resurrection.

Second, Paul, and indeed all the New Testament, makes a distinction between an *appearance* of Jesus and a *vision* of Jesus. The appearances of Jesus soon ceased, but visions of Jesus continued in the early church. Now the question is: What is the difference between an appearance and a vision? The answer of the New Testament seems to be clear: A vision, though caused by God, was purely in the mind, while an appearance took place "out there" in the external world.

Compare Stephen's vision of Jesus in Acts 7 with the resurrection appearances of Jesus. Though Stephen saw an identifiable, bodily image, what he saw was a vision of a man, not a man who was physically there, for no one else present experienced anything at all. By contrast the resurrection appearances took place in the world "out there" and could be experienced by anybody present. Paul could rightly regard his experience on the Damascus road as an appearance, even though it took place after Jesus' ascension, because it involved manifestations in the external world like the light and the voice, which Paul's companions also experienced to varying degrees. Thus, the

In 1 Corinthians 15:44, the Greek word translated as "natural" in NIV, NKJV, KJV, and NASB is *psychikos*, or "soul-ish," from the word *psyche*, or "soul." The word translated as "spiritual" is *pneumatikos*. Paul is not talking of physical vs. ethereal bodies, but of soul-led vs. Spirit-led bodies. This is clear when we look at 1 Corinthians 2:14, where Paul uses the same words, *psychikos* and *pneumatikos*, to describe different sorts of people in Corinth. The contrast is not one of materiality but of orientation.

distinction between a vision and an appearance of Jesus also implies that the resurrection appearances were physical.

2. *The gospel accounts show that the appearances were physical and bodily.* Again, two points deserve to be made.

First, every resurrection appearance related in the gospels is a physical, bodily appearance. The unanimous testimony of the gospels in this regard is quite impressive. If *none* of the appearances was originally a physical, bodily appearance, then it's very strange that we have a completely unanimous testimony in the gospels that *all* of them were physical, with no trace of the supposed original, nonphysical appearances. Such a thoroughgoing corruption of oral tradition in so short a time, while the original eyewitnesses were still about, is most unlikely.

"But he's alive spiritually!
He appeared to me in a vision!
Mary saw him too — didn't you,
Mary — tell them!"

Second, if all the appearances were originally nonphysical visions, then we're at a complete loss to explain the rise of the gospel accounts. For physical, bodily appearances would be foolishness to Gentiles and a stumbling block to Jews, since neither could accept physical resurrection from the dead. The Greek mentality regarded the death of the physical body as "good riddance," since the physical body was an impediment to the soul. The Jewish mentality precluded any physical resurrection to glory and immortality prior to the general resurrection at the end of the world. So both parties would have been very skeptical about tales of real, bodily appearances of someone risen from the dead. But both would have been quite happy to accept stories of visionary appearances of the deceased. If the original appearances were just visions, then, it becomes inexplicable why a unanimous tradition of physical appearances would develop.

TALK ABOUT IT

Why does Jesus' bodily resurrection matter to Christians? What difference would it make if Jesus simply lives on as a spirit and has no body?

To be perfectly candid, the only grounds for denying the physical, bodily nature of the postmortem appearances of Jesus is philosophical, not historical: Such appearances would be miracles of the most stupendous proportions, and that many critics cannot swallow. But in that case we need to retrace our steps to think again about the evidence for the existence of

God. If God exists, there's no good reason to be skeptical about miracles. As the agnostic Australian philosopher Peter Slezak nicely put it in our debate, for a God who is able to create the entire universe, the odd resurrection would be child's play!

So on the basis of these three lines of evidence, we can conclude that the fact of Jesus' postmortem appearances to various individuals and groups under a variety of circumstances is firmly established historically and, moreover, that these appearances were bodily and physical.

The Fact of the Origin of the Christian Faith

The third fact to be explained is the very origin of the Christian faith. We all know that Christianity sprang into being sometime midway through the first century AD. Why did it come into existence? What caused this movement to begin? Even skeptical New Testament scholars recognize that the Christian faith owes its origin to the belief of the earliest disciples that God had raised Jesus of Nazareth from the dead. In fact, they pinned nearly everything on this belief.

To take just one example: their belief that Jesus was the Messiah. Jews had no conception of a Messiah who, instead of triumphing over Israel's enemies, would be shamefully executed by them as a criminal. Messiah was supposed to be a triumphant figure who would command the respect of Jew and Gentile alike and who would establish the throne of David in Jerusalem. A Messiah who failed to deliver and to reign, who was defeated, humiliated, and slain by His enemies, is a contradiction in terms. Nowhere do Jewish texts speak of such a "Messiah." Therefore, it's difficult to overemphasize what a disaster the crucifixion was for the disciples' faith. Jesus' death on the cross spelled the humiliating end for any hopes they had entertained that He was the Messiah.

> ### TALK ABOUT IT
>
> Which of the lines of evidence in this chapter do you find most convincing personally? How do you think non-Christians you know would respond to the various lines of evidence? Which would be most compelling for them?

But the belief in the resurrection of Jesus reversed the catastrophe of the crucifixion. Because God had raised Jesus from the dead, He was seen to be Messiah after all. Thus, Peter proclaims in Acts 2:23–36: "This man … God raised…. Let the entire house of Israel know with certainty that God has made him both Lord and Messiah, this Jesus whom you crucified." It was on the basis of belief in His resurrection that the disciples could believe that Jesus was the Messiah.

It's no surprise, therefore, that belief in Jesus' resurrection was universal in the early Christian church. The traditional formula quoted in 1 Corinthians 15:3–7, in which the gospel is defined as the death, burial, resurrection, and appearances of Christ, shows that this understanding of the gospel goes right back to the very beginning of the church in Jerusalem.

Thus, the origin of Christianity hinges on the belief of the earliest disciples that God had raised Jesus from the dead. But the question is: How does one explain the origin of that belief? As R. H. Fuller says, even the most skeptical critic must posit some mysterious X to get the movement going. But what was that X?

Summary

Now we're ready to summarize all three of our points:

First, we saw that numerous lines of historical evidence prove that the tomb of Jesus was found empty by a group of His women followers.

Second, we saw that several lines of historical evidence establish that on numerous occasions and in different places various individuals and groups saw appearances of Jesus alive from the dead.

And finally, third, we saw that the very origin of the Christian faith depends on the belief of the earliest disciples that God had raised Jesus of Nazareth from the dead.

One of the things that most astonished me after completing my research in Munich was the realization that these three great, independently established facts represent *the majority view* of New Testament critics today.

The only point of serious disagreement would be on the physical nature of the resurrection appearances. But the state of current scholarship strongly supports the three facts as I have stated them.

These are not the conclusions of conservative or evangelical scholarship; these are the conclusions of mainstream New Testament criticism. As we saw, the wide majority of scholars who have written on the subject accept the fact of the empty tomb; virtually no one today denies that the earliest disciples experienced postmortem appearances of Jesus; and far and away most scholars agree that the earliest disciples at least believed that God had raised Jesus from the dead. It is the critic who would deny these facts that today finds himself on the defensive.

So don't be misled by unbelievers who want to quibble about inconsistencies in the circumstantial details of the gospel accounts. Our case for Jesus' resurrection doesn't depend on such details. All four gospels agree that:

> Jesus of Nazareth was crucified in Jerusalem by Roman authority during the Passover Feast, having been arrested and convicted on charges of blasphemy by the Jewish Sanhedrin and then slandered before the governor Pilate on charges of treason. He died within several hours and was buried Friday afternoon by Joseph of Arimathea in a tomb, which was shut with a stone. Certain female followers of Jesus, including Mary Magdalene, having observed his interment, visited his tomb early on Sunday morning, only to find it empty. Thereafter, Jesus appeared alive from the dead to the disciples, including Peter, who then became proclaimers of the message of His resurrection.

All four gospels attest to these facts. Many more details can be supplied by adding facts that are attested by three out of four.

So minor discrepancies don't affect our case. Historians expect to find inconsistencies even in the most reliable sources. No historian simply throws out a source because it has inconsistencies. Otherwise we'd have to be skeptical about all secular historical narratives that also contain such inconsistencies, which is wholly unreasonable. Moreover, in this case the inconsistencies aren't even within a single source; they're between independent sources. But obviously, it doesn't follow from an inconsistency between two independent sources that both sources are wrong. At worst, one is wrong if they can't be harmonized.

The remaining issue, then, is how the three established facts I've stated are best explained.

Explaining the Evidence

We come, then, to the second step in our case: determining which explanation of the evidence is the best. Historians weigh various factors in assessing competing hypotheses. Some of the most important are as follows:

1. The best explanation will have greater *explanatory scope* than other explanations. That is, it will explain more of the evidence.

2. The best explanation will have greater *explanatory power* than other explanations. That is, it will make the evidence more probable.

3. The best explanation will be *more plausible* than other explanations. That is, it will fit better with true background beliefs.

4. The best explanation will be less *contrived* than other explanations. That is, it won't require adopting as many new beliefs that have no independent evidence.

5. The best explanation will be *disconfirmed by fewer accepted beliefs* than other explanations. That is, it won't conflict with as many accepted beliefs.

6. The best explanation will meet conditions 1–5 so much better than the others that there's little chance that one of the other explanations, after further investigation, will do better in meeting these conditions.

Since a hypothesis may do really well in meeting some conditions but not so well in meeting others, figuring out which hypothesis is the best explanation may often be difficult and requires skill. But if the explanatory scope and power of a hypothesis are very great, so that it does a much better job in explaining a wide variety of facts, then it's likely to be the true explanation.

So let's apply these tests to the typical hypotheses that have been offered down through history to explain the empty tomb, postmortem appearances, and origin of the disciples' belief in Jesus' resurrection, and let's see if they do better or as well in explaining these facts as the resurrection hypothesis.

Conspiracy Hypothesis

According to this hypothesis, the disciples stole the body of Jesus and lied about His appearances, thus faking the resurrection. This was the very first counterexplanation for the empty tomb, as we've seen, and it was revived during the eighteenth century by European deists. Today, however, this explanation has been completely given up by modern scholarship. Let's see how it fares when assessed by the standard criteria for testing historical hypotheses.

1. *Explanatory scope.* The conspiracy hypothesis meets this condition pretty well, for it offers explanations of the empty tomb (the disciples stole the body), the postmortem appearances (the disciples lied about these), and the origin of the disciples' (supposed) belief in Jesus' resurrection (again, they lied).

2. *Explanatory power.* Here doubts begin to arise about the conspiracy hypothesis. Take the empty tomb, for example. If the disciples stole Jesus' corpse, then it would be utterly pointless to fabricate a story about *women* finding the tomb to be empty. Such a story would not be the sort of tale Jewish men would invent. Moreover, the simplicity of the story is not well explained by the conspiracy hypothesis—where are the scriptural proof texts, the evidence of fulfilled prophecy? Why isn't Jesus described as emerging from the tomb, as in later forgeries like the Gospel of Peter? Neither is the dispute with nonbelieving Jews well explained. Why isn't Matthew's guard already there in Mark's story? Even in Matthew's story the guard is set too late:

The body could have already been stolen before the guard arrived on Saturday morning, so that they were guarding, unbeknownst to them, an empty tomb! For a fail-safe alibi against theft of the body, see again the forged Gospel of Peter, where the guard is set immediately upon interment of the corpse.

As for the appearance stories, similar problems arise. A fabricator would probably describe Jesus' resurrection appearances in terms of Old Testament visions of God and descriptions of the end-time resurrection (as in Daniel 12:2). But then Jesus should appear to the disciples in dazzling glory. And why not a description of the resurrection itself? Why no appearances to Caiaphas the high priest or to the villains on the Sanhedrin, as Jesus predicted? They could be then branded as the real liars for denying that Jesus did appear to them!

"Okay, so here's the plan: We get the body out of the tomb
and stash it somewhere, and then we come back
and tell a story that will probably get us all killed.
So who's with me on this?"

But the explanatory power of the conspiracy hypothesis is undoubtedly weakest when it comes to the origin of the disciples' belief in Jesus' resurrection. For the hypothesis is really a denial of that fact; it seeks to explain the mere semblance of belief on the disciples' part. But as critics have universally recognized, you can't plausibly deny that the earliest disciples at least sincerely *believed* that Jesus was risen from the dead. They staked their very lives on that conviction. The transformation in the lives of the disciples is not credibly explained by the hypothesis of a conspiracy. This shortcoming alone has been enough in the minds of most scholars to sink the old conspiracy hypothesis forever.

3. *Plausibility.* The real Achilles' heel of the conspiracy hypothesis is, however, its implausibility. One might mention here objections to the unbelievable complexity of such a conspiracy or the supposed psychological state of the disciples; but the overriding problem that dwarfs all others is that it is wholly anachronistic to suppose that first-century Jews intended to hoax Jesus' resurrection.

The conspiracy hypothesis views the disciples' situation through the rearview mirror of Christian history rather than through the eyes of a first-century Jew. There was no expectation of a Messiah who, instead of establishing David's throne and subduing Israel's enemies, would be shamefully executed by the Gentiles as a criminal. Moreover, the idea of resurrection was just unconnected with the idea of Messiah and even incompatible with it, since Messiah was not supposed to be killed. As N. T. Wright nicely puts it, if you're a first-century Jew, and your favorite Messiah got himself crucified, then you've basically got two choices: Either you go home or else you get yourself a new Messiah. But the idea of stealing Jesus' corpse and saying that God had raised him from the dead is hardly one that would have entered the minds of the disciples.

It has been suggested that the idea of Jesus' resurrection could have originated through the influence of pagan mythology. Back around the turn of the nineteenth to the twentieth century, scholars in comparative religion collected parallels to Christian beliefs in other religious movements, and some thought to explain Christian beliefs, including the belief in Jesus' resurrection, as the result of the influence of such myths. The movement soon collapsed, however, principally due to two factors:

First, scholars came to realize that the parallels are false. The ancient world was a virtual fruit basket of myths of various gods and heroes. Comparative studies in religion require sensitivity to their similarities and differences, or distortion and confusion inevitably result. Unfortunately, those who were eager to find parallels to Jesus' resurrection failed to exercise such sensitivity.

Many of the alleged parallels are actually stories of the *assumption* of the hero into heaven (Hercules, Romulus). Others are *disappearance* stories, which claim that the hero has vanished into a higher sphere (Apollonius of Tyana, Empedocles). Still others are *seasonal symbols* for the crop cycle, as the vegetation dies in the dry season and comes back to life in the rainy season (Tammuz, Osiris, Adonis). Some are *political expressions* of emperor worship (Julius Caesar, Caesar Augustus).

None of these is parallel to the Jewish idea of the resurrection of the dead. Indeed, most scholars have come to doubt whether, properly speaking, there really were *any* myths of dying and rising gods at all. For example, in the myth of Osiris, which was one of the best-known symbolic seasonal myths, Osiris doesn't really come back to life but simply continues to exist in the realm of the departed.

In general, scholars have come to realize that pagan mythology is simply the wrong interpretive context for understanding Jesus of Nazareth. Jesus and His disciples were first-century Israelite Jews, and it is against that background that they must be understood. The collapse of the alleged parallels is just one indication that pagan mythology is the wrong interpretive context for understanding the disciples' belief in Jesus' resurrection.

Second, there's no causal connection between pagan myths and the origin of the disciples' belief in Jesus' resurrection. Jews were familiar with the seasonal deities (Ezek. 8:14–15) and found them abhorrent. Therefore, there's no trace of cults of dying and rising gods in first-century Israel. In any case it's highly unlikely that the original disciples would have come up with the idea that Jesus of Nazareth was risen from the dead because they had heard

pagan myths about dying and rising seasonal gods. Contemporary scholars have therefore abandoned this approach.

But maybe the disciples could have come up with the idea of Jesus' resurrection on the basis of Jewish influences? Again, this is unlikely. For the Jewish conception of resurrection differed in at least two fundamental respects from the resurrection of Jesus.

First, in Jewish thinking the resurrection to glory and immortality always occurred *after* the end of the world. Jews had no idea of a resurrection within history. That's why, I think, the disciples had so much trouble understanding Jesus' predictions of His own resurrection. They thought He was talking about the resurrection at the end of the world. Look at Mark 9:9–11 (NASB), for example.

> As they were coming down from the mountain, He gave them orders not to relate to anyone what they had seen, until the Son of Man rose from the dead. They seized upon that statement, discussing with one another what rising from the dead meant. They asked Him, saying, "Why is it that the scribes say that Elijah must come first?"

Here Jesus predicts His resurrection, and what do the disciples ask? "Why is it that the scribes say that Elijah must come first?" In first-century Judaism it was believed the prophet Elijah would come again before the great and terrible day of the Lord, the judgment day when the dead would be raised. The disciples could not understand the idea of a resurrection occurring within history prior to the end of the world. Hence, Jesus' predictions only confused them.

Thus, given the Jewish conception of the resurrection, the disciples after Jesus' crucifixion would not have come up with the idea that He had been already raised. They would have only looked forward to the resurrection at the last day and perhaps, in keeping with Jewish custom, preserved His tomb as a shrine where His bones could rest until the resurrection.

Second, in Jewish thinking the resurrection was always the resurrection of *all* the righteous dead. They had no idea of the resurrection of an isolated individual. Moreover, not only was there no connection between the individual believer's resurrection and the prior resurrection of the Messiah, there existed no belief in the Messiah's prior resurrection at all. That's why we find no examples of other messianic movements claiming that their executed leader was risen from the dead. Wright has been insistent upon this point. "The followers of the first-century messianic movements … were fanatically committed to the cause…. In no other case, however, right across the century before Jesus and the century after him, do we hear of any Jewish group saying that their executed leader had been raised again from the dead."[7]

TALK ABOUT IT

How does this historical background help you understand incidents such as those described in Mark 8:31–32 and Acts 17:16–18, 32?

Jews had no idea of the resurrection of an isolated individual, especially of the Messiah. Therefore, after Jesus' crucifixion, all the disciples could do was wait with longing for the general resurrection of the dead to see their Master again.

Notice that this point undermines not only conspiracy theories, which suppose that the disciples *insincerely* proclaimed Jesus' resurrection, but also any theory that suggests that, on the basis of pagan or Jewish influences, they *sincerely* came to believe in and preached His resurrection.

4. *Less contrived.* Like all conspiracy theories of history, the conspiracy hypothesis is contrived in supposing that what all the evidence seems to point to is, in fact, mere appearance only, to be explained away by hypotheses for which there is no evidence. Specifically, it postulates motives and ideas in the minds of the earliest disciples and actions on their part for which there is not a shred of evidence. It can become even more contrived, as hypotheses have to be multiplied to deal with objections to the theory; for example, how to account for the appearance to the five hundred brethren or the women's role in the empty tomb and appearance stories.

5. *Disconfirmed by fewer accepted beliefs.* The conspiracy hypothesis tends to be disconfirmed by our general knowledge of conspiracies, their instability and tendency to unravel. Moreover, it is disconfirmed by accepted beliefs such as the sincerity of the disciples, the nature of first-century Jewish messianic expectations, and so on.

6. *Exceeds other hypotheses in fulfilling conditions 1–5.* The conspiracy hypothesis obviously fails to meet this condition, since there are better hypotheses (such as the hallucination hypothesis), which don't dismiss the disciples' belief in Jesus' resurrection as a blatant lie.

No scholar would defend the conspiracy hypothesis today. The only place you read about such things is in the popular, sensationalist press or Internet fantasies.

Apparent Death Hypothesis

A second explanation was the apparent death hypothesis. Critics around the beginning of the nineteenth century claimed that Jesus was not completely dead when He was taken down from the cross. He revived in the tomb and escaped to convince His disciples He had risen from the dead. Today this hypothesis has also been almost completely given up. Once again, let's apply our criteria for the best explanation:

1. *Explanatory scope.* The apparent death hypothesis also provides explanations for the empty tomb, postmortem appearances, and origin of the disciples' belief in Jesus' resurrection.

2. *Explanatory power.* Here the theory begins to founder. Some versions of the apparent death hypothesis were really variations on the conspiracy hypothesis. Instead of stealing the body, the disciples (along with Jesus Himself!) were supposed to have conspired to fake Jesus' death on the cross. In such cases, the theory shares all the weaknesses of the conspiracy hypothesis. A nonconspiratorial version of the theory was that Jesus just happened to survive the crucifixion, though the guards thought He was dead. Such a version of the hypothesis is also saddled with insurmountable difficulties:

How do you explain the empty tomb, since a man sealed inside a tomb could not move the stone so as to escape? How do you explain the postmortem appearances, since the appearance of a half-dead man desperately in need of medical attention would hardly have elicited in the disciples the conclusion that He was the risen Lord and conqueror of death? How do you explain the origin of the disciples' belief in Jesus' resurrection, since seeing Him again would lead them to conclude merely that He hadn't died? They wouldn't think that He was, contrary to Jewish thought (as well as their own eyes), gloriously risen from the dead.

3. *Plausibility*. Here again the theory fails miserably. Roman executioners could be relied upon to ensure that their victims were dead. Since the exact moment of death by crucifixion is uncertain, executioners could ensure death by a spear thrust into the victim's side. This is what happened to Jesus (John 19:34). Moreover, what the theory suggests is virtually physically impossible. The Jewish historian Josephus tells of how he had three acquaintances who had been crucified removed from their crosses, but despite the best medical attention two of the three died anyway (*Life* 75:420–21). The extent of Jesus' tortures was such that He could never have survived the crucifixion and entombment. The suggestion that a man so critically wounded then went on to appear to the disciples on various occasions in Jerusalem and Galilee is pure fantasy.

4. *Less contrived*. The apparent death hypothesis, especially in its conspiratorial versions, can become enormously contrived. We're invited to imagine secret societies, stealthily administered potions, conspiratorial alliances between Jesus' disciples and members of the Sanhedrin, and so forth, all with nary a scrap of evidence in support.

5. *Disconfirmed by fewer accepted beliefs*. The apparent death hypothesis is massively disconfirmed by medical facts concerning what would happen to a person who has been scourged and crucified. It is also disconfirmed by the unanimous evidence that Jesus did not continue among His disciples after His death.

6. *Exceeds other hypotheses in fulfilling conditions 1–5.* This theory also is hardly a standout! For that reason it has virtually no defenders among New Testament historians today.

Displaced Body Hypothesis

In one of the few modern Jewish attempts to deal with the facts concerning Jesus' resurrection, Joseph Klausner in 1922 proposed that Joseph of Arimathea placed Jesus' body in his tomb temporarily, due to the lateness of the hour and the closeness of his own family tomb to the place of Jesus' execution. But then he moved the corpse later to the criminals' common graveyard. Unaware of the displacement of the body, the disciples upon finding the tomb empty inferred that Jesus was risen from the dead. Although no scholars defend Klausner's hypothesis today, I have seen attempts by popular authors to revive it. In light of what has already been said of other theories, its shortcomings are evident:

1. *Explanatory scope.* The displaced body hypothesis has narrow explanatory scope. It tries to explain the empty tomb but says nothing about the postmortem appearances and the origin of the disciples' belief in Jesus' resurrection. Independent hypotheses must be adopted to explain the full scope of the evidence.

2. *Explanatory power.* Klausner's hypothesis has no explanatory power with regard to either the appearances or the origin of the Christian faith. As for the empty tomb, the hypothesis faces an obvious problem: Since Joseph and any servants with him knew what they had done with the corpse, the theory is at a loss to explain why the disciples' error wasn't corrected once they began to proclaim Jesus' resurrection—unless, that is, one resorts to contrived conjectures to save the day, such as Joseph and his servants' sudden deaths!

It might be said that Jesus' corpse would have no longer been identifiable. But this assertion is not, in fact, true. Jewish burial practices typically involved digging up the bones of the deceased a year later and placing them in an ossuary. So grave sites, even for criminals, were carefully noted. But, in any case, the objection misses the point. The point is that the earliest Jewish-Christian disputes about the resurrection were not over the location of Jesus' grave or the identity of the corpse but over why the tomb was empty. Had Joseph displaced the body, the Jewish-Christian controversy would have taken a quite different course.

3. *Plausibility.* The hypothesis is implausible for a number of reasons. So far as we can rely on Jewish sources, the criminals' graveyard was only fifty to six hundred yards from the site of Jesus' crucifixion. Jewish practice, furthermore, was to bury executed criminals on the day of their execution, so that's what Joseph would have wanted to accomplish. Therefore, Joseph could and would have placed the body directly in the criminals' graveyard, thereby eliminating any need to move it later or defile his own family tomb. Indeed, Jewish law did not even *permit* the body to be moved later, except to the family tomb. Joseph had adequate time for a simple burial, which probably included washing the corpse and wrapping it up in a sheet with dry spices.

4. *Less contrived.* The theory is mildly contrived in ascribing to Joseph motives and activities for which we have no evidence at all. It becomes really contrived if we have to start inventing things like Joseph's sudden death in order to save the hypothesis.

5. *Disconfirmed by fewer accepted beliefs.* The theory suffers disconfirmation from what we know about Jewish burial procedures for criminals mentioned above.

6. *Exceeds other hypotheses in fulfilling conditions 1–5.* Again, no historian seems to share this estimation.

Hallucination Hypothesis

In his book *The Life of Jesus, Critically Examined* (1835), David Strauss proposed that the resurrection appearances were merely hallucinations on the part of the disciples. The most prominent defender of this view today is the German New Testament critic Gerd Lüdemann. How does the hallucination hypothesis fare when assessed by our criteria?

1. *Explanatory scope*. The hallucination hypothesis has narrow explanatory scope. It says nothing to explain the empty tomb. Therefore, one must either deny the fact of the empty tomb (and, therefore, the burial as well) or else conjoin some *independent* hypothesis to the hallucination hypothesis to account for the empty tomb.

Again, the hallucination hypothesis says nothing to explain the origin of the disciples' belief in Jesus' resurrection. Some scholars have made a great deal out of the alleged similarities between the postmortem appearances of Jesus and visions of the recently departed on the part of the bereaved. But the overriding lesson of such intriguing stories is that the bereaved do *not* conclude that the deceased has returned physically to life as a result of such experiences, however real and tangible they may seem—rather the deceased is seen in the afterlife. As Wright observes, for someone in the ancient world, visions of the deceased are not evidence that the person is alive, but evidence that he is dead!

Moreover, in a Jewish context other, more appropriate interpretations of such experiences than resurrection are close to hand. Given the current Jewish beliefs about life after death, the disciples, if they were to project hallucinations of Jesus, would have seen Jesus in heaven or in Abraham's bosom, where the souls of the righteous dead were believed to abide until the final resurrection. And such visions would not have led to belief in Jesus' resurrection. At the most, it would have only led the disciples to say that Jesus had been assumed into heaven, not raised from the dead.

In the Old Testament, figures such as Enoch and Elijah were portrayed as not having died but as having been taken directly into heaven. In an extrabiblical Jewish writing called The Testament of Job (40), the story is told of two children killed in the collapse of a house. When the rescuers clear away the rubble, the bodies of the children are nowhere to be found. Meanwhile, their mother sees a vision of the two children glorified in heaven,

Resurrection is the raising up of a dead man in the space-time universe to glory and immortality. *Assumption* is the taking of someone bodily out of this world into heaven. *Revivification* is the return of a dead man to the mortal life. Second Kings 2:1–12 describes the assumption of Elijah into heaven. John 11:1–44 describes the revivification of Lazarus by Jesus. Note the differences between the two events and Jesus' resurrection.

where they have been taken up by God. It needs to be emphasized that for the Jew an assumption into heaven is not the same as a resurrection. Assumption is the taking of someone bodily out of this world into heaven. Resurrection is the raising up of a dead man in the space-time universe. They are distinct ideas.

Given Jewish beliefs concerning assumption and resurrection, the disciples, having seen heavenly visions of Jesus, would not have preached that Jesus had been raised from the dead. At the very most, the empty tomb and hallucinations of Jesus would have caused them to believe in the assumption of Jesus into glory, for this was consistent with their Jewish frame of thought. But they wouldn't have come to believe that Jesus had been raised from the dead, for this contradicted Jewish beliefs about the resurrection of the dead, as we have seen. Thus, even given hallucinations, belief in Jesus' resurrection remains unexplained.

2. *Explanatory power.* The hallucination hypothesis obviously does nothing to explain the empty tomb and the origin of the disciples' belief in Jesus' resurrection. But it arguably has weak explanatory power even when it comes to the appearances. Suppose that Peter was one of those individuals who experienced a vision of a deceased loved one or experienced a guilt-induced vision, as Lüdemann imagines. Would this suffice to explain the resurrection appearances? Not really, for the diversity of the appearances bursts the bounds of anything found in the psychological casebooks. Jesus appeared not just one time, but many times; not at just one locale and circumstance, but at a variety of places and under a variety of circumstances; not to just one individual, but to different persons; not just to individuals, but to various groups; not just to believers, but to unbelievers and even enemies. Positing a chain reaction among the disciples won't solve the problem because people like James and Paul don't stand in the chain. Those who would explain the resurrection appearances psychologically are compelled to construct a composite picture by cobbling together different unrelated cases of hallucinatory experiences, which only serves to underline the fact that there's nothing like the resurrection appearances in the psychological casebooks.

3. *Plausibility.* Lüdemann attempts to make his hallucination hypothesis plausible by a psychoanalysis of Peter and Paul. He believes they both labored under guilt complexes that found release in hallucinations of Jesus. But Lüdemann's psychoanalysis is implausible for three reasons: *First,* Lüdemann's use of depth psychology is based upon certain theories of Jung and Freud, which are highly disputed. *Second,* there's insufficient data to do a psychoanalysis of Peter and Paul. Psychoanalysis is difficult enough to carry out even with patients on the psychoanalyst's couch, so to speak, but it's next to impossible with historical figures. For that reason the attempt to write psychobiography is rejected by historians today. Finally, *third,* the evidence we do have suggests that Paul did *not* struggle with a guilt complex as Lüdemann supposes. Nearly fifty years ago the Swedish scholar Krister Stendahl pointed out that Western readers have tended to interpret Paul in light of Martin Luther's struggles with guilt and sin. But Paul (or Saul) the Pharisee experienced no such struggle. Stendahl writes:

> Contrast Paul, a very happy and successful Jew, one who can say "As to righteousness under the Law (I was) blameless" (Phil. 3:6). That *is* what he says. He experiences no troubles, no problems, no qualms of conscience. He is a star pupil, the student to get the thousand dollar graduate scholarship in Gamaliel's Seminary.… Nowhere in Paul's writings is there any indication … that psychologically Paul had some problem of conscience.[8]

In order to justify his portrait of a guilt-ridden Paul, Lüdemann is forced to interpret Romans 7 in terms of Paul's pre-Christian experience. But this interpretation is rejected by almost all commentators since the late 1920s. So Lüdemann's psychoanalysis is positively implausible.

A second respect in which the hallucination hypothesis is implausible is its taking the resurrection appearances to be merely visionary experiences. Lüdemann recognizes that the hallucination hypothesis depends on the presupposition that what Paul experienced on the Damascus road was the same as what all the *other* disciples experienced. But this presupposition is groundless. In including himself in the list of eyewitnesses to Christ's resurrection appearances, Paul is in no way implying that they were all just like the appearance to him. Many of Paul's opponents in Corinth denied that he was a true apostle, so Paul is anxious to include himself along with the other apostles who had seen Christ. Paul is trying to bring his experience up to the objectivity and reality of theirs, not to pull their experience down to the level of merely visionary experiences.

So the hallucination hypothesis suffers from implausibility with respect to its psychoanalysis of the witnesses and its blanket reduction of the appearances to visionary experiences.

4. *Less contrived.* Lüdemann's version of the hallucination hypothesis is contrived in a number of ways: For example, it assumes that the disciples fled back to Galilee after Jesus' arrest, that Peter was so obsessed with guilt that he projected a hallucination of Jesus, that the other disciples were also prone to hallucinations, and that Paul had a struggle with the Jewish law and a secret attraction to Christianity.

5. *Disconfirmed by fewer accepted beliefs.* Some of the accepted beliefs of New Testament scholars today tend to disconfirm the hallucination hypothesis, at least as Lüdemann presents it; for example, the beliefs that Jesus was laid in a tomb by Joseph of Arimathea, that Jesus' tomb was discovered empty by women, that psychoanalysis of historical figures is not feasible, that Paul was basically content with his life under the Jewish law, and that the New Testament makes a distinction between a mere vision and a resurrection appearance.

TALK ABOUT IT

Why do you suppose the hallucination hypothesis is today the most prominent hypothesis among those who deny Jesus' resurrection?

6. *Exceeds other hypotheses in fulfilling conditions 1–5.* The hallucination hypothesis remains a live option today and in that respect has outstripped its naturalistic rivals. But the question is whether it outstrips the resurrection hypothesis.

🙠 On Guard

The Resurrection Hypothesis

We've seen how poorly the typical explanations of the empty tomb, the postmortem appearances, and the origin of the disciples' faith fare when assessed by standard criteria for testing historical hypotheses. They're especially weak when it comes to explanatory scope and power and are often highly implausible.

But does the resurrection hypothesis do any better at explaining the evidence? Is it a better explanation than the implausible naturalistic explanations offered in the past? In order to answer these questions, let's apply our same criteria to the hypothesis that "God raised Jesus from the dead."

1. *Explanatory scope.* The resurrection hypothesis has greater explanatory scope than some rival explanations like the hallucination hypothesis or the displaced body hypothesis by explaining all three of the main facts at issue, whereas these rival hypotheses explain only one.

2. *Explanatory power.* This is perhaps the greatest strength of the resurrection hypothesis. The conspiracy hypothesis and the apparent death hypothesis, for example, just do not convincingly account for the empty tomb, resurrection appearances, and origin of the Christian faith; on these theories the evidence (for example, the transformation of the disciples) becomes very improbable. By contrast, on the hypothesis of Jesus' resurrection it seems extremely probable that the tomb should be empty, that the disciples should see appearances of Jesus alive, and that they should come to believe in His resurrection.

3. *Plausibility.* The plausibility of Jesus' resurrection grows exponentially once we consider it in its historical context, namely, Jesus' unparalleled life and radical personal claims, and in its philosophical context, namely, the evidence for God's existence. Once one embraces the view that God exists, the hypothesis that God would raise Jesus from the dead is no more implausible than its rivals.

4. *Less contrived.* The resurrection hypothesis possesses great explanatory scope and power, but some scholars have charged that it is contrived. Being

contrived, you'll recall, is a matter of how many new suppositions a hypothesis must make that are not implied by existing knowledge.

So defined, however, it's hard to see why the resurrection hypothesis is extraordinarily contrived. It requires only one new supposition: that God exists. Surely its rival hypotheses require many new suppositions. For example, the conspiracy hypothesis requires us to suppose that the moral character of the disciples was defective, which is certainly not implied by already existing knowledge; the apparent death hypothesis requires the supposition that the centurion's lance thrust into Jesus' side was just a superficial poke or is an unhistorical detail in the narrative, which again goes beyond existing knowledge; the hallucination hypothesis requires us to suppose some sort of emotional preparation of the disciples which predisposed them to project visions of Jesus alive, which is not implied by our knowledge. Such examples could be multiplied.

Moreover, for the person who *already* believes in God, the resurrection hypothesis doesn't even introduce the new supposition of God's existence, since that's already implied by his existing knowledge. So the resurrection hypothesis cannot be said to be contrived simply by virtue of the number of new suppositions it introduces.

If our hypothesis is contrived, then, it must be for some other reasons. Scientific hypotheses regularly include the supposition of the existence of new entities, such as quarks, strings, gravitons, black holes, and the like, without those theories being characterized as contrived. Philosophers of science have found it notoriously difficult to explain what it is exactly that makes a hypothesis contrived. There seems to be an air of artificiality about a hypothesis deemed to be contrived, which can be sensed by those who are seasoned practitioners of the relevant science.

Now I think the sense of discomfort that many people, *even Christians*, feel about appealing to God as part of an explanatory hypothesis for some phenomenon in the world is that so doing has this air of artificiality. It just seems too easy when confronted with some unexplained phenomenon to throw up one's hands and say, "God did it!" Is the hypothesis that "God raised Jesus from the dead" contrived in this sense?

I don't think so. A supernatural explanation of the empty tomb, the resurrection appearances, and the origin of the Christian faith can scarcely be said to be contrived given the context of Jesus' own unparalleled life, ministry, and personal claims. A supernatural hypothesis readily fits into such a context. It's also precisely because of this historical context that the resurrection hypothesis doesn't seem contrived when compared to miraculous explanations of other sorts: for example, that a "psychological miracle" occurred, causing normal men and women to become conspirators and liars who would be willingly martyred for their lies; or that a "biological miracle" occurred, which prevented Jesus' dying on the cross (despite the spear-thrust through his chest, and so forth). It is *these* miraculous hypotheses that strike us as artificial and contrived, not the resurrection hypothesis, which makes abundantly good sense in the context of Jesus' ministry and radical personal claims. Thus, it seems to me that the resurrection hypothesis cannot be characterized as excessively contrived.

5. *Disconfirmed by fewer accepted beliefs.* I can't think of any accepted beliefs that disconfirm the resurrection hypothesis—unless one thinks of, say, "Dead men do not rise" as disconfirmatory. But this generalization based on what naturally happens when people die does nothing to disconfirm the hypothesis that *God* raised Jesus from the dead. We may consistently believe *both* that men do not rise naturally from the dead *and* that God raised Jesus from the dead. By contrast, rival theories are disconfirmed by accepted beliefs about, for example, the instability of conspiracies, the likelihood of death as a result of crucifixion, the psychological characteristics of hallucinatory experiences, and so forth, as we have seen.

6. *Exceeds other hypotheses in fulfilling conditions 1–5.* There's certainly little chance of any of the rival hypotheses' ever exceeding the resurrection hypothesis in fulfilling the above conditions. The bewilderment of contemporary scholarship when confronted with the facts of the empty

tomb, the resurrection appearances, and the origin of the Christian faith suggests that no better rival is anywhere on the horizon. Once you give up the prejudice against miracles, it's hard to deny that the resurrection of Jesus is the best explanation of the facts.

Conclusion

In conclusion, then, three great, independently established facts—the empty tomb, the resurrection appearances, and the origin of the Christian faith—all point to the same marvelous conclusion: that God raised Jesus from the dead. Given that God exists, this conclusion cannot be barred to anyone seeking the meaning to existence.

1. John A. T. Robinson, *The Human Face of God* (Philadelphia: Westminster, 1973), 131.
2. Jacob Kremer, *Die Osterevangelien—Geschichten um Geschichte* (Stuttgart: Katholisches Bibelwerk, 1977), 49–50.
3. Gary Habermas, "Experience of the Risen Jesus: The Foundational Historical Issue in the Early Proclamation of the Resurrection," *Dialog* 45 (2006): 292.
4. C. H. Dodd, *More New Testament Studies* (Manchester: University of Manchester, 1968), 128.
5. Hans Grass, *Ostergeschehen und Osterberichte*, 4th ed. (Göttingen: Vandenhoeck & Ruprecht, 1974), 80.
6. Gerd Lüdemann, *What Really Happened to Jesus?*, trans. John Bowden (Louisville, KY: Westminster John Knox Press, 1995), 80.
7. N. T. Wright, *Sewanee Theological Review*, 41.2, 1998.
8. Kristen Stendahl, *Paul Among Jews and Gentiles* (Philadelphia: Fortress, 1976), 12–13.

I. Determining the evidence to be explained

    A. Jesus' tomb was found empty by a group of His women followers on the first day of the week following His crucifixion.

        1. The historical reliability of the story of Jesus' burial supports the empty tomb.

        2. The story of Jesus' empty tomb is independently reported in very early sources.

        3. Mark's story is simple and lacks legendary development.

        4. The tomb was discovered empty by women.

        5. The earliest Jewish response to the disciples presupposes the empty tomb.

    B. Various individuals and groups on different occasions and under varying circumstances experienced appearances of Jesus alive.

        1. Paul's list of eyewitnesses to Jesus' resurrection appearances guarantees that such appearances occurred.

        2. The gospel accounts provide multiple, independent reports of postmortem appearances of Jesus.

        3. The resurrection appearances were physical, bodily appearances.

    C. The first disciples came sincerely to believe in Jesus' resurrection despite every predisposition to the contrary.

        1. Jews had no expectation of a Messiah who instead of triumphing over Israel's enemies would be shamefully executed by them as a criminal.

        2. Jewish beliefs about the afterlife preclude anyone's rising from the dead to glory and immortality before the resurrection at the end of the world.

II. Explaining the evidence

    A. Rival explanations do not fare well when assessed by the standard criteria for the best explanation, such as explanatory scope, explanatory power, plausibility, being contrived, disconfirmation by accepted beliefs, and outstripping its rivals in meeting these criteria.

1. Conspiracy theory

2. Apparent death theory

3. Displaced body theory

4. Hallucination theory

B. The resurrection theory when judged by these same criteria emerges as the best explanation.

CHAPTER 10

IS JESUS THE ONLY WAY TO GOD?

*There is salvation in no one else, for there is no other name under heaven
given among men by which we must be saved. (Acts 4:12 RSV)*

I often speak at major Canadian universities on the existence of God. I typically present a cumulative case climaxing in Jesus' resurrection. After one of my talks, one slightly irate student wrote on her comment card, "I was with you until you got to the stuff about Jesus. God is *not* the Christian God!"

This attitude is pervasive in Western culture today. Most people are happy to agree that God exists; but in our pluralistic society it has become politically incorrect to claim that God has revealed Himself decisively in Jesus.

New Testament Teaching

And yet this is exactly what the New Testament clearly teaches. Take the letters of the apostle Paul, for example. He invites his Gentile converts to recall their pre-Christian days: "Remember that you were at that time without Christ, being aliens from the commonwealth of Israel, and strangers to the covenants of promise, *having no hope and without God* in the world." (Eph. 2:12).

It's the burden of the opening chapters of Paul's letter to the Romans to show that this desolate condition is the general situation of mankind. Paul explains that God's power and deity are made known through the created order around us, so that all men are without excuse (1:20), and that God has written His moral law upon all men's hearts, so that they are morally responsible before Him (2:15). Although God offers eternal life to all who will respond in an appropriate way to God's general revelation in nature and conscience (2:7), the sad fact is that rather than worship and serve their Creator, people ignore God and flout His moral law (1:21–32). The conclusion: All men are under the power of sin (3:9–12).

Worse, Paul goes on to explain that no one can redeem himself by means of righteous living (3:19–20). We are therefore utterly helpless. Fortunately, however, God has provided a means of escape: Jesus Christ has died for the sins of mankind, thereby satisfying the demands of God's justice and facilitating reconciliation with God (3:21–26). By means of His atoning death salvation is made available as a gift to be received by faith.

Perpetua was a young mother who was arrested in the early third century AD for refusing to acknowledge other gods besides Christ. She and several others were sentenced to be torn to pieces by wild animals. While in prison she wrote an account of her experience, which survives to this day.

The logic of the New Testament is clear: The *universality of sin* and the *uniqueness of Christ's atoning death* entail that there is no salvation apart from Christ. As the apostles proclaimed, "There is salvation in no one else, for there

is no other name under heaven given among men by which we must be saved" (Acts 4:12 RSV).

This particularistic doctrine of salvation through Christ alone was just as scandalous in the polytheistic world of the Roman Empire as in contemporary Western culture. Early Christians were often subjected to severe persecution, torture, and death because they refused to embrace a pluralistic approach to religions. In time, however, as Christianity grew and became the official religion of the Roman Empire, the scandal receded. Indeed, for medieval thinkers like Augustine and Aquinas, one of the marks of the true church was its universality. To them it seemed inconceivable that the great edifice of the Christian church, filling all of civilization, should be founded on a falsehood.

The Demise of the Traditional Doctrine

The demise of this doctrine came with the so-called Expansion of Europe, that is, the three centuries of exploration and discovery from about 1450 until 1750. Through the travels and voyages of men like Marco Polo, Christopher Columbus, and Ferdinand Magellan, new civilizations and whole new worlds were discovered that knew nothing of the Christian faith. The realization that much of the world's population lay outside the bounds of Christianity had a twofold impact upon people's religious thinking.

First, it tended to relativize religious beliefs. People realized that far from being the universal religion of mankind, Christianity was largely confined to western Europe, a corner of the globe. No particular religion, it seemed, could make a claim to universal validity; each society seemed to have its own religion suited to its peculiar needs.

Second, it made Christianity's claim to be the only way of salvation seem narrow and cruel. Enlightenment rationalists like Voltaire taunted the Christians of his day with the prospect of millions of Chinese doomed to hell for not having believed in Christ, when they had not so much as even heard of Christ.

In our own day, the influx into Western nations of immigrants from former colonies and the advances in telecommunications that have served to shrink the world to a global village have heightened our awareness of the religious diversity of mankind. As a result, religious pluralism—the view that there are many roads to God—has today become once again the conventional wisdom.

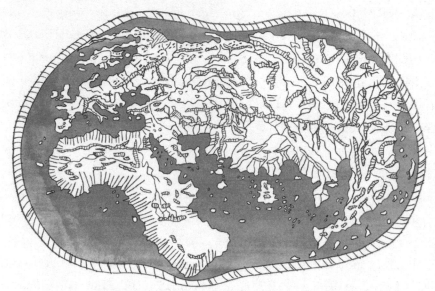

Henricus Martellus's 1489 world map showed increasing knowledge of Asia and of Africa's west coast. Soon the New World was added to such maps.

The Problem Posed by Religious Diversity

But what, exactly, is the problem posed by mankind's religious diversity? And for whom is this supposed to be a problem? When you read the literature on this issue, the recurring challenge seems to be laid at the doorstep of the Christian particularist, the person who says Christ is the only way to God. The phenomenon of religious diversity is taken to imply the truth of pluralism, and the main debate then becomes the question of which form of pluralism is the most plausible. But why think that Christian particularism is untenable in the face of religious diversity? What exactly seems to be the problem?

Fallacious Arguments for Pluralism

When you examine the arguments on behalf of pluralism, you'll find many of them to be almost textbook examples of informal fallacies.

Argument ad Hominem

For example, it's frequently asserted that it's arrogant and immoral to hold to any kind of religious particularism because you then have to regard everybody who disagrees with you as mistaken. Therefore, religious particularism is false.

Recall the definitions of formal and informal fallacies from chapter 3, page 57.

This seems to be a textbook example of the logical fallacy known as "argument *ad hominem*," which tries to invalidate a position by attacking the character of those who hold to it. This is a fallacy because the truth of a position is independent of the moral character of those who believe it. To illustrate: Imagine a medical scientist who finally discovers an AIDS vaccine that really works. Suppose, moreover, that this fellow is really full of himself. He boasts openly of his discovery, he claims that he deserves the Nobel Prize, he looks down on his colleagues as mental midgets because they didn't discover the vaccine, and so on. Clearly, he's arrogant and immoral in his behavior. But does that do anything to undermine the truth of his claim to have discovered the sole AIDS vaccine? More pointedly, if you had AIDS, would you refuse to take his vaccine because he is arrogant and immoral? I hope not! The truth of a position is independent of the character of those who hold it. In the same way, even if it were the case that all religious particularists were arrogant and immoral, that would do nothing to prove that their particular views are false.

Not only that, but why think that arrogance and immorality are necessary conditions of being a particularist? Suppose I've done all I can to discover the truth about God. Suppose I've studied various religions; I've sincerely sought God in prayer. Suppose as a result of my search I'm convinced that Christianity is true, and so I humbly embrace Christian faith as an undeserved gift of God. Am I arrogant and immoral for believing what I sincerely think is true? What else can I do but believe it? I think it's *true*!

Finally, and even more fundamentally, this objection is a double-edged sword. For the pluralist also believes that *his* view is right and that all those adherents to particularistic religious traditions are *wrong*. Therefore, if holding to a view that many others disagree with means you're arrogant and immoral, then the pluralist himself would be convicted of arrogance and immorality.

TALK ABOUT IT

Do you think it's arrogant for a religious pluralist to believe that his view is right and all religious particularists are wrong? Explain.

Genetic Fallacy

Or to give another example, it's frequently alleged that Christian particularism can't be correct because religious beliefs are culturally relative. For example, if you had been born in Pakistan, you would likely have been a Muslim. Therefore your belief in Christianity is false or unjustified.

But again this seems to be a textbook example of what's called the "genetic fallacy." This is trying to invalidate a position by criticizing the way a person came to hold that position. The fact that your beliefs depend upon where and when you were born has no relevance to the *truth* of those beliefs. If you had been born in ancient Greece, you would probably have believed that the sun orbits the Earth. Does that imply that your belief that the Earth orbits the sun is therefore false or unjustified? Obviously not!

And once again, the pluralist pulls the rug from beneath his own feet: For had the pluralist been born in Pakistan, then he would likely have been a religious particularist! Thus, on his own analysis his pluralism is merely the product of his being born in late twentieth-century Western society and is therefore false or unjustified.

The Problem with Christian Particularism

Thus, some of the arguments you frequently hear against Christian particularism are pretty unimpressive. But don't think that because such

fallacious arguments are often given on behalf of religious pluralism therefore pluralism doesn't pose a serious challenge to Christian belief. On the contrary, I think it does. But clearing away these fallacious arguments can help us to get to the real problem lurking in the background.

The real problem concerns the fate of unbelievers outside of one's own particular religious tradition. Christian particularism consigns such persons to hell, which pluralists take to be unconscionable.

Nowhere is this problem better illustrated than in the life of my own doctoral mentor, John Hick. Professor Hick began his career as a relatively conservative Christian theologian. His first book was entitled *Christianity at the Centre*. But as he began to study the other world religions and to become acquainted with many of their saintly followers, he found it simply inconceivable that such good people should be on their way to hell. He realized what that meant. Somehow he had to get Jesus Christ out of the center. So long as Christ's incarnation and atoning death were retained, Christ could not be successfully marginalized. Hick therefore came to edit *The Myth of God Incarnate*, in which he argues that these central Christian doctrines are not true but mere myths. He wrote:

> The problem which has come to the surface in the encounter of Christianity with the other world religions is this: If Jesus was literally God incarnate, and if it is by his death alone that men can be saved, and by their response to him alone that they can appropriate that salvation, then the only doorway to eternal life is Christian faith. It would follow from this that the large majority of the human race so far have not been saved. But is it credible that the loving God and Father of all men has decreed that only those born within one particular thread of human history shall be saved?[1]

This is the real problem raised by the religious diversity of mankind: the fate of those who stand outside the Christian tradition.

Is Hell the Problem?

But what exactly is the problem here supposed to be? What's the problem with holding that salvation is available only through Christ? Is it supposed to be simply that a loving God wouldn't send people to hell?

TALK ABOUT IT

How easy is it for you to respond coolly and rationally, rather than emotionally, to the idea that people who have never heard about Christ will face eternal suffering? What helps you do that? What makes it harder?

I don't think so. The Bible says that God wills the salvation of every human being: "The Lord is … not willing that *any* should perish but that *all* should come to repentance" (2 Peter 3:9 NKJV). Or again, He "desires *all men* to be saved and to come to the knowledge of the truth" (1 Tim. 2:4 RSV). God says through the prophet Ezekiel:

Have I any pleasure in the death of the wicked, says the Lord GOD, and not rather that he should turn from his way and live?… For I have no pleasure in the death of any one, says the Lord GOD; so turn, and live!… Say to them, As I live, says the Lord GOD, I have no pleasure in the death of the wicked, but that the wicked turn from his way and live; turn back, turn back from your evil ways; for why will you die? (Ezek. 18:23, 32; 33:11 RSV)

Here God literally pleads with people to turn back from their self-destructive course of action and be saved.

Thus, in a sense, God doesn't *send* anybody to hell. His desire is that everyone be saved, and He seeks to draw all persons to Himself. If we make a free and well-informed decision to reject Christ's sacrifice for our sin, then God has no choice but to give us what we deserve. God will not send us to hell—but we shall send ourselves.

Our eternal destiny thus lies in our own hands. It's a matter of our free choice where we shall spend eternity. Those who are lost, therefore, are self-condemned; they separate themselves from God despite God's will and every effort to save them, and God grieves over their loss.

Does the Punishment Fit the Crime?

Now the pluralist might admit that given human freedom God can't guarantee that everyone will be saved. Some people might freely condemn themselves by rejecting God's offer of salvation. But, he might argue, it would be unjust of God to condemn such people *forever*. For even terrible sins like those of the Nazi torturers in the death camps still deserve only a finite punishment. Therefore, at most hell could be a sort of purgatory, lasting an appropriate length of time for each person before that person is released and admitted into heaven. Eventually hell would be emptied and heaven filled. Thus, ironically, hell is incompatible, not with God's love, but with His justice. The objection charges that God is unjust because the punishment doesn't fit the crime.

But, again, this doesn't seem to me to be the real problem. For the objection seems flawed in at least two ways:

First, the objection equivocates between *every* sin we commit and *all* the sins we commit. We could agree that every individual sin that a person commits deserves only a finite punishment. But it doesn't follow from this that *all* of a person's sins taken together as a whole deserve only a finite punishment. If a person commits an infinite number of sins, then the sum total of all such sins deserves infinite punishment.

Now, of course, nobody commits an infinite number of sins in the earthly life. But what about in the afterlife? Insofar as the inhabitants of hell continue to hate God and reject Him, they continue to sin and so accrue to themselves more guilt and more punishment. In a real sense, then, hell is *self-perpetuating*. In such a case, every sin has a finite punishment, but because sinning goes on forever, so does the punishment.

Second, why think that every sin does have only a finite punishment? We could agree that sins like theft, lying, adultery, and so forth are only of finite consequence and so deserve only a finite punishment. But, in a sense, these sins aren't what separates someone from God. For Christ has died for those sins; the penalty for those sins has been paid. One has only to accept Christ as Savior to be completely free and cleansed of those sins.

The medieval Italian poet
Dante Alighieri wrote a
poem called *Inferno* that
depicts hell with gothic
gruesomeness. But Dante
carefully chose each type
of suffering to illustrate his
belief that the punishment
for the sin is the sin itself.
That is, each person's sin
has formed his soul in such
a way that he creates his
own agony. For example,
Satan stands at the bottom
of hell encased chest-high
in ice. What freezes the ice
is the endless flapping of his
batlike wings. The flapping
expresses his will: "I *will*
fly to the heights of heaven
and be equal to God on my
own terms." If he could just
humble himself and stop
flapping, the ice would melt
and he would be free. But he
never does.

But the refusal to accept Christ and His sacrifice seems to be a sin of a different order altogether. For this sin repudiates God's provision for sin and so decisively separates someone from God and His salvation. To reject Christ is to reject God Himself. And in light of who God is, this is a sin of infinite gravity and proportion and therefore plausibly deserves infinite punishment. We should not, therefore, think of hell primarily as punishment for the array of sins of finite consequence that we've committed, but as the just penalty for a sin of infinite consequence, namely the rejection of God Himself.

Is the Problem Lack of Information?

But perhaps the problem is supposed to be that a loving God wouldn't send people to hell because they were *uninformed* or *misinformed* about Christ. People who have never heard of Christ or have been given a distorted picture of Christ can't be expected to place their faith in Christ.

But again, this doesn't seem to me to be the heart of the problem. For according to the Bible, God doesn't judge people who have never heard of Christ on the basis of whether they've placed their faith in Christ. Rather God judges them on the basis of the light of God's general revelation in nature and conscience that they do have. The offer of Romans 2:7—"To those who by patiently doing good seek for glory and honor and immortality, he will give eternal life"—is a bona fide offer of salvation. Someone who senses his need of forgiveness through his guilty conscience and flings himself upon the mercy of the God revealed in nature may find salvation. This is not to say that people can be saved apart from Christ. Rather it's to say that the benefits of Christ's atoning death can be applied to people without their conscious knowledge of Christ.

Such persons would be like certain people mentioned in the Old Testament such as Job and Melchizedek, who were saved only through Christ but who had no conscious knowledge of Christ. They weren't even members of the covenant family of Israel, and yet they clearly enjoyed a personal relationship with God. Similarly, there could be modern-day Jobs living

among that percentage of the world's population that has yet to hear the gospel of Christ.

Unfortunately, the testimony of the New Testament, as we've seen, is that people don't generally measure up even to these much lower standards of general revelation. So there are little grounds for optimism about there being many people, if any at all, who will actually be saved through their response to general revelation alone. Nonetheless, the point remains that salvation is *universally accessible* through God's general revelation in nature and conscience. So the problem posed by religious diversity can't be simply that God would not condemn persons who are uninformed or misinformed about Christ.

The Real Problem

Rather it seems to me that the real problem is this: If God is all-knowing, then He knew who would freely receive the gospel and who would not. But then certain very difficult questions arise:

(1) Why didn't God bring the gospel to people who He knew *would* accept it if they heard it, even though they reject the light of general revelation that they do have?

To illustrate: Imagine a North American Indian living prior to the arrival of Christian missionaries. Let's call him Walking Bear. Let's suppose that as Walking Bear looks up at the heavens at night and as he sees the intricacy and beauty of nature around him, he senses that all of this has been made by the Great Spirit. Furthermore, as Walking Bear looks into his own heart, he senses there the moral law, telling him that all men are brothers made by the Great Spirit and therefore we ought to live in love for one another.

But suppose that instead of worshipping the Great Spirit and living in love for his fellow man, Walking Bear ignores the Great Spirit and creates totems of other spirits and that rather than loving his fellow man he lives in selfishness and cruelty toward others. In such a case Walking Bear would be justly condemned before God on the basis of his failure to respond to God's general revelation in nature and conscience.

GENERAL VS. SPECIAL
REVELATION

Theologians distinguish between God's general revelation and His special revelation. These differ in that the former is more general than the latter both in terms of its availability and in terms of the information it imparts. God's existence and power are generally revealed in nature, and His fundamental moral law is instinctively grasped by persons everywhere at all times. God specially reveals Himself to specific people at certain times through His Word and supremely through Jesus Christ. The question then arises: How will God judge those who have experienced His general revelation in nature and conscience but have not known His special revelation?

But now suppose that if only the missionaries had arrived, then Walking Bear would have believed the gospel and been saved! In that case his salvation or damnation seems to be the result of bad luck. Through no fault of his own he just happened to be born at a time and place in history when the gospel was not yet available. His condemnation is just; but would an all-loving God allow people's eternal destiny to hinge on historical and geographical accident?

(2) More fundamentally, why did God even create the world, when He knew that so many people would not believe the gospel and be lost? Since creation is a free act of God, why not simply refrain from creating any free creatures at all?

(3) Even more radically, why didn't God create a world in which everyone freely believes the gospel and is saved? Such a world must be logically possible, since people are free to believe or not believe. So why didn't God create a world in which every person freely chooses to place his faith in Christ and be saved?

What's the Christian supposed to say in answer to these questions? Does Christianity make God out to be cruel and unloving?

The Problem Analyzed

In order to answer these questions it will be helpful to examine more closely the logical structure of the problem before us. The problem seems to be very similar to the logical version of the problem of suffering that we examined in chapter 7. The pluralist seems to be claiming that it's impossible for God to be all-powerful and all-loving and yet for some people to never hear the gospel and be lost. That is to say, the pluralist claims that the following statements are logically inconsistent:

1. God is all-powerful and all-loving.

2. Some people never hear the gospel and are lost.

Thus, Christian particularism is logically incoherent.

Is There an Inconsistency?

But now we need to ask, why think that 1 and 2 are logically inconsistent? After all, there's no *explicit* contradiction between them. But if the pluralist is claiming that 1 and 2 are *implicitly* contradictory, he must be assuming some hidden premises that would serve to bring out this contradiction and make it explicit. The question is, what are those hidden premises?

I must say that I've never seen any attempt on the part of religious pluralists to identify those hidden assumptions. But let's try to help the pluralist out a bit. It seems to me that he must be assuming something like the following:

3. If God is all-powerful, He can create a world in which everybody hears the gospel and is freely saved.

4. If God is all-loving, He prefers a world in which everybody hears the gospel and is freely saved.

Since, according to 1, God is both all-powerful and all-loving, it follows that He can create a world of universal salvation and that He prefers such a world. Therefore such a world exists, in contradiction to 2.

Now both of the hidden premises must be necessarily true if the pluralist is to prove the logical incompatibility of 1 and 2. So the question is, are these assumptions necessarily true?

Consider 3: It seems uncontroversial that God could create a world in which everybody hears the gospel. That's no big deal. But so long as people are free, there's no guarantee that everybody in such a world would be freely saved. In fact, when you think about it, there's no reason to think that the balance between saved and lost in such a world would be any better than the balance in the actual world!

It is logically impossible to *make* someone *freely* do something. Being all-powerful does not mean having the ability to do the logically impossible. So there's no guarantee that a possible world in which everyone hears the gospel and is freely saved is feasible for God to create. For all we know, in any world of free people that God could create, some people would freely reject His

saving grace and be lost. Hence, 3 is not necessarily true, and so the pluralist's argument is fallacious.

But what about 4? Is it necessarily true? Let's suppose for the sake of argument that there are possible worlds that are feasible for God in which everyone hears the gospel and freely accepts it. Does God's being all-loving compel Him to prefer one of these worlds over a world in which some persons are lost?

Not necessarily; for the worlds involving universal salvation might have other, *overriding* deficiencies that make them less preferable. For example, suppose that the only worlds in which everybody freely believes the gospel and is saved are worlds with only a handful of people in them, say, three or four. If God were to create any more people, then at least one of them would have freely rejected His grace and been lost. Must He prefer one of these sparsely populated worlds over a world in which multitudes believe in the gospel and are saved, even though that implies that other persons freely reject His grace and are lost?

TALK ABOUT IT

Are people raised in Christian homes getting more grace for salvation than people raised in communities where the gospel is unknown? If not, why not? If so, is this a failure of love on God's part?

That's far from obvious. So long as God gives sufficient grace for salvation to all persons He creates, God seems no less loving for preferring a more populous world, even though that implies that some people would freely resist His every effort to save them and be damned. Thus, the pluralist's second assumption is also not necessarily true, so that his argument is revealed to be doubly fallacious.

So neither of the pluralist's assumptions seems to be necessarily true. Unless the pluralist can suggest some other premises, we have no reason to think that 1 and 2 are logically incompatible.

There Is No Inconsistency

But we can push the argument a notch further. We can show positively that it's entirely possible that God is all-powerful and all-loving and that many persons never hear the gospel and are lost.

As a good and loving God, God wants as many people as possible to be saved and as few as possible to be lost. His goal, then, is to achieve an optimal balance between these, to create no more of the lost than is necessary to attain a certain number of the saved. But it's possible that the actual world (which includes the future as well as the present and past) has such a balance. It's possible that in order to create this many people who will be saved, God also had to create this many people who will be lost. It's possible that had God created a world in which fewer people go to hell, then even fewer people would have gone to heaven. It's possible that in order to achieve a multitude of saints, God had to accept a multitude of sinners.

It might be objected that an all-loving God would not create people who He knew *will be* lost, but who *would have been* saved if only they had heard the gospel. But how do we know there *are* any such persons? It's reasonable to assume that many people who never hear the gospel wouldn't have believed the gospel even if they had heard it. Suppose, then, that God in His mercy has so providentially ordered the world that *all* persons who never hear the gospel are precisely such people. God is too good to allow someone to be lost due to historical or geographical accident.

In that case, anybody who never hears the gospel and is lost would have rejected the gospel and been lost even if he had heard it. No one could stand before God on the judgment day and complain, "All right, God, so I didn't respond to Your general revelation in nature and conscience! But if only I had heard the gospel, then I would have believed!"

For God will say, "No, I knew that even if you had heard the gospel, you wouldn't have believed it. Therefore, My judgment of you on the basis of nature and conscience—which you willingly turned your back on—is neither unfair nor unloving."

Thus, it's possible that:

> 5. God has created a world that has an optimal balance between saved and lost, and those who never hear the gospel and are lost would not have believed in it even if they had heard it.

Providence is the doctrine that God orders events in history so that His purposes are achieved. The challenge is doing this while respecting human freedom. Some theologians abridge God's providence; some curtail human freedom. A better way is to say that God takes human free choices into account in His planning. He does this by knowing how every possible person would freely choose in whatever nondetermining circumstances God might place him in. By creating certain persons in certain circumstances, God knows exactly how they will freely choose and can plan accordingly. On this view everything that happens is either directly willed by God or permitted by God, including where and when people are born.

So long as 5 is even *possibly true*, it shows that there's no inconsistency between an all-powerful, all-loving God and some people's never hearing the gospel and being lost.

On this basis we're now prepared to offer *possible* answers to the three difficult questions that prompted this inquiry. To take them in reverse order:

(3) Why didn't God create a world in which everyone freely believes the gospel and is saved?

Answer: It may not be feasible for God to create such a world. If such a world were feasible, then (all else being equal) God would have created it. But given His will to create *free* creatures, God had to accept that some would freely reject Him and His every effort to save them and be lost.

(2) Why did God even create the world, when He knew that so many people would not believe the gospel and be lost?

Answer: God wanted to share His love and fellowship with created persons. He knew this meant that many would freely reject Him and be lost. But He also knew that many others would freely receive His grace and be saved. The happiness and blessedness of those who would freely embrace His love should not be precluded by those who would freely spurn Him. Persons who would freely reject God and His love should not be allowed, in effect, to hold a sort of veto power over which worlds God is free to create. In His mercy God has providentially ordered the world to achieve an optimal balance between saved and lost by maximizing the number of those who freely accept Him and minimizing the number of those who would not.

(1) Why didn't God bring the gospel to people who He knew would accept it if they heard it, even though they reject the light of general revelation that they do have?

Answer: There are no such people. God in His providence has so arranged the world that those who would respond to the gospel if they heard it, do hear it. The sovereign God has so ordered human history that as the gospel spreads out from first-century Palestine, He places people in its path who would believe it if they heard it. Once the gospel reaches a people, God

providentially places there persons who He knew would respond to it if they heard it. In His love and mercy, God ensures that no one who would believe the gospel if he heard it is born at a time and place in history where he fails to hear it. Those who don't respond to God's general revelation in nature and conscience and never hear the gospel wouldn't respond to it if they did hear it. Hence, no one is lost because of historical or geographical accident. Anyone who wants *or even would want* to be saved will be saved.

I want to emphasize that these are just *possible* answers to the questions we posed. But so long as they're even possible, they show that there's no incompatibility between God's being all-powerful and all-loving and some people's never hearing the gospel and being lost.

Furthermore, these answers are attractive because they also seem to be biblical as well. In his open-air address to the Athenian philosophers gathered on the Areopagus, Paul declared:

> The God who made the world and everything in it is the Lord of heaven and earth and … gives all men life and breath and everything else. From one man he made every nation of men, that they should inhabit the whole earth; and he determined *the times* set for them and *the exact places* where they should live. God did this so that men would seek him and perhaps reach out for him and find him, though he is not far from each one of us. "For in him we live and move and have our being." (Acts 17:24–28 NIV)

This sounds exactly like the conclusion to which I have come through purely philosophical reflection on the question!

Plausibility of the Solution

Now the pluralist might concede the logical *possibility* of God's being all-powerful and all-loving and some people's never hearing the gospel and being lost but insist that these two facts are nonetheless *improbable* with respect to each other. People by and large seem to believe in the religion of the culture in which they were raised. But in that case, the pluralist might argue, it's highly probable that if many of those who never hear the gospel had been raised in a Christian culture, they would have believed the gospel and been saved. Thus, the hypothesis I've offered is highly implausible.

Now it would, indeed, be fantastically improbable that by happenstance alone it just turned out that all those who never hear the gospel and are lost are persons who would not have believed the gospel even if they had heard it. But that's not the hypothesis! The hypothesis is that a provident God has so arranged the world. Given a God endowed with knowledge of how every person would freely respond to His grace in whatever circumstances God might place him, it's not at all implausible that God has ordered the world in the way described.

Such a world wouldn't look outwardly any different from a world where the circumstances of a person's birth are a matter of happenstance. We can agree that people generally adopt the religion of their culture and that if many of those born into non-Christian cultures had been born in a Christian society instead, they would have become nominally or culturally Christian. But that's not to say that they would have been saved. It's a simple empirical fact that there are no distinguishing psychological or sociological traits between persons who receive Christ and persons who don't. There's no way to predict accurately by examining a person whether and under what circumstances that person would believe in Christ for salvation. Since a world providentially ordered by God in the way I suggest would appear outwardly identical to a world in which one's birth is a matter of historical and geographical accident, it's hard to see how the hypothesis I've defended can be said to be improbable—apart from a demonstration that the existence of a God endowed with such knowledge is implausible. And I don't know of any such demonstration.

Conclusion

In conclusion, then, pluralists haven't been able to show any logical inconsistency in Christian particularism. On the contrary, we've been able to prove that such a position is logically coherent. More than that, I think such a view is not only possible, but plausible as well. Therefore mankind's religious diversity doesn't undermine the Christian gospel of salvation through Christ alone.

In fact, for those of us who are Christians, I think that what I've said helps to put the proper perspective on Christian missions: It's our duty as Christians to proclaim the gospel to the whole world, trusting that God has so providentially ordered things that through us the good news will come to persons who God knew would accept it if they heard it. Our compassion toward those in other world religions is expressed, not by pretending they are not lost without Christ, but by supporting and making every effort ourselves to communicate to them the life-giving message of Christ.

It's my hope that the material contained in this book will help you to become a more effective communicator of the gospel to a lost and dying world. Review it, memorize the premises of the arguments, discuss the issues with Christian friends, and then as occasion arises share it with others when you find yourself called upon to give an answer for the hope within.

1. John Hick, "Jesus and the World Religions,: in *The Myth of God Incarnate*, ed. John Hick (London: SCM, 1977), 180.

> Then Jesus came to them and said, "All authority in heaven and on earth has been given to me. Therefore go and make disciples of all nations, baptizing them in the name of the Father and of the Son and of the Holy Spirit, and teaching them to obey everything I have commanded you. And surely I am with you always, to the very end of the age." (Matt. 28:18–20 NIV)

RELIGIOUS PLURALISM OBJECTION

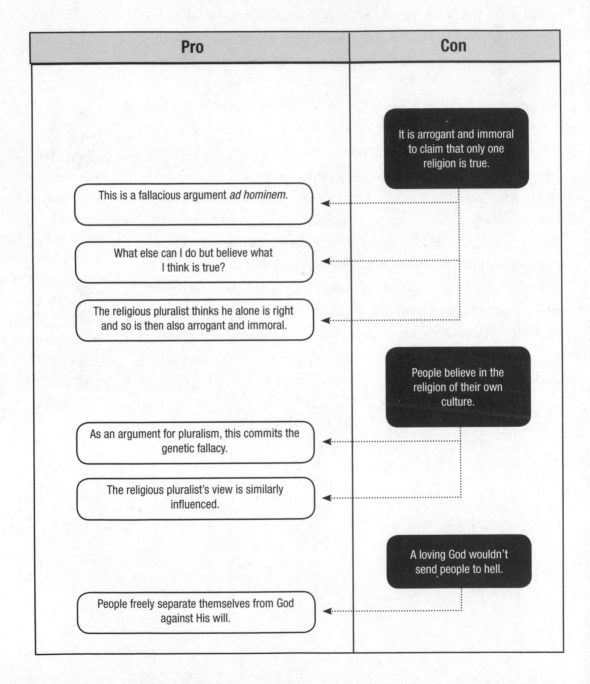

Pro	Con
	It is arrogant and immoral to claim that only one religion is true.
This is a fallacious argument *ad hominem.*	
What else can I do but believe what I think is true?	
The religious pluralist thinks he alone is right and so is then also arrogant and immoral.	
	People believe in the religion of their own culture.
As an argument for pluralism, this commits the genetic fallacy.	
The religious pluralist's view is similarly influenced.	
	A loving God wouldn't send people to hell.
People freely separate themselves from God against His will.	

RELIGIOUS PLURALISM OBJECTION (cont.)

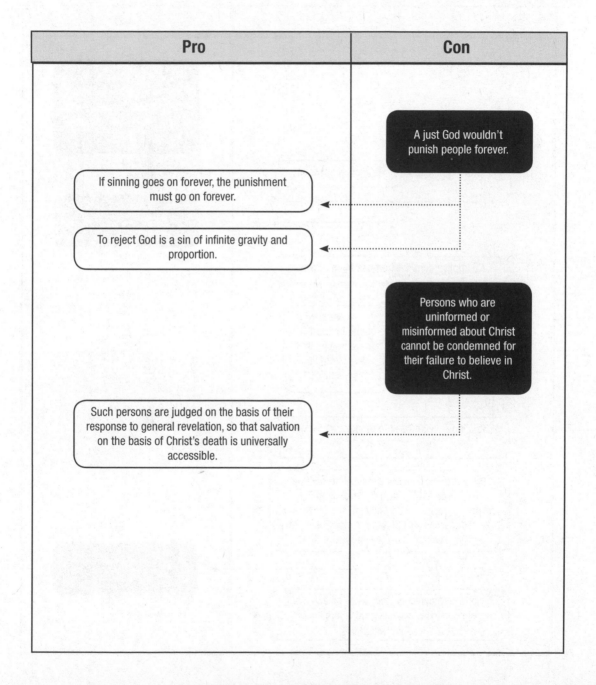

Pro	Con
	A just God wouldn't punish people forever.
If sinning goes on forever, the punishment must go on forever.	
To reject God is a sin of infinite gravity and proportion.	
	Persons who are uninformed or misinformed about Christ cannot be condemned for their failure to believe in Christ.
Such persons are judged on the basis of their response to general revelation, so that salvation on the basis of Christ's death is universally accessible.	

RELIGIOUS PLURALISM OBJECTION (cont.)

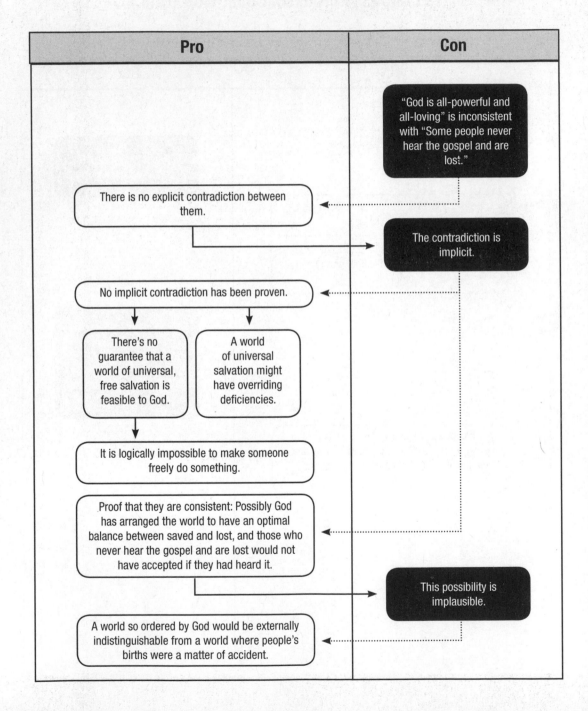

Pro	Con
	"God is all-powerful and all-loving" is inconsistent with "Some people never hear the gospel and are lost."
There is no explicit contradiction between them.	
	The contradiction is implicit.
No implicit contradiction has been proven.	
There's no guarantee that a world of universal, free salvation is feasible to God.	A world of universal salvation might have overriding deficiencies.
It is logically impossible to make someone freely do something.	
Proof that they are consistent: Possibly God has arranged the world to have an optimal balance between saved and lost, and those who never hear the gospel and are lost would not have accepted if they had heard it.	
	This possibility is implausible.
A world so ordered by God would be externally indistinguishable from a world where people's births were a matter of accident.